The China Dream
and the China Path

Series on Chinese Economics Research

(ISSN: 2251-1644)

Series Editors: Yang Mu *(Lee Kuan Yew School of Public Policies, NUS)*
Fan Gang *(Peking University, China)*

Published:

Vol. 1: China's State-Owned Enterprises: Nature, Performance and Reform
by Sheng Hong and Zhao Nong

Vol. 2: Food Security and Farm Land Protection in China
by Mao Yushi, Zhao Nong and Yang Xiaojing

Vol. 3: The Micro-Analysis of Regional Economy in China:
A Perspective of Firm Relocation
by Wei Houkai, Wang Yeqiang and Bai Mei

Vol. 4: The China Dream and the China Path
by Zhou Tianyong

Series on Chinese Economics Research – Vol. 4

The China Dream and the China Path

Zhou Tianyong

Party School of the Central Committee of Communist Party of China, China

社会科学文献出版社
SOCIAL SCIENCES ACADEMIC PRESS (CHINA)

World Scientific

Published by

World Scientific Publishing Co. Pte. Ltd.

5 Toh Tuck Link, Singapore 596224

USA office: 27 Warren Street, Suite 401-402, Hackensack, NJ 07601

UK office: 57 Shelton Street, Covent Garden, London WC2H 9HE

Library of Congress Cataloging-in-Publication Data
Zhou, Tianyong, 1958–
   [Zhongguo meng yu Zhongguo dao lu. English]
   The China dream and the China path / Zhou Tianyong, Party School of the Central
Committee of Communist Party of China, China.
     pages cm. -- (Series on Chinese economics research, ISSN 2251-1644 ; vol. 4)
   Translation of Zhongguo meng yu Zhongguo dao lu.
   Includes bibliographical references.
   ISBN 978-9814472661
   1. China--Economic policy--2000–   2. China--Economic conditions--2000–   I. Title.
   HC427.95.Z467313 2014
   330.951--dc23
                         2013031942

British Library Cataloguing-in-Publication Data ·
A catalogue record for this book is available from the British Library.

中国梦与中国道路
Originally published in Chinese by Social Sciences Academic Press (China).
Copyright © 2011 Social Sciences Academic Press (China).

China Book International provided funding for the translation of this book.

Translator: Jiang Hang

Copyright © 2014 by World Scientific Publishing Co. Pte. Ltd.

In-house Editor: Zheng Danjun

Typeset by Stallion Press
Email: enquiries@stallionpress.com

Printed in Singapore.

Foreword by Zheng Xinli

In 2009, Professor Zhou Tianyong wrote a book entitled *China's Way Out*, where he discussed China's achievements made over the three decades after the reform and opening up. He also analyzed the causes of the problems and weaknesses in the economic and social development of previous years, as well as the possible risks and problems in future development. In addition, he compared the route and process for China's development with those of India, Latin America, Japan, and Korea. It was after reading the proof of this valuable book that I agreed to write the preface. The following year, I received his other book entitled *Chinese Dream and China's Road* that answers the question of China's "way out" after the reform, aroused by the previous book, including solutions to the future problems of population, resources, and environment. Professor Zhou Tianyong proposed a comprehensive, long-term, and extensive strategic plan for China's development, reform, and employment over the next three decades. This book examines, in detail, what steps China should take during the next 30 years. In my opinion, this is one of the finest books on basic Chinese policies I have ever had the pleasure of reading.

Since the reform and opening up, China has made unprecedented achievements in economic and social development. While ushering in a new age, China has maintained sound development by seizing opportunities, overcoming difficulties, avoiding risks, and achieving scientific development in the first decade of the 21st century. The rapid development and rise of Chinese economy is an unstoppable trend in the 12th five-year plan period. In fact, some predict this rapid development will continue well past the 12th five-year plan period. Meanwhile, it should also be noted that the social and economic development of China has encountered many difficulties and challenges, with both long-term and short-term problems in the economy concerning employment, system reforms, and development. These issues are integrally linked, making it even more difficult to find effective solutions to these problems. The year 2011 marked the 90th anniversary of the founding of the Communist Party of China (CPC), which was also the first year of the 12th five-year plan. The 18th Congress of CPC will be held in 2012. Therefore, at this critical development transformation period, it is of great importance for academic, political, industrial, and all other circles to pragmatically reflect on past achievements and experiences in order to plan future development in a rational and systematic manner. I believe that the publication of this book will promote and direct more scholars to actively research major problems related to the future of China and its people.

During the critical transformation period, a more cohesive, optimistic, and ambitious common perspective is necessary for future societal development. This common perspective shall also embody the goal of socialist politics with Chinese characteristics. The foremost objective in the late 1970s was to eliminate poverty and lay out a road to prosperity through hard work, which precisely outlined the ideological basis for civilians actively responding to and participating in the reform and opening-up. As China has ushered into a new era and a new life for its people, the interest demands of the people have significantly changed during the current transformation period. The base for the formulation of correct development strategies and the new objective forces for development lie in understanding the change of people's interest demand, respecting the objective law for economic and social development, and summarizing and extracting the new common perspective on social development. Professor Zhou Tianyong has proposed the idea of the "Chinese dream" and carried out a systematic in-depth analysis. According to Professor Zhou, the "Chinese dream" includes living in urban areas, living and working in contentment, social security, equal public service, beautiful ecological environment, family security, and favorable spiritual life, that collectively represent people's longing for a better life in the future, reflect the direction of social reform and progress, and highlight the livelihood issue that currently calls for a solution.

As demonstrated by development practices, a correct development path is an important factor toward realizing the "Chinese dream." The path and method for development in the past three decades since the reform and opening-up have been widely recognized and acclaimed, both at home and abroad. In fact, China has developed a productive development path, maintained rapid growth of national economy for more than 30 years, constantly improved citizens livelihood, and significantly enhanced comprehensive national strength by focusing on developing productivity, reforming both the state-owned and collective economic system, adjusting and optimizing the industrial structure, gradually propelling political system reform, and adopting the strategy of opening-up. However, when focusing on the course of development, some obvious weaknesses can be seen in the early stages of development, such as the excessive distortion of economic structure, comparatively lagging urbanization, the increasing gap between the rich and the poor, and the high consumption of resources and environment. The development road shall be appropriately adjusted based on the new development background, development tasks, and people's demand for loans and interests. This is an important issue, covering a wide range of subjects and complicated relations, such as how to adjust the development road? What direction should the development road take? How to break from the constraints exerted by the current interest pattern? In this book, Professor Zhou has summarized the achievements, experiences, and shortcomings of the previous development road and proposed his individual insight on the adjustment of China's development road and ideological improvement. The new development road shall focus on the following: adjusting urban and rural structure; realizing free residence and movement of population; creating public service for all urban inhabitants and favorable housing for migrants; assigning importance to the adjustment of industrial structure and vigorously promoting the third industry; emphasizing the business structure and vigorously developing small enterprises; carrying out the strategy of science and technological advancement; improving competitiveness; and building an innovation-oriented country. Since reform is the most important objective for determining China's future path, propelling reform is the key to achieving China's goal. The most urgent reform issue is to temper controls on entrepreneurship and employment. The most crucial reform issue is to promote the fiscal and taxation system, which is the focal point of the second reform.

The realization of the Chinese dream needs both constant economic development and progress in all aspects of society. Along with the increase in economic production and improvement in people's living standards, the key factors for selecting China's course turn to the constraints of resources and environment and the decrease of the gap between the rich and poor. According to Professor Zhou, if the development mode remains unchanged, there will be no evading of the issues of resources and environment. China shall conquer the constraints of resources and environment by improving technologies, adjusting urban, rural, and industrial structure, changing consumption style, and establishing market and governance systems that rationally utilize resources and environment, thereby moving towards sustainable development. The essential requirement of socialism, with China's characteristics, is to eliminate polarization and achieve common prosperity. However, China shall not follow the old path in achieving common prosperity, but shall be free from fixed idea modes, such as: "more state-owned economy and less private economy" and "more planned economy and less market economy". China should recognize the reason for income inequality in a scientific and comprehensive way; deliberate the question from a higher level based on economic laws and tendencies such as social transformation, economic structure change and regional population flow; encourage business startups; improve employment; adjust the employment structure; avoid the rise of the Gini coefficient in the transformation from agricultural society to urban society; actively mobilize the mechanisms and forces of self-balanced income distribution; and promote rational income distribution.

Professor Zhou has conducted an in-depth study on some long-standing, major issues in China's development strategies, proposed numerous influential views on policy making, published a series of works, and has successfully generated widespread influence on the society with his commitment, academic courage, solid theoretical basis and all his energy. As is often emphasized, one might be a master in his own special field, but it is quite difficult to research on such a large subject as national development plans and strategies, without wide research perspectives, proficient knowledge, and absolute dedication. After reading this book, I find that Professor Zhou has two essential bases for writing such a book that exhibits his proficient knowledge on economics and a familiarity with the practices of development, reform and people's livelihood in China, including a knowledge and understanding of many professional fields. I believe Zhou Tianyong's expansive knowledge has created a book that will provide a helpful reference in policy making, while his spirit and research method will produce a profound influence in the current academic world. This book is a valuable resource for anyone concerned with the future and prospect of China over the next 30 years.

Zheng Xinli
First Deputy Director of the China Center
for International Economic Exchanges
6 March 2013

Foreword by Li Junru

This is the second time I have written a preface to a book by Zhou Tianyong, and I am very surprised and delighted by the proof of *Chinese Dream and China's Road*. The first time I wrote a preface for Zhou Tianyong was for his book *Assault Fortified Positions*, which discussed the reform of the Chinese political system. I was surprised to find that a scholar who had long committed himself to economic research was engaged in the controversial issue of the political system. Indeed, in *Chinese Dream and China's Road*, he surprised me again in the same way. However, this time, it was as a scholar who had long been dedicated to empirical studies and who in recent times has begun to concentrate on the macro economic problem of the "Chinese dream and China's road." Zhou Tianyang is a scholar that continues to astound and capture his audience.

This book has also struck a very personal chord with me. In 2006, I wrote a book entitled Chinese Dream, which was published in Chinese, English, French, and Spanish. The book was inspired by Zheng Bijian, a great thinker of the Communist Party of China (CPC), who had once discussed an idea called the "Chinese dream." However, Zheng Bijian and I primarily stated that China aimed to realize the dream of modernization by insisting on peaceful development based on both domestic and foreign general conditions, while Zhou Tianyong postulates that Chinese people's pursuit and dream of economic and social development is based on the research of China's development road.

It is evident that, despite different research perspectives, Zhou Tianyong adopts the same thoughts as Zheng Bijian and myself. We all hope that the "Chinese dream" acts as the moral support and motivation for China in its peaceful rise to power and becomes the foundation for rejuvenating the Chinese nation, and the gateway to China's success.

First, the main goal of the "Chinese dream" is the Chinese people's pursuit for modernization, i.e., to realize the modernization of China while carrying forth the national spirit and independent innovation based on the exchange of various civilizations in the first half of the 21st century. Therefore, the Chinese dream is considered to be the rehabilitation of the Chinese civilization with an enlightened idea, method, and image. Zhou Tianyong further details the "Chinese dream" as the personal desire and spiritual demand of living in urban areas that provides housing facilities, employment, social security, and a beautiful living environment, which practically links the overall pursuit of Chinese people to the pursuit of an individual. As mentioned by Zhou Tianyong, what pushes the Chinese to continue to make such painstaking efforts in the 21st century are the following: Chinese people's dreams and desires about their lives and development in the 21st century; their responsibilities, trust, hopes, and dreams of a secured future that includes well being of their families, society, and the country; and their pursuit of the vision and the ideal of China.

In addition, the Chinese believe that the "Chinese dream" will be realized based on the unique "China's development road," developed under the reform and opening up after lengthy exploration and various hardships. This refers to peaceful development achieved by holding consideration for its own people and other nations. On the proposed road to modernization, China plans to do the following: join the global economic development efforts while independently realizing industrialization and modernization; learn from achievements made by various civilizations and carry forth these traditional advantages to the Chinese civilization; promote economic and cultural exchange within the world; and form the pattern of "you in me, me in you." Meanwhile, China will be conscious of the difficulties of other countries and depend mainly on itself to solve national problems. The Chinese people are determined to realize the "Chinese dream" through peaceful development, as mentioned above. In terms of domestic economy, politics, culture, and society, China is committed to building socialism with Chinese characteristics. In this road to modernization, China will abide by the leadership of CPC, based on the practical position of the primary stage of socialism, and follow the basic line of "one central task, two basic points," according to the overall layout of the harmonious promotion of economic, political, cultural, and social construction, while reaching the goal of modernization, including prosperity, democracy, civilization, and harmony. Under this framework, Zhou Tianyong further details the specific requirements of China's development road based on economic analysis, which includes adjusting the urban and rural structures, adjusting the industrial and enterprise structures, and transforming the development method; carrying out the strategy of science and technological advancement; overcoming the obstruction of interested parties, while firmly promoting reform and developing the mechanism and system for structure adjustment and development promotion; and profoundly enhancing the political, social, and cultural system reform. He also conducts an in-depth, detailed analysis and demonstration on how China shall follow its path in the 21st century and proposes several practical ideas and strategies for key development issues. Though these proposals will be proved by practices, he undoubtedly provides readers with precious references for the ideas and direction of China's future social and economic development.

History has and will continue, to teach and demonstrate that no one can prevent the realization of the "Chinese dream" and "China's development road," except the Chinese themselves. The Chinese have struggled for two centuries to realize the "Chinese dream" of modernization. In the first century, in order to create the proper political and social environment for industrialization and modernization, the Chinese strove for national independence and the liberation of their own people. In the second century, the Chinese strove for national prosperity and happiness into people's lives in order to realize the dream of industrialization and modernization. The first century has respectively proven that no single person or power could prevent the Chinese from gaining independence, while the past sixty years of the second century, especially the past three decades have demonstrated that no single person or world power could prevent China from gaining strength.

In the academic environment that focuses on rapid and short-term issues, Zhou Tianyong's in-depth analysis on this great topic reveals his deep feelings for China and its people, as well as his strong sense of duty as an ethical economist. I hope that readers can feel his passion emanating from his book. I also believe that the production of this book will contribute to the presentation of the "Chinese dream" and creation of the Chinese spirit, and provide theoretical and logic support to China's important policy making.

More importantly, I hope that the Chinese people will not allow their pride of past achievements or a few negativities that came across in their pursuit of harmonious development, to prevent them from achieving their dreams. In order to realize the "Chinese dream," the Chinese must seize strategic opportunities, bravely handle challenges, and turn their hopes into realities.

Li Junru
Former Vice Principal of the Party School
of the Central Committee of CPC
17 March 2013

Contents

Chapter 1

Chinese Dream for the 21st Century

During February 2010 until the beginning of 2011, I conducted research on the following: How to adjust the development structure? How to remove the constraints put in place by resources and environment? How to reform the fiscal and tax systems? How to practically narrow the income gap between the rich and poor? How to prevent polarization and realize common prosperity? and, How to further reform the land, finance, and state-owned economy? This book, as the result of my efforts, largely aims to propose a road map for future development, reform and opening of China and design a practical road and comprehensive overall plan.

This chapter focuses on the Chinese dreams of the 21st century. I will explain the significant achievements made over the past three decades since the late 1970s under the leadership of CPC, based on the spirit of reform and opening up that originated from China's dream to achieve development and modernization.

1. Introduction: Equitable Analysis of the Achievements in the Past Three Decades

Despite some achievements, the first 30 years of the foundation of the People's Republic of China did not see significant economic growth.

Unfortunately, CPC did not change from a party of revolutionary struggle to a party of economic construction. After the foundation of the country, China still placed class conflicts as the central task of the party and regarded the commodity economy that stressed on developing productivity and improving people's living standard as capitalism. Even though China had waged arduous struggles in economic development, they were seen to have wasted 30 years in economic development and scientific and technological progress, and were listed as the lowest of all countries and economies in economic development and modernization in the first three decades.

Thirty years ago, Deng Xiaoping led the party and all Chinese out of chaos and took steps to modernize. In terms of the willingness and actions of the governing party and the government's presence in the structure of agricultural society, Deng Xiaoping's actions were unprecedented.

In the following 30 years, CPC has gradually transformed itself from a party of revolution and struggle to a party of governance and economic development, additionally placing economic development as the unswerving central task of the party. Chinese economy has developed at an annual growth rate of 9.7%, while its GDP per capita 30 years ago, which was only two-third of India's GDP per capita, grew from about 200 U.S. dollars (USD) to 3,000 USD in 2008, which is now three times that of India. Some have equated this fantastic growth as a miracle.

Urbanization, considered an important symbol of the country's transformation from a backward agricultural society to a modern society, improved from less than 18% at the beginning of the reform and opening up to 45% in 2008. China has initially stepped from the agricultural society to industrial and urban society and entered the medium term of urbanization.

In the past three decades, industrialization of China has been rapidly and favorably promoted, thus ushering its entrance into advanced industrialization period. Along with a stronger industrial system, the advancement of the heavy and chemical industrial foundation has seen constant progress in terms of equipment, technology, and scale. Household electrical appliances, mobile phones, computers, and the auto industry and its facilities have met the increasing demands of 1.3 billion people and reached world levels, including the foreign-capital enterprises in China. The industrial structure has been adjusted, optimized, and upgraded.

A modern traffic system has also taken shape in China. The exceptional development of high-speed railways, light rails, classed highways, city subways, formation of power, oil, and gas transmission networks, and the establishment and upgradation of high-speed information network have laid the foundation for the completion of the first phase of modernization and further development of the second stage of modernization.

In the past 30 years, China has also made every effort to improve science and technology, reducing the gap with developed countries from about 50 years to 10 years. Though China may have been several decades, or even a hundred years, behind the level of developed countries at the beginning of reform and opening up, China has reduced this gap with breakthroughs in many fields, including mobile communications, high-speed railway technologies, mainframe computers, new energies, large aircraft manufacture, large hydroelectric power and gas generators, and seed-breeding of grains. China has also reached or even surpassed international levels in many aspects.

Thirty years ago, foreign scholars, politicians, and public opinion generally believed that CPC could not solve the food shortage problem of China's population, totaling about 1 billion people. However, in those 30 years, CPC did not only solve the food shortage problem, but also significantly improved people's living standards. The Engel coefficient of urban residents has dropped from 57.5% in 1978 to 37.9% in 2008, while the coefficient of rural residents has declined from 67.7% in 1978 to 43% in 2008. Dramatic changes have occurred in the living standards of rural and urban residents. Laborious household chores that included lighting kerosene lamps, chopping wood, lighting the stove, making noodles and washing clothes by hand, carrying water, and sewing clothes have essentially disappeared. Family properties and appliances, such as watches, bicycles, radios, and sewing machines, have been replaced by mobile phones, televisions, electric washing machines, refrigerators and cars. In addition, electricity, water, gas, and internet networks have helped to facilitate and ease people's lives. The absolute poverty population dropped from 250 million at the beginning of reform and opening up to about 20 million today.

Since the 1970s, China has essentially completed the transformation from a planned economy to a socialist market economy and established a society full of enthusiasm for future development. The market adjusts the commodity supply and demand and price of more than 99% of commodities, and the market systems for commodities, capitals, technologies, real estate, and foreign exchange have been formed. China also reformed the ownership structure of "(concerning the people's commune) large in size and collective in nature" to a pattern of fair competition and common development of different ownerships. Currently, more than 75% of labor in China is working in private enterprises, limited liability companies, joint-stock companies, and foreign-owned enterprises. Despite some new problems in the relations between local and central authorities, the fiscal and tax systems have been adjusted, which enabled both central control and enthusiasm for local development. The competitive economic development among provinces has become an important driving force for the economic adjustment and growth of China.

Regarding foreign relations, China, once a closed society, has now opened itself to the world. China has refocused its attention from the development strategy of import substitution to export orientation and export substitution, established an overall opening of multi-level and wide range (including allowing foreign investment, establishing special zones and opening coastal, frontier and inland areas), commenced bilateral, multilateral, and economic zone cooperation for common development, started the exchange rate control, and finally formed the exchange rate market under the administration. In these 30 years, China has obtained enormous benefits from opening up to the world by introducing foreign investment and technologies, learning advanced foreign enterprise systems and management and exportation of products created by domestic surplus labor force. The current economic and political status of China in the world is drastically different from that in 1978.

In the past 30 years, China has welcomed the return of Hong Kong and Macao as special administrative regions and maintained favorable development in the economic and cultural relations with Taiwan. Despite some financial hardships after their return, the economic development of Hong Kong and Macao have not been restricted, but have seen more dynamic growth based on the integration with mainland China's economy. Mainland China and Taiwan have established trade and travel relations, and conducted cultural exchanges, and thus further strengthened the economic, cultural, and national ties between both sides of the straits. People from both sides are increasingly conscious of them belonging to the Chinese nation and family.

In the past three decades, especially the first 10 years of the 21st century, CPC has attached great importance to public service and people's livelihood and exerted efforts to establish a society with a modern security and welfare system, in addition to economic development. The finance expenditure, which had mainly concentrated on basic construction, has expanded to include public service and social security, including education, health care, agriculture, ecological environment, and urban traffic. China's recent achievements include (1) establishing the minimum living system for low-income urban and rural residents thus eliminating the existence of jobless urban families; (2) exempting the agricultural tax and tax on native products of agriculture and forestry and providing subsidies to peasants for planting crops and purchasing agricultural implements and high-quality seeds; (3) establishing new cooperative medical care system in rural areas and pilot endowment security system in some rural areas; (4) expanding the social security network by building a medical security system and endowment security system for preschool children, students, and unemployed people in urban areas; (5) strengthening the transfer payment in old liberated areas, areas of ethnic minorities, outlying areas and other less-developed areas and applying special policies to facilitate the development of these places; and (6) controlling the housing prices in cities and establishing the housing guarantee system to solve the housing problem of middle and low-income residents. Though the social security and welfare system is still weak, incomplete in coverage and cannot meet the requirements of all urban and rural residents, the party and the government have begun to improve the situation and are insisting on establishing a modern country of vigor in creativity, work, public service, and social security for all people in the next ten years.

China has made significant achievements in recent history, especially when compared to other developing countries and as well as to previous periods in Chinese history. Despite the large population, new issues, and historical problems, the painstaking efforts of Chinese Communists and Chinese people in the 30 years since the reform and opening up in achieving modernization cannot be denied.

2. Introduction: Why do we put Forward and Discuss Chinese Dreams?

About 300 years ago, Puritan immigrants from England traveled across the Atlantic Ocean on the *Mayflower* to Plymouth, Massachusetts in search of religious and political freedom. This was the birth of the "American Dream". The "American Dream" encompassed a belief that all people had equal opportunities to achieve their dreams. The "American Dream" refers to an ideal where everyone can achieve a better life through hard work, and obtain prosperity based on their own work, courage, creativity, and determination, and not merely by depending upon other people or belonging to a particular social class. According to my interpretation of the "America Dream," it represents the spirit of economic success and entrepreneurship. Many European immigrants settled in America in search of their "American dream." (Baidu Baike, 2010).

Therefore, what is the source of Chinese dreams? Does the Chinese spirit drive the "Chinese Dream?" We believe there is, and there must be.

Since the 20th century, with the spirit of "survival of the fittest" and the underlying perpetual need for self-improvement, the Chinese tirelessly fought against foreign forces and finally founded the People's Republic of China in 1949. In the late 1970s when China's economic development was far behind many other countries, the

Chinese initiated actions toward reform and opening up. They concentrated on the construction based on their spirit of self-improvement, overcame the constraints of a large population, lack of resources, low productivity, and increased GDP per capita from 200 USD in 1978 to 4,100 USD in 2010 through the three-decade efforts, raising from the global bottom two or three to medium–lower level. In the last century, the Chinese have depended on their Chinese spirit in state's foundation and construction. Though the Chinese spirit has not been clearly defined, it is rooted in several hundred millions people's dream of independence, state's foundation, economic prosperity, and greater power.

After 30 years, since the reform and opening up and the first decade of the 21st century, China seeks to adjust the direction and explore a new road of social harmony and scientific development according to the new world pattern, situation, and problems in the future.

It is important to note that China needs to establish its own path for future development. A common perspective shall be formed among the party, government, and citizens on the methods to follow China's own way and the necessity for structure adjustment and reform. A strong, united Chinese spirit in the 21st century is necessary for a nation with such a huge population to achieve greatness. The Chinese spirit is rooted in the hopes and dreams of the Chinese people, a population that accounts for 1/6–1/5 of the world's population. A nation without desire and hope for the future will definitely lose its ambition and spirit. Then, will the spiritual source be able to sustain Chinese motivation to endure such efforts in the 21st century? I believe the Chinese dream is rooted in people's obligations, trust, hopes and dreams for themselves, families, society and country in the future, and the pursuit for the vision and ideal of China.

3. The Dream of Several Hundred Million Chinese: Becoming a Townsman

As China is undergoing the transformation from a rural and agricultural society to an urban and industrial society, hundreds of millions of peasants are working to realize their dreams. The older rural population is sacrificing all they have to enable school education for their children so they can move away from the rural areas, while the younger population aspires to becoming townsmen and live in urban areas. Urban families also make sacrifices for their children to attend a university, pursue master's degree, and even send their children to study abroad. Although their hopes and dreams may differ, both the old and young generations, hope and struggle to achieve success in economic and social status.

3.1. *Countrymen's dream of becoming townsmen*

Hundreds of millions of countrymen are dreaming of becoming townsmen. Urbanization is irresistible, according to the economic and social development process. Throughout history, the development of human civilization is actually the transition from a rural and agricultural economy to an urban economy. What are the dreams of the 200 million peasant-workers and four to 500 million peasants who are moving to cities? They dream of getting a job of rational income in the city or starting their own businesses; renting a proper home and eventually, after several years of hard work, buying a house in the city for their families; enabling themselves and their children to obtain education, the same as other urban residents; enjoying the same medical care and endowment system; not being despised by urban residents and the system; and sharing equal rights with other urban citizens. Chinese peasants, as many as 800 million, are dreaming of becoming townsmen in the next two or three decades. This has never been seen in the world history at such a large scale, with such strong flexibility and momentum.

3.2. *Dream of new villagers of peasants remaining in rural areas*

In many rural families, the middle-aged and elderly population make many sacrifices to send their children to school, who will most likely go to cities after obtaining their education. They sacrifice their own hopes so that their children may become townsmen and live a better life. But what about the dreams of the middle and old-aged? They also wish to do farming, forestry, husbandry and fishing which will earn them a satisfactory income to enroll themselves into medical care and endowment system, enjoy public facilities and services such as basic transportation, gas supply, water supply, power supply, communications, medical care, education, refuse and sewage disposal, communicate often with their children living in cities, and reunite with their children every year, as per their customs. The middle-aged and elderly would hope that they live a better life when they become older, enjoy a fair and just life, maintain good relations with their neighbors, live in a harmonious village, and inherit the cultural heritages. This is the dream of hundreds of millions of peasants remaining in the rural areas. The number may reduce from the current 700 million to 200–300 million in the future. I will name this as "the dream of new villagers under modernization". Though fewer and fewer people are still holding on to this dream, the large scale, strong requirement, huge demand, high cost and heavy burden of the dream can hardly be seen in any other part of the world.

4. The Dream of Good Living and Work

As calculated by 30% of the registered household population, China has 400 million native urban residents. Since more and more people who transfer to cities establish permanent residences, the population of urban residents may reach 80% (1.2 billion) in 2040. This ideal, which is to increase urban residents from 400 million to as many as 1.2 billion, is rarely seen in other developing nations.

Although the dreams of 400 million to 1.2 billion individual urban residents vary, their dreams are the driving forces for the economic and social development in the next three decades. It then raises the question — what hopes and dreams do they have?

4.1. *Dream of housing: comfortable, proper, and self-owned*

The most important dream of every Chinese urban family is to own a comfortable and proper house in the city. Many people have realized this dream, but a significant number of urban residents are still living in small houses under poor conditions. These urban residents are dreaming of ideal houses. Within several years of employment, many students that graduate from junior colleges and special secondary schools; or demobilized or transferred soldiers, live in poor conditions and struggle to make ends meet, and these numbers continue to increase. They strive to fulfill their dreams of buying their own houses by saving as much as they can, even if it is only a few dollars. For those living in small rented rooms, renting houses in villages within cities, or suburban peasant families working several hours every day, buying a house may be their first and ultimate dream. Eighty five percent of urban citizens cannot buy their own houses, but can only rent houses from 15% of urban residents. This is not in accordance with the cultural traditions of China or the socialist value of common prosperity. It is definitely not the Chinese dream.

Currently, a huge gap exists between supply and demand of urban housing. The area of urban residence in 2010 equaled 11.2 billion m², so the area of urban residence per capita is only 17.5 m² if the urban population reaches 640 million by the end of 2010. It is estimated that 200 million are peasants migrating to cities. Based on the standard of 20 m² for every peasant and 30 m² for every urban resident, a total area of 17.2 billion m² is needed. According to the average level, the gap in residence demand reaches 6 billion m² without regard to a family with several houses or one large house.

Unbalanced distribution of housing property. According to my small-scale investigation and assessment, the distribution of housing property is as follows: the 200 million peasants migrating to cities and 75.2 million urban residents, accounting for 43% of the overall urban population, do not own, but rent houses in the cities. Based on a conservative estimate, among the 640 million urban residents, 1% has an average residence area of 130 m², reaching a total of 832 million m²; 2% has an average residence area of 65 m², reaching a total of 832 million m²; 5% has an average residence area of 40 m², reaching a total of 1.28 billion m²; 25% has an average residence area of 30 m², reaching a total of 4.8 billion m²; 20% has an average residence area of 20 m², reaching a total of 2.56 billion m²; and 10% has an average residence area of 14 m², reaching a total of 896 million m². The 33% of urban residents who own an average area of residence (above 30 m²) possess 69.14% of urban housing properties. This is only my personal estimate based on the current materials of different communities in various regions. An overall census on housing shall be conducted to obtain a more comprehensive idea on the urban residence area among different categories of residents.

As previously stated, the gap, as big as 6 billion m², is unique to other countries in the world. The gap may even be as much as 10 billion if the uneven distribution is taken into consideration. Against the distinctive and severe reality, how can China fill in such a gap in few years based on the related elements including the ideal, systems, financial resources, housing prices, and land resources? Will the dream of meeting the housing needs of 1.2 billion urban residents be realized in the next three decades?

Can the government satisfy the enormous demand for residence area by only building low-rent housing or economically affordable housing? The government should figure out a method that is low in cost, stimulates people's enthusiasm, and avoid bankruptcy of the government. The housing of the high-income group shall be solved fully by the market adjustment. The market shall mainly solve housing for the moderate-income group, while the government shall control the ratio of housing price to income. The government shall ensure that the growth of housing price would be slower than the growth of income, meanwhile encouraging the circulation of residential, forest, and arable lands, so as to promote the property income of rural residents as part of the payment capacity for houses in the cities. Housing for the low-income group shall be solved by affordable, government-supplied houses. I believe that, through modernization based on well-thought processes, rational systems, and mechanisms, solving the housing problem will not be difficult.

4.2. *Dream of employment and entrepreneurship: living and success*

Jobs are the main source of income and livelihood for most urban residents, while entrepreneurship is the road to wealth and success for city people, especially young and middle-aged. A number of city people, especially university graduates and transferred former soldiers, are looking forward to a stable job of favorable income, enough to obtain social security. Other city people want to invest in a factory, run a company, or register a clinic. Some others aspire to run their own businesses, take investment risks, open the market, and accomplish their own success. There are also others who want to become investors, enterprise partners, professional managers, lawyers, doctors, civil servants, researchers, engineers, scientists, professors, etc., to realize their ideals through life-long learning, practices, and great efforts in their own fields. This is the dream of about 1.2 billion Chinese residents who would be living in urban areas in the next three decades. Their unremitting and endless pursuit of these dreams will create social wealth, satisfy their own living needs, help more and more people to live a better life, and enable the country to prosper and garner more power internationally.

During modernization, Europe was faced with severe overpopulation due to the bankruptcy of agriculture and the rise of organic composition of industrial capital. However, Europe transferred their people by invading other countries and exploring the new continent of America. Most of them who stayed or got transferred to colonial and semi-colonial countries in Asia, Africa, and Latin America, had realized their dreams of employment and entrepreneurship. The "American Dream", refers to the dream of employment and entrepreneurship of those who transferred from Europe to North America.

The Chinese dream of employment and entrepreneurship features unique characteristics. First, in terms of the trends in labor supply in China, the current labor supply in the agricultural industry is very serious, owing to the fewer cultivated land per capita, faster agricultural modernization, and low labor productivity, so middle-aged and young labors, especially the new population of labor forces in rural areas every year, constantly fly away to the cities. In the following five years, the annual flow will reach approximately 10 million. Second, graduates from high schools, junior colleges, and special secondary schools, demobilized soldiers, incoming labor forces, and existing labor forces seeking new jobs owing to enterprise bankruptcy and industrial structure adjustments, would supply another 10 million labor force. In the next three decades, the labor forces demanding employment will increase from the current 300 million to 700 million. The annual increase of labor forces will reach 13.3 million in cities.

In terms of the structure of demand on labor forces, first, the scale of Chinese civil servants and public institutions is already too big to provide additional employment, owing to the heavy tax expenses. Second, the industry is weaker in absorbing labor forces due to the rising income wage levels, standardization of social security, endowment and medical care guarantee, increase in labor cost, rise of the organic composition of capital, and even some declining industries may extrude labor forces in the future. Third, rural areas and agricultural industry cannot receive labor forces, but extrude labor forces to cities every year. Fourth, China's third industry cannot absorb as many labor forces as other similar countries since China's urbanization is backward and service industry remains prejudiced both in the previous and current systems. Fifth, the local government is more willing to develop large and extra large enterprises that comparatively absorb less labor forces for the sake of GDP and taxation, but ignores the development of small and micro enterprises that can receive a large amount of labor forces. In addition, small businesses run against the urban management and construction, which objectively inhibit and prejudice small and micro enterprises, and suffer from the registration permission, tax burden, various inspections, fines and difficulties in financing, which systematically deprive them from having smooth development in China.

Unlike the industrialization process of Euro–American countries, it is impossible for China to export a large population, so China is destined to solve the demands of employment and entrepreneurship in its own land. This means that the Chinese have to realize their dreams of employment and entrepreneurship at home. Under the uncommon excessive supply of labor and extremely unfavorable development mode and system environment for employment and entrepreneurship, will hundreds of millions of urban citizens find jobs? Will 1.2 billion Chinese urban residents live an affluent life through employment and entrepreneurship and succeed in their future careers? Can they realize their dreams of employment and entrepreneurship?

Nations with greater population density such as Japan, Korea, and Taiwan in East Asia have successfully solved the employment of the surplus labor forces in rural areas in their transformation of the dual structure and maintained very low, long-term unemployment rate. It is crucial that they adopt labor intensive industry-oriented industrialization strategy that can absorb large amounts of employments in their foreign relations, apply small enterprise-based measures that can also receive numerous labor forces in terms of the enterprise scale, and enact policies to facilitate the service industry regarding the industrial structure. China shall learn from their methods to solve the surplus labor forces in their urbanization. China is fully capable of realizing full employment by developing middle and small sized enterprises and service industries, without following European countries' way of solving surplus population and labor forces in industrialization, i.e., to invade other countries, or exporting a large amount of the population and labor forces to the outside world.

5. Dream of Social Security

Once people are satisfied with the current living standards, they would seek higher standards of living. The dream of safety and harmony of peasants remaining in rural areas has been previously discussed, while the dream of safety and harmony of urban residents in a more complicated environment will be discussed going forward.

From the late 20th century to the early 21st century, an integral part of the dream of Chinese people in the fierce transformation of economic and social dual structure is to ensure the safety of their lives in case of aging and accidents. This applies to the old, unemployed, sick and disabled group; peasants moving to cities; and healthy urban residents of regular employment who are preparing for the possibility of unemployment, retirement, sickness, and accidental injuries.

Since there has been no social security system in Chinese history, only the family's land and their son could guarantee a rural family's future and defend them from unexpected life occurrences. In the three decades after liberation, China planned to prevent the risks of the old, sick, and disabled through planned economy and public ownership. Meanwhile, China emphasized production and expanded reproduction by applying the social risk funds and the pension for workers in factories, machines, and streets. It was only since the 1990s that China started to learn and establish the modern social security system for both urban and rural areas.

What are the dreams of the urban residents that live comfortably? The basic standards of those living comfortably refers to giving support to the old, providing medical care to the sick, supplying aid to the disabled, and giving relief to the poor. Modern city life differs from a traditional rural life with regard to the structure of the family, financial accumulation, working mode, and marketing degree of commodities and service. Therefore, a modern aid and security mode for the old, sick, unemployed, disabled, and poor shall be built in accordance with the current family structure, life mode, and market economy. This means to withdraw money from individual income and working unit as the security capital when they are healthy and able to work, establish a personal account and mutual assistance fund, and distribute capital for the sick, the old, and anyone needing help. Modern urban residents' dream of living safely means to protect the old and vulnerable from worrying about their life in the fierce competition of the market economy. China should transform into a economy that offers modern social security network, where the young and adults can be self-reliant, and the sick, disabled, old, unemployed, and helpless depend on state and society.

As estimated by professionals, the conservative capital demands for social security shall be 10 trillion RMB (without considering unemployment security), compared to the 2.5 trillion RMB accumulated by various social security funds according to the audit administration at the end of 2008. It was pointed out that "the main cause for the capital insufficiency lies in the low wages and high employment, since the company is the main body for pension." According to the author, the problem is rooted in low wage, no social security, non-people-oriented spirit, and appropriating the investment on the reproduction of labors to the expanded reproduction of fixed assets. Under the system of combining social mutual assistance and personal account, local social security departments apply the capital in the personal account in current payment, leaving the personal account useless (Wen Rujun, 2010). The potential capital gap is estimated to exceed 30 trillion RMB if the new debts incurred by appropriating the personal account, unpaid old "implicit debts" and the increasing coverage and level of the urban and rural social security are taken into consideration.

The dream of secured living of 1.3–1.55 billion people in Chinese rural and urban areas can be accomplished by establishing a social security network covering both rural and urban areas. How will China establish this network?

Without a doubt, social security shall be expanded to all the citizens, but the level of social security shall be confirmed according to the capability of the state. The author believes that the gap of social security capital will be gradually closed and the level of social security will be improved, along with the expanding Chinese economic scale, increasing financial income, and socialization of the state-owned assets.

6. Dream of Public Service

As society is transforming from a self-sufficient rural society and agricultural economy to an open urban society and modern economy, more and more demands and labor services of families and individuals are socialized, with non-public goods provided by the market, including household electrical appliances, cars, and public and quasi-public goods provided by the government, such as street lamps, roads, water supply and sewage, police, gas, and education. According to the theory of institutional economics, every family shall transfer part of its right and submit a certain amount of taxes to the government for institutions because affairs related to the government, army, diplomacy, administration of justice, police, education, medical care, traffic, water supply, and sewage will be mainly solved by these institutions. Therefore, the large-scale and professional public service can reduce the transaction cost to meet the living and development demands. The individual costs of hiring a teacher for tuitions, a doctor to treat family, a lawyer to settle disputes are huge, so all families gather together to select public institutions, establish a government, build schools, fund the police office, court and hospitals and build roads with the taxpayers' money. This is the economic cause for the formation of the state, government, and other public institutions. Everyone is living under the basic premise of public service and relations in the modern, market, industrialized and urban society, including Chinese urban residents.

What, then, are the dreams of both native and new urban residents on public service and social security?

The first is the dream of pursuing good education. Throughout Chinese history, most families would hope for good education, employment, family, prosperity honor for their children. This desire among Chinese has lasted through the present times, despite a few changes. Every family, in both rural and urban areas, hope that their children would complete their formal education and obtain a bachelor, master or doctorate's degree. Thirty years ago, they may have wished for their children to work as a worker, soldier, driver, or for the government. A few decades later, they wished their children to become a doctor, engineer, an artist, etc. Later in the history, they may have preferred their child to become a scientist, bank staff, security company worker, etc. Currently, they hope their children would become a civil servant or lawyer, or work in a government-sponsored institution, large or monopolistic state-owned enterprises, or finance institutions. The ideal career changed with the time, but generally, every family and older generation hoped their children would find a job that paid well, gave them a good social status and respect, and gave them a better life. Many rural families or urban low-income families are burdened with debts incurred when sending their children to university. These are the sacrifices that are made to achieve the dream of pursuing a good education in China. The dream leads to great demands on public service, which requires the government to build more schools, provide favorable education, expand the compulsory education to cover from kindergarten to high school including higher and secondary education for agricultural, standard and military schools, lower the tuition for non-compulsory education and provide each family with fair educational resources. Chinese people also wish the government to provide the following educational service: aid in both selecting a school and for the fee in selecting a school, help children from non-registered households in Beijing that are unable to take the college entrance examination, provide aid for the kindergarten attendance fee, and help with expensive tuitions.

The second is the dream of convenient and inexpensive medical care. Before the foundation of the People's Republic of China, the poor medical conditions in both rural and urban areas led to high disease mortality, especially high infant mortality, and short or average life span. Many people could not afford medical care so they turned to "folk prescriptions" from folk doctors. After liberation, the public health and medical care system was gradually established and most urban and rural residents received service from the urban medical care system and rural cooperative medical care system. Despite the low level, the medical care service at that time was featured with large coverage and low cost. Since the reform and opening up, the traditional medical care service system under the state-owned and planned economy disappeared and the public medical care service system under the market economy has not been appropriately built. Even the over-market reform was applied to the medical care service upon the administrative monopoly of medical care resources, so many villages lacked a quality medical care service institute and many peasants had to travel to cities to see a doctor. The medical care institutes in cities were also very crowded, so it was more and more inconvenient and expensive for urban residents to see a doctor. A considerable number of rural and urban residents endured depletion in their quality of life and livelihood because of illness. Some even died or became disabled due to sham doctors and medicines in some areas.

In addition, the government should also invest or direct the construction of more medium- or large-scaled and community hospitals, increase medical care resource supplies, relieve the current difficulties of seeing a doctor in a timely manner, control the price of medical care and medicines, regulate medical care and medicines, eliminate the practice of fake doctors and medicines, prevent people from paying a high cost to cure common diseases due to misinformation from the medicine supplier, and prevent death due to fake doctors and medicines. Generally, people's dream of obtaining convenient and inexpensive medical care refers to being able to go to see a doctor in a timely manner with safe treatment and low cost, which is also people's hope for the government with regards to the public service of medical care.

The third is the dream of convenient travel and communications. In rural society and agricultural economy, people often did not need to travel far for work and communication, owing to the closeness of a self-sufficient economy and society. Modernization of agriculture, industrialization, and urbanization significantly changes the distance and time traveled for work, shopping, and communication. It has become an integral part of residents' lives whether or not travel between the residence and working place is convenient, and whether it is convenient and rapid to go to school, shopping, or to see doctor. A car for each family is an important part of the American dream. Unlike America, before the reform and opening up of China, it was an impossible fantasy for each Chinese family to own a car. However, the Chinese dream of owning a car has been brought to fruition. More and more cars are owned by ordinary families.

Since the reform and opening up, especially in the 1990s, the rapid development of city roads, common roads, and highways in China brought increasingly favorable conditions for the realization of the dream of "car travel". However, America has a relatively lower population than China, but is slightly larger in land area, so its resources per capita are much greater than China and its average population of cities is much less than China. Americans could realize their dream of car ownership under their specific circumstances, but how about China? Another 200 million mu (Chinese unit, about 13.3 million ha), or even more, of cultivated lands will be utilized to build common roads and highways, if every family has two to three cars in addition to the non-household cars for the party, government, government-sponsored institutes, associations, and enterprises. Sixty percent of newly discovered petroleum in the world needs to be distributed to China. Moreover, the exhaust gas of cars will further pollute the cities, causing them to become darker and cloudier. In some countries with a large, dense population, driving a car may be considered a slower mode of transportation than walking. The roads will become severely congested, and it will take as long as two hours, on average, to travel from home to work.

Therefore, to replicate the American-dream of owning a car will definitely be restrained in China by its large population, comparatively small space, and insufficient resources. Local governments will provide a diversified public transportation system in order to lower the cost, enable more convenient modes of travel, and significantly shorten the traveling time in order to save it for the family and recreation.

In the 1950s, Chinese people described that their definition of an ideal communist society is the provider of "electricity, light, and telephone for every family". At present, along with the productivity and progress in science and technological development, China has realized electrization and entered the "information technology age" by applying wireless communication technology, computer network, and TV rebroadcasting and receiving in large scale. The previously fixed telephones have been mostly replaced by wireless mobile telephones; and print media, audio communication, networks, and TV are widely utilized. Currently, everyone, old or young, male or female, has a mobile phone regardless of their jobs, while computers are popular in cities and TVs have become an integral part of people's lives. Even convenient communications, networks, and video information have been realized that are beyond the imagination. People are looking forward to lower expenses on mobile communications, networks, and TVs.

7. Dream of a Beautiful Ecological Environment and Family Safety

In the past, Chinese people imagined modernization as steel works and tall chimneys, steam engines, fertilizer and farm chemicals, reclamation of grassland, wetlands, lakes and forests, fertile land, and cities of reinforced concrete and matchbox-type houses. During the industrialization, petro agriculture, industrialized production, and living goods, such as chemicals, caused great damage to the ecology and environment, and threatened people's safe living. Furthermore, urban population, unemployment, increasing social conflicts and the development of motor vehicles also contributes to the risks posed to individual, family property, and personal safety.

Information convenience has been realized beyond people's imagination and the traditional dream of modernization, which will be realized in two or three decades, brings about another dream: to maintain a beautiful and safe ecological environment for our living and workplace, and a social environment of personal and property safety, along with the promotion of modernization.

The first is the dream of safe drinking water and food. People are dreaming of unpolluted water, no harmful substances in mineral spring water, no chemicals in drinks, no fake wine, no harmful substances, such as melamine in milk, no whitening agent in noodles, no residue of pesticides or fertilizers, and no additives in grains and vegetables. Safe water and food is an integral part of urban residents' dream of safe living.

The second is the dream of clean and oxygen-enriched air. People are dreaming of a clear, blue sky, white clouds, little dust or sand in the air, industrial exhaust gas meeting the discharge standard, industries exhaust gas and dust far from the cities, the use of advanced technologies to significantly decrease emission, well-developed public traffic, reducing tail gas of cars so that it meets standards, initiation of a smoke-free environment, decreasing the number of smokers, reducing second-hand smoke, establishment of clean air, high visibility, high vegetation cover rate, rich oxygen in air and decreasing the occurrence rate of consumption.

The third is the dream of a quiet and calm environment. In a traditional agricultural society, people lived in villages, woke at sunrise, arrived home at sunset, and utilized animal labor to cultivate their lands and to carry things, so people were always living and working in a quiet environment, both day and night. However, the urban and industrial society is filled with typical city sounds: automobile engines, sounds from construction areas and factories, police cars, fire engines, ambulances and service car alarms, and the voices of people talking on the streets. Noise pollution continues during the night. People dream of living in a city with less noise, more trees, quieter streets, friendly neighborhood and work places.

The fourth is the dream of a healthy and clean environment in the communities, streets, and workplaces. In a traditional agricultural society, soils, woods, and potteries are mainly applied in ecological fertilizer and irrigation, so the environment might not be clean. However, less degradable paper, glass, plastics, metal, chemical fibers, and mineral construction materials in an urban and industrialized society also greatly pollute the environment. People living and working in cities are dreaming of cleaner streets, communities, and workplaces; underground sewage discharge and constructive treatment; industrial and domestic sewage that does not pollute crops; clean odorless water and lakes that shall be kept at Grade I; timely clearance and transportation of industrial and domestic garbage; refuse dumps far from communities for close treatment and sealed cleaning vehicles that securely transport garbage and prevent the garbage from being sprinkled on streets. This is urban residents' dream of clean environment in the living and work areas.

The fifth is the dream of garden, marsh, and landscape. People in cities are surrounded by steel, cement, glass, asphalt roads and other constructions, but they are looking toward a future with forests, rivers, lakes, and marshes in cities. They dream of trees, grasslands, mountains, water, birds, insects, and animals, and enjoying beautiful flowers and plants throughout the year. They are looking forward to the day when they can enjoy gardens, marshes, and woods after their working hours. This is the dream of all modern urban residents — to live in a city of favorable ecology.

The sixth is the dream of a secured family and work life. In many villages, especially in traditional Chinese agricultural society, people did not take anything left by others on the road, left doors open, respected the elderly, loved the young, and lived in harmony with one another. The urban and industrial society has changed all these things and made living less safe. Therefore, people living in cities hope that the adults and children return home safely without traffic or accidents; sustain no personal injuries when students travel to and from school; children and adults will not be abducted, robbed, or extorted; homes will not burn down or be vandalized. People also hope housing quality would meet the standard for secure houses. The old-aged and children wish not to be cheated by illegal businesses, find help when they run into danger, and the party involved in the accident and his relatives, especially the judges, shall not burden the responsibility and fees of medical care onto the aide. This is urban residents' dream of living and working safely in cities.

8. Dream of a Spiritual Life

In addition to the material dreams, the Chinese also dream of having a colorful spiritual life. Chinese residents have varying dreams of spiritual life, owing to the differences in living environment, educational background, regions and nations, as long as they all belong to one Chinese nation, they pursue the same dreams of a spiritual life.

The civilization in China has been multi-national, multi-regional, multi-periodical, and extremely diversified, owing to its long history and vast territory. Chinese civilization was developed from the farming culture in the central plains, later amalgamated with the hunting and nomadic culture in the North and West and thus sowing the seeds of the formation of Chinese culture. The culture is also based on the South–North exchanges and East–West integration; and developed from numerous schools of thinkers, in particular, by Confucius, Mencius's and Marxist's theories, that led to the coexistence and integration of Taoism, Buddhism, Islam, Christianity and Catholicism. Chinese culture was also impacted by the ideology formed at the foundation of the state. Later, the liberation of ideology and introduction of western values in the late 1970s impacted upon the traditional cultural values and led to the rise of Sinology. Sinology refers to the traditional collective idea and culture of state-owned system, planned economy and equitable distribution, encouragement to individual and private enterprises after the reform and opening up that enables market competition and survival of the fittest. Chinese culture has come a long way starting initially from the large family culture of four generations under the same roof to the rise of smaller families — single child and single person sort of family types. In the past, present, and future, the Chinese civilization and spirit has seen unprecedented changes along with the development in communications, lifestyle and human communication expansion. Distinguished from many other countries, Chinese culture and spirit features diversity, variability, and integration, and advances with the times.

What is the present state of Chinese culture and spirit, i.e., the cultural and value systems of modern Chinese people, and the dream of a spiritual life in the global modern civilization pattern? To live up to the dream of a spiritual life, the Chinese people hope to live with dignity, achieve success in their chosen careers, and gain respect from their families, relatives and community; they also hope to be able to sustain social relations and go beyond the constraints in rational and legal behaviors; ensure fair opportunities and just distribution of property; give full play to individual innovation and creation under flexible conditions for science and innovation. It is hoped that spiritualism would also be achieved when Chinese encourage equality among all people, and nurture relationships irrespective of the religious beliefs of others in the community. Helping others and be helped by others and believing in a fair and just administration, judicature, media, and spreading kindness and restraining evil thoughts are other characteristics of spirituality. By inheriting the essence of Chinese culture, including thriftiness, hard work, respect toward the elderly and care toward the younger people, one can display loyalty to country and people. One can also earn from advance foreign cultures on how to form a modern and advance Chinese culture and civilization; and live and work in a harmonious society with mutual aid, understanding, and containment between government and civilians, and an overall peaceful environment. In summary, Chinese people's dream of a spiritual life in the 21st century is to live and work in a free, democratic, fair, just, harmonious society of mutual aid, where they can freely explore their talents, under the leadership of the CPC.

China shall correctly deal with the relations between the Chinese traditional culture and modern civilization, and between the Chinese culture and foreign cultures, and inherit and develop fine cultural traditions. According to most academic circles, traditional Chinese culture refers to the culture of lengthy history, extensive knowledge, profound scholarship, and fine traditions and features unique national characters created by Chinese nations and their ancestors residing in China, intrinsically inherited and developed by the Chinese nation from age to age. Who are the Chinese? The Chinese refer to the human group with historical origins in various regions of China, sharing common characteristics in their communications, languages, ideology, habits, social customs, and behavioral norms who have inherited thousands of years of lasting traditional culture and civilization, and includes members of the Chinese nation formed in the territory of China. The Chinese must inherit the Chinese culture, which differentiates them from Russians, Japanese, British, Germans, French, and Indians.

Traditions followed by our ancestors have shortcomings and shall advance with modernization. However, should the Chinese completely abandon their traditional culture by adopting a modern spiritual life under the influence of foreign lifestyle, cultures, religions, and logic? I believe the answer will be, and should be, No. Otherwise, the Chinese will lose the characteristics that make them inherently Chinese. Therefore, the Chinese shall pursue the dream of attaining a modern spiritual life by learning the best practices from the advance foreign culture and civilization, simultaneously holding on to the best of their own fine culture and civilization from their ancestors.

Traditional Chinese culture pursues benevolent interpersonal concordance of common benefits, emphasizes respect and care for others, advocates mutual consideration and aid of people, and aims to establish a harmonious and compassionate atmosphere. Chinese culture concentrates on "harmony without sameness" and stresses social harmony. It attaches importance to the respect and love between different generations and cultivates harmony within the family and interpersonal relations. It also puts forth the idea of "prized peacefulness," pursues harmonious interpersonal relations, coordinated mind and body harmony between man and nature, upholds the "humanity, justice, propriety, wisdom and faith, as well as temperate, kind, courteous, restrained and magnanimous dignities". and looks forward to the ideal society of "harmonious relations, equal status for everyone and public spirit".

The traditional Chinese culture also includes honesty, morality, thriftiness, and spiritual retreat. Honesty is practiced in everyday conduct and in formal exchanges, i.e., treating people and handling matters sincerely, acting truthfully, and keeping promises. Different than the "theory of original sin" of the West, Chinese traditional culture is based on "good human nature". The honesty in Chinese culture is a kind of ethnic, the root of human nature, while the credibility in the West is a "contract" ethic. China shall persist in the basis of "good human nature," meanwhile, learning from the western culture of the improvisation of market economy where it constrains people to keep promises by law and contract.

The tradition of hard work and thriftiness is inherent in Chinese culture. Their ancestors left them with a poem that reads, "Every grain is the product of toiling". In terms of the financial crisis in Europe and America, Chinese residents and government prefer to manage money by deposit, compared to the European and American residents and government managing money by borrowing. The Chinese lifestyle of deposit, accumulation, and investment contributes to the rapid growth of the Chinese economy over the past 30 years. More importantly, owing to its large population and depleting resources, China should develop the tradition of frugality as prescribed in Chinese culture, pursue a simple and comfortable lifestyle, and establish a conservation-minded society.

In traditional Chinese culture, Confucianism summarized a complete system of moral cultivation and confirmed its essential importance. It also directed the moral cultivation and provided many specific and practical methods, such as determination, learning, self-control, self-examination, practicing, self-restraint in privacy, and following discipline, in order to build noble and moral people.

Traditional Chinese culture focuses on persistence, toughness, and ceaseless struggle, as well as the broad-mindedness. A Chinese proverb goes, "As heaven's movement is ever vigorous, so must a gentleman ceaselessly strive along". It is the persistent struggle of many families and individuals, despite frustrations and setbacks along the way that contribute to the development of the Chinese nation in its 5,000 year history. The Chinese shall accept others with joy, treats their lives kindly, focus on the positive, find beauty in life, discover beneficial things for humanity and themselves, maintain friendly relationships with others, seek common grounds, accept existing differences, and pursue common development.[1]

When the Chinese advance with modern civilization and learn foreign cultures, they shall also inherit the best practices from other cultural traditions, including language, ways of thinking, ideology, culture, habits, social customs, communications, and moral norms. It is these significant characteristics that distinguish the Chinese from others and the key to strengthening the unity of Chinese nations, realizing the rejuvenation of Chinese nations in the 21st century, and maintaining long-term prosperity.

9. Conclusion: Summary of Chinese Dreams

In conclusion, what are the dreams of the 1.34 to 1.55 billion Chinese people in the 21st century? They are dreaming of living and working in peace and contentment, and achieving success in careers through hard work. They wish to become urbanized by working and residing in cities, pay taxes in a honest and rational way in the hope that the government will provide, establish and construct satisfying public service, social security and public facilities. They hope that the ecology would be preserved rendering clean air. They desire a life in a free, democratic, equal, fair, just, righteous, orderly and harmonious society, and work together with other Chinese people to build a strong socialist country of prosperity, great power, security, and to develop into a beautiful environment by the middle of the 21st century and realize the rejuvenation of Chinese nations based on the Chinese spirit rooted in their dreams and efforts for over 40 years.

---

[1] The three passages above were from *Baidu Baike*, Baidu Wenda, and relevant documents from the Bureau of Theory of the Propaganda Department of CPC Central Committee.

Bibliography

Baidu Baike. American Dreams. Available at baike.baidu.com/view/77925. htm. Accessed on 19 December 2010.

Local Social Security Departments Applying Personal Account in Current Payment. *China Times,* 31 May 2009.

Minich Tierny (2010). *Chinese Dragon and American Dreams.* Washington, D.C.: Atlantic Monthly.

Wen Rujun (2010). Suggestion to fill in the one trillion gap in Chinese social security funds with the profits of state-owned enterprises. *Legal Evening News,* 24 August 2010.

Zhou Tianyong, C Wang Changjiang, and Anling Wang (2008). Assault fortified positions: Report on the research of Chinese political system reform. Xinjiang: Construction Corps Press.

Zhou Tianyong (2010). *China's Way Out.* Beijing: People's Daily Press.

Chapter 2

China's Development Road to Realizing Chinese Dreams

Each country or nation has its own unique dreams, and each country needs the correct road to realize its ideal, with its dreams as the main driving force. If a wrong road is chosen, the driving force will be greatly weakened, or even become destructive, like that of the Cultural Revolution. Chinese dreams and the Chinese spirit based on these dreams have been discussed as above. Then, the question remains, how will China's development road be chosen in order to give full play to Chinese spiritual force? The author will first discuss the development road and the meaning of the development mode in terms of development economics, summarize the development road of China in the previous three decades after the reform and opening up, as well as its achievements, faults and problems, and finally propose how to adjust this development road.

1. Development Road of Developing Countries

There are quite a number of publications on the study of development roads and methods. However, in terms of development economics, only a few rational discussions on the development road have been systematically conducted. In more than 60 years after World War II, developing countries have adopted different systems,

29

development roads and modes. In terms of the rich accumulated materials for development and preparation of its theory, further theoretical research on the development road and mode is necessary to summarize the past and direct the future. The primary task for the innovation of development economics is to deepen the research on the development road and mode.

1.1. *Theoretical explanation on the development road and development mode*

Development road and development mode are seen as interchangeable terms in most researches despite their academic distinctions. Many publications have discussed the development road and mode and proposed their own definitions for each. They are part of development economics study which includes economics, philosophy, sociology, politics, and history and refers to various combinations of economic, societal, and political patterns of a country or a region.

The development road and mode shall be categorized in both static and dynamic perspectives. From the static perspective, development mode refers to the combination of economic structures, political systems, and social cultures, etc., while in a dynamic view, development mode refers to the growth process of the development road, transformation of dualistic structure, target selection of different stages, evolution of political systems, and social and cultural progress. The development roads and modes shall be comprehensively categorized from single and multiple aspects. The development road and mode sometimes refer to the pattern or process of a project, such as the development mode of export-orientation or import substitution. However, they sometimes refer to the pattern or process of an aspect or the comprehensive combination of several projects and aspects. The categorization of the development road and mode shall be conducted in terms of common characters and individual characters. Based on some common characteristics, all the development modes of developing countries refer to the transformation of its rural society or its agricultural economy to an urban society and modern economy. According to William Lewis, the common characteristic of developing countries lies in the dualistic economic mode, also known as the transformation road. Other than its common character, the development roads can be divided into: the road of East Asia, road of Latin America, road of South Asia, and road of China. In terms of the dualistic economic mode, there are development roads of different characteristics; while there are common modes of various countries and regions. Finally, the development road and mode shall be categorized based on subjective selection, path dependence, and condition constraints.

1.2. Practical meaning of the development road

What is China's path for development taking into consideration, the economics, the influence of politics and society on economic development, and the role of such a development road? It shall include the following based on economic theory and practical meaning:

The ways and means to promote urbanization in economic development. In order to realize modernization, which is the core of economic development, developing countries should transfer the rural population to urban areas in order to promote urbanization. However, how will they be transferred to cities? What can they do in cities? Where will they live? How can they abandon rural areas leaving behind their existing employment, income, assets, and adapt themselves into cities? How will these barriers be removed? For example, India and some Latin American countries promoted and realized urbanization by (a) allowing free migration and polarization based on low-cost areas, (b) the bankruptcy of small-scale peasant economy, and (c) generating abundant of informal employment opportunities for peasants in cities. In contrast, Japan, Korea, and Taiwan in East Asia adopted more civilized ways and means to promote and realize urbanization. However, Chinese customs and measures for urbanization are different to the modes of India, Latin America, and East Asia, where people are not allowed to migrate freely. Peasants suffer an increased loss of assets when they abandon their rural areas. The cost of urban housing increases at a higher rate than their incomes with the majority of the population from rural areas being unable to sustain in the cities.

The ways and measures to promote industrialization and industrial upgrade in economic development. Another important part of economic development is to realize industrialization. For example, China and the former Soviet Union enhanced industrialization by giving priority to heavy and chemical industries and lowering the prices of agricultural products to accumulate industrial funds. However, this industrialization model led to high accumulation, imbalance between the accumulation and investment against consumption, and low living standards. Some developing countries followed the rules of upgrading their industrial structure by seeking guidance from their governments and started from the development of light industry before turning to heavy and chemical industry. Ultimately, they avoided damages to agricultural development, accumulated funds for the development of heavy and chemical industry, and thus upgraded their industrial structure. In the process of industrialization, some countries focused more on education, investment and accumulation in human capital, while the progress of knowledge and technology played an important role in the research, development, design, transformation, and upgrading of the industry, which greatly improved the competitiveness of their industries and products globally. Other countries, especially China, paid more attention to the investment in material capital, but ignored education, knowledge, and technology and thus took no account of the investment in education and human capital. China had once disregarded education, science, and technology and ended up contributing little to the growth of its economy. This led to low global competitiveness of its industry and products, listing China under countries and regions of low industrialization. Some other countries and regions, in their process of industrialization, gave priority to the development of leading sectors before turning to other related sectors, and developed the industry before the investment in, and construction of, infrastructure. Some other countries and regions developed all types of industries at the same time and simultaneously invested in industry and infrastructure for coordination. Other countries and regions invested in and constructed infrastructures even before the industrial development.

The utilization mode of industrialization elements and the scale structure of enterprises in economic development. States can only promote economic growth based on elements such as labor, capital, land, resources, and technology in terms of elemental structure in the industrialization process. Different countries and regions have different element endowment, a different combination of investments on elements, and different combinations and consumption of resources.

Centralized or decentralized development mode to promote modernization. Economic development refers to the geographical process of centralizing population, labor, other production factors, productivity, and market. However, there is still no clear idea of the difference between centralization and decentralization and their positive and negative roles in economic development. Based on the principles of economics, a centralized development mode can significantly promote economic growth without an increase in the investment. Enterprises of large-scale industries need a scale economy to reduce fixed costs. The population should be centralized in small towns and cities to form the market room and capacity for the third industry. The population, including peasants, should be centralized in multi-layer buildings to save land and lower the cost of public service. Industrial enterprises would need to be centralized in order to externally economize and reduce external costs, such as electricity, road, storage, and infrastructure. Centralized industries would facilitate the labor division, coordination, and market share and frequently generate the industry cluster of aggregation effect. Centralized population, industry, and commerce will facilitate the centralized treatment of the population, lower the investment on facilities such as sewer lines, decrease the cost of environmental protection, and improve economic performance. Cultivated lands should be centralized for large-scale planting to facilitate mechanization and adequate irrigation and lower the apportioned cost of agricultural production.

Traditional urbanization mode or modern urbanization mode of network systems. Development economics shall advance with time. Along with the development of traffic, communications, and electronic network technologies, the transformation of the dualistic structure originally from rural areas to urban areas, has now become the transformation of a rural society to an urban system of networks, and from a traditional industrial economy to a knowledge-, technology-, and network-based economy. The economic incentive of the urban network systems is that they must minimize the cost and maximize the production. A modern economy includes seamlessly integrated networks in highways, expressways, railways, power generation and distribution, oil and gas pipelines, water-bound transport, air-bound transport, water supply, postal service, commerce, gas pipes, fixed telephone services, mobile communication, wired television, financial services, international internet, etc. The urban network system, formed by the connections of fluid objects and nodes is the compound network and economic system integrated with various networks. Therefore, China should pay particular attention to the construction of networks and urban systems in its economic development, in order to establish a city band, agglomeration, and circle and find the systematic network-centered development mode for big, medium, and small cities.

Sustainable development. Two modes exist in relation to development and population, resources, ecology, and environment: the unsustainable development mode of unlimited population expansion and endless consumption of resources, ecology, and environment; and the sustainable development mode, which refers why the present generation will not achieve development at the cost of consumption of, or incurring damages to, resources, ecology and environment that the next generation will live on, but maintain biodiversity, enable the continuous utilization of resources, and ensure the ecology and environment suitable for the habitation, living, and work of people. The simple economic definition for sustainability is to maintain the natural resource base at a certain level and enable the resource production at least equal to the current level in the future. This requires the renewability of renewable resources, stable non-renewable resources or reserves, or the effective replacement of other resources. In addition, a balance should also be reached between an economy's ability to purify pollution and the disposal of pollutants that cannot be purified.

Internal and external modes in economic development. Each country or region will certainly relate to the external economy during its industrialization. Based on different degrees of connections, it can be divided into the development mode of domestic orientation and of external orientation. Correspondingly, regarding the relations between internal development and external relations, industrialization roads can be divided into import substitution and export orientation.

Many countries had once followed the industrialization road of import substitution. In particular, China had established its own industrialization system and followed the typical development road of industrialization based on import substitution under its extremely low proportion of external trade in GDP. As approved by practices for several decades, nearly all countries adopting import substitution have failed, especially when compared to the success achieved by countries and regions following export orientation industrialization, such as Japan, Korea, Taiwan, Singapore, and Hong Kong. China won worldwide recognition for its economic success after implementing its industrialization strategy of export orientation in 1978 following reforms and opening up.

The mode to realize fair distribution of income and wealth in economic development. The goal of socialist countries, including the countries of welfare society system on the "third road", is the fair distribution of income and wealth based on their core social value; while capitalist countries also establish this system to adjust the distribution of income and wealth by social security, public service, levying benefits, and wealth tax and transfer payment in order to maintain social stability. It is an important aspect of the research on economic development modes to discuss the measures that shall be taken by developing countries to pursue the fair distribution of income and wealth among all people and share development achievements with all of them during the process of modernization.

Selection of political systems and economic systems and the combination mode in economic development. In the three decades after the foundation of New China, it suffered worse economic growth rates owing to the combination of the planned and state-owned economic system and centralized political system, in addition to the constant political campaigns. However, in the 30 years after reform and opening up, China has seen an unprecedented rapid economic growth based on the centralized political system, reform of the planned and state-owned and collective economy, and the market economy system. Japan, South Korea, and Taiwan had rationally adopted the combination of a centralized political system and market economic system in their transformation of dualistic structure, thus achieving phenomenal economic growth, while other countries and regions, such as South Korea and Taiwan, had realized industrialization based on their efforts. However, their economic growth rate had significantly declined once when they began to apply democracy. Therefore, it is crucial for development that developing countries confirm the nature of their political and economic systems during the transformation of the dualistic structure.

2. Achievements, Faults, and Problems of China's Development Road Since 1978

Before the reform, China did not have an understanding of the development road, because it had not grasped the true meaning of development.

2.1. *China's development road after reform and opening up and its achievements*

How does one understand and summarize China's development road in the 30 years after 1978 in terms of development economics? According to the author, its theoretical and practical content shall be summarized thus: (a) to develop productivity and emphasize progress in science and technology as the primary productive force; (b) to reform the state-owned and collective economic system, change the method of resource allocation, and promote economic development with new systems and mechanisms; (c) to combine the centralized political system and market economic system that was gradually formed during the reform, so as to provide a stable political and social environment for the development and mobilize the vitality and movement of economic development; (d) to gradually adjust the relationship between agriculture and industry; heavy and light industry; and establish a favorable circulation between agriculture and industry; and investment and consumption, and (e) in order to promote the growth rate, to adopt the strategy of opening up, transfer the comparative disadvantage of huge surplus of labor forces to the comparative advantage of export orientation, and introduce capital and technologies. China's development road has maintained a high national economic growth rate for 30 years since reform and opening up. This is also summarized as the Beijing consensus on development.

2.2. Problems and faults in China's development road in the previous 30 years

In recent years, domestic and foreign academic circles have attached great importance to the development road of China, also called as the Chinese mode. Here, we will discuss the problems in the previous China's development road or Chinese pattern and the necessary adjustments taken.

2.2.1. Structural deviation and distortion of the development road

Theoretically, the development mode refers to the ways, means, and approaches of economic development. The irrational structure of the primary, secondary, and tertiary industries may result from an improper development method. The inconsistency between the development approach in one aspect and the development approach in another aspect often leads to problems in the development mode, including structural deviation. The biggest problem of Chinese economic development lies in structural deviation and distortion, which is presented in the following aspects:

(1) The derivative and distortion between the production structure of the three industries and labor employment structure. (2) Derivatives among the development level, urbanization level, and proportion of the service industry, i.e., the advanced industrialization against the lagging urbanization. Lagging urbanization leads to population dispersion, problems in the consumption method and market capacity, slow development of the service industry and inhibits the transfer of excessive labor from the primary industry to the tertiary industry. (3) The derivative and distortion among the economic development level, enterprise size and structure and the number of enterprises per 1,000 people. Owing to comparatively fewer small enterprises that can largely absorb labor forces, the transfer of surplus labor forces from agriculture is slow, while the growth of residents' income is slower than the growth of capital and finance. 4) The derivative between economic aggregate and industrial competitiveness. First, the contribution rate of technical progress to economic growth maintains around 40%, much lower than 65% of developed countries. Second, some industries that need to improve concentration ratio are still scattered and disorderly, and when compared to other countries they have no competitive edge. Third, the industrial system is still low in standardization. Fourth, domestic industries employ a large number of laborers, with lower skills and intellect, transferred from rural areas, leading to the unfavorable implementation of production regulations and standards, as well as production and product quality.

Due to these derivatives, China has only few products of core competitiveness in global trade, but mainly exports products of low added value, so the export is greatly subject to the adverse effect of trade protection, including standards, low carbon, and environmental protection. Some of its products have consumed huge national resources, leaving heavy pollution in China. The unbalanced trade, comparative value rise of the Renminbi, and comparative devaluation of the USD results in the prejudice of export surplus.

2.2.2. *Faults and risks in the previous China's development road*

According to rational opinion, China has unconsciously committed four major faults in the previous 30-year development road: (1) It did not promote urbanization in a timely manner; (2) It selected a type of land and housing system that expropriated peasants' interests and raised housing prices; (3) It did not place high importance to the development of small enterprises that could have solved the biggest problem of unemployment in China, but instead placed restrictions on it, with no support from the system or policies to support employment; and (4) It did not design or establish the system of "budget-design", which could have controlled the expansion of party administered organizations and personnel, and managed the expenses of these organizations in the centralized political system under the leadership of CPC.

It is clear that, in order to build a modern country of resource conservation, social stability, wealth, global competitiveness, and favorable ecological environment by 2040, China must make major adjustments on the previous development mode, select a more scientific development road, and firmly carry out major reforms, including the reform of finance and tax system.

3. The Key to China's Development Road: Firmly Propelling Reform

It is necessary to mention that the adjustments in the development road are often interfered by route dependence, interest obstruction, and unfavorable systems. Therefore, an indepth adjustment of the development road can only be carried out and realized by liberating minds, reforming systems, establishing mechanisms, and by designing and proposing systematic policies which will be further discussed in this chapter.

3.1. *The most urgent reform: Relaxing restrictions on entrepreneurship and employment*

Hundreds of millions of people transfer from rural areas to cities in search of the Chinese dream. What can they do? What skills do they have? The most important thing is to encourage employment. At the same time, starting own business is essential to employment, as the new businesses will lead to more employment opportunities. Urban residents' dreams of entrepreneurship and employment are integrated. It is the most important method for the urbanization of hundreds of millions of people and their struggle for a happy life. Only through employment can income be realized, the wage can be increased along with the rise of labor demands, and people's living can be guaranteed and improved. Large and small enterprises play different roles in economic and social development. The large enterprises raise the power of the country, while small enterprises absorb more labor forces, thereby solving the unemployment problem, also leading to increase in salaries, improvements in people's lives, and finally stabilizing the society. A society without sufficient small enterprise development will definitely become a society of high unemployment, difficult livelihood, and fierce conflicts. The Chinese dreams cannot be realized without entrepreneurship and employment generation schemes as without them, people's ideals will turn to disappointment, leading to an unstable society.

If the party and government want to enable hundreds of millions of Chinese to realize their ideals, they should attach higher importance to the development of small enterprises, and formulate strategies to create positive environment for entrepreneurial system and policy-making. A relaxed environment for system and policy-making is very important for the development of small enterprises. Therefore, system reform and formulating appropriate policies are necessary.

3.2. *The most crucial reform: Fiscal and taxation system*

The fiscal and taxation system reform is the core of Chinese system reform, which relates to both economic and political mechanisms. It is also the condition for the solution to many economic and social problems in the future. Fiscal and taxation system reform is difficult since it is related to the interests of every resident, stratum, party, government, and government-sponsored organization. Therefore, despite an ideal proposal, it is difficult to implement in the name of all interest-related parties. However, without reforms in the fiscal and taxation system, there is certainly no future of Chinese reform and it will be difficult to establish China as a fair and just modern country of favorable management.

China must adjust and reform the taxation structure, encourage entrepreneurship, employment, and inhibit speculation, obtain profits based on assets, and adjust resource wastage and environmental pollution. The main targets of taxation are enterprises in the current Chinese taxation structure. In fact, China is actually adopting a taxation policy that encourages benefits based on assets, pollution, and wastage of resources, instead of encouraging entrepreneurship or accumulating wealth. The taxation structure runs counter to the value of common prosperity of socialism and scientific thought of development in terms of results.

3.3. *The inevitable reform: Land system*

In recent years, village renovation schemes have been propelled in various regions in order to obtain permission to build on land from the housing sites of peasants. The land removal and the balance between occupying and compensation, on the one hand, have explored a large area of land for construction, but on the other hand, have led to huge social conflicts. The current occupying area in villages has amounted to 270 million mu. Villages utilize most lands inefficiently, leading to a massive waste of land, including good quality agricultural land. If 100 million mu of land can be sorted out, will it play a positive role in saving agricultural land and promoting urbanization?

Then, how should China reform? First, China should abolish the government's monopoly on land trade and cancel the administrative "bidding" of land. Second, land-use rights can be extended in order to promote the reformation of land system, based on the state owned and collective land system. Third, the correct confirmation certificate should be issued on the long-term use of land period. The terms "collective land" and "state-owned land" are both legally deemed as approximation to property ownership, with the same property right attributes to all properties, such as inheritance, trade, mortgage, investment, and rent. Fourth, the government should no longer collect a land transfer fee and cancel expenses on land development and commercial housing, consolidate some taxes, and start to collect the value annex tax and housing tax upon land usage and housing transactions. Generally, the reform route can be summarized as extending the term, giving the property right, entering the market, and replacing the fees with taxes.

The goal of the complete reformation of the land system is to form a competitive market of land supply, therefore, reducing the land price, and inhibit the speculation demands on and stabilize the prices of houses. The inexhaustible and sustainable local finance shall be established for the future government. Local governments are prevented from accumulating lands, wasting lands, or misusing lands based on expansion of land finance. The current land finance collects money from low-income populations, and the low-income populations are forced to buy houses at high prices. These people are actually paying taxes for the government with loans. Therefore, the reform on current land management system shall be carried out as soon as possible. Especially in the 12th five-year plan, the reformation in land management will be given as much attention as the reformation of the fiscal and taxation systems, so as to avoid risks in the future and maintain favorable operation and development.

3.4. *Indispensable reform: Price of resources*

The price of resources will increase owing to the shortage in the supply of resources. In accordance with the constraints from resources and environment, the establishment of the living and consumption method will be forced by high prices and high taxation in order to control pollution and wastage for the sake of future generations. Under the circumstances of low prices in the usage of resources, environment, traditional production, living technologies and methods based on consumption of resources and environment, the nation will be trapped in the resource and environmental disaster in the long-term.

The direction and goal should be to rationalize the prices of resources and resource products. The author believes that the second price reform would concentrate upon rationalizing the price system for resources and resource products. The key to the reform is to properly handle the relationship between the reformation in the prices of resources and resource products and the bearing ability of people, bearing ability of enterprises, and rise of consumer prices. China should continue to promote the reform on the price system for resources and resource products for the sake of long-term benefits.

3.5. Reform required by social vitality and fair distribution: Reform on state-owned economy

Many complaints have been raised from academic circles on the reformation of state-owned enterprises, such as "the progress of state-owned enterprises would lead to backwardness of private enterprises", the hegemony of state-owned enterprises, and irrational distribution. How, then, will China continue to deepen the reform?

The capital should be further socialized. The overall direction of the reform on large state-owned enterprises is not to turn state-owned assets to family or individual assets, or enhance the state-owned assets, but to further socialize the state-owned assets to become social assets. The role of the further socialization of state-owned assets includes the following: (1) The state-owned economy would exit from the competitive fields; (2) It would continue to improvise the modern enterprise system. The administration structure of the enterprise would be further improved and the market, instead of organization departments, shall select the leaders, including the chairman and general manager. Socialized companies can be deemed as public companies, and the performance of leaders and other aspects shall be under public supervision. First, the administration and contributor supervision, and assets operation shall be separated. Second, a reform on the budget and profit distribution of state-owned assets shall be carried out. Third, the democratic supervision on state-owned assets shall be promoted.

4. Principles of China's Development Road and Governance Strategies

Discussions on the achievements, experiences, faults, and problems in the previous 30 years development road, as well as the risks in the future, can be found in my book *China's Way Out*. In the next 30 or 40 years, some crucial principles must be followed on how to choose a more scientific development road, how to adjust the current development road, and how to avoid some risks in the development process.

4.1. *Principle of Chinese dreams and China's development road*

The Chinese dream in the 21st century is the dream of prosperity for Chinese people and country, which would be supported by resources, environment, and wealth. However, China should not establish a society of low competitiveness, high deficit and debt, and unsustainable development. Therefore, the following important principles should be abided.

The principle of balance between competitiveness and social equity. The first is to pursue competitiveness, vitality, and encourage entrepreneurship and employment. Second, the economic development of a state, competitiveness of national economy, entrepreneurship, and employment should be the basis of social equity. The third should be to positively manage the relations between the taxation structure, and the level and encouragement to investments, entrepreneurship and employment.

The principle of balance between affluent life, resources, and the environment. Wealth is based on resources and environment. Different countries have different resource endowments. Owing to the huge population, China owns comparatively less resources, especially the space and land resources per capita and the narrow environment for each person. Therefore, some living methods and wealth forms, such as American-style houses, cannot be realized in China. China cannot learn and directly copy the lifestyles of other countries.

The principle of balance between welfare society and the productivity and fiscal capacity. The content of many Chinese dreams relate to a welfare society, where the government provides better public service, social security, and payment transfer. However, the basis of the welfare society is the productivity, or, more specifically, fiscal capacity. Many problems have occurred in the North European, Latin American, and American welfare systems, leading to social disorder. China must draw lessons from these countries in the construction of a welfare society. Before issuing a policy that benefits people, China should carefully contribute financial resources and conduct a feasibility study for sustainable development.

4.2. Realization of the Chinese dream: Governance according to popular will

On behalf of all Chinese people's benefits, CPC assumes power for the people, but what should CPC actually do? The author believes that the most important action is to govern the state according to people's ideals, desires, and hopes. The result for governance, according to popularity poll, will depends on how well CPC can realize the demands and ideals of the people.

In this context, popularity refers to the dream of more than a billion people, their ideals about material and spiritual life, and their demands and hopes for work and living. It does not necessarily mean that the party and government would support the livelihood and welfare of all people to realize their dreams and satisfy their demands. The government does not create wealth; only individuals can create wealth and thus support the government through taxes. Any government that wants to support its citizens by creating wealth for them will only incur an overprinting of currency, runaway inflation, bankruptcy, financial storms, and economic risks. Therefore, the party and government that wants to assume power for its people, do not simply give them wealth, but should design the correct development road, formulate accurate development strategies, construct a system full of vitality, create a flexible environment for individuals to create their own wealth, stimulate the enthusiasm of hundreds of millions of people in entrepreneurship, innovation, investment, and employment and turn people's dreams of a better life into productivity in order to positively build and develop China.

4.3. *China's development road: Scientific governance*

The adjustment of the development road would require a change in the mode of thinking, i.e., emancipating the mind.

First, the objective laws and tendencies of economic and social development should be followed. The previous anti-urbanization policy in China, which advocated the development of industry and service industry in rural areas, ran counter to the objective tendency of economic and social development, leading to great losses. Second, passion cannot replace objective laws. People should not become involved in practices of high cost and low benefits solely based on passion, without regard to laws in economic and social development. Third, experiences alone cannot answer all the problems in state governance, while new conditions and problems should be understood primarily. People cannot think and make decisions based on experiences alone, since stages vary in economic and social development. Fourth, a long-term point of view is necessary for the governance of the state and the regions. In addition to correctly handling daily affairs, the governance of a country or a region requires some considerations over some long-term, strategic, and overall problems. Fifth, the correct ideas and strategies should be integrated as a proposal, jointly implemented by various departments and stages. The current problems in China may include the inability to transfer good ideas and concepts into strategic plans; the inability to establish good strategic proposals as implementation plans, laws, and regulations; and the inability for good proposals, laws and regulations to be carried out.

Bibliography

Baidu Baike. American Dreams. Available at baike.baidu.com/view/77925. htm. Accessed on 7 January 2011.

Germing A. Schubert (2010). Promises from the East. *Hong Kong Asian Times Online* (The article had made comments on Wang Hailun's article of "Chinese Dreams: The Rise of Biggest Middle Class in World and Its Influence," while all major medias reported, "What Will Chinese Dreams Bring to China?")

Li Junru (2006). *Chinese Dreams: China of Peaceful Development.* Beijing: New World Press.

Zhao Qizheng (2010). China's Mode is Exactly China's Case. ifeng.com. Available at http://finance.ifeng.com/news/special/china-way/20101116/2893237.shtml. Accessed on 17 November 2010.

Zhou Tianyong (2006). *New Development Economics.* Beijing: Renmin University Press.

Zhou Tianyong (2010). *China's Way Out.* Beijing: People's Daily Press.

Note: Relevant data mentioned in the article comes from the website of the State Statistics Bureau.

Chapter 3

Selection of Development Road: Material Structural Adjustment and Competitiveness Promotion

What is the meaning of development economics? It refers to the process of transformation from an agricultural rural economy to an urbanized modern economy. It is presented as: improving productivity and increasing GDP per capita in terms of the development level; constant transfer from rural population to urban population, raising the urbanization rate and increasing the added value of service, trade, and employment rate in terms of rural and urban structure; improving the quality of economic and social development, such as the populations' growing cultural quality and prolonging average life; full employment of labor and an affluent and stable life; and the country realizing modernization and becoming a super power. The development road is the process and the development mode is the method by which to reach these goals. Did China previously develop scientific plans for its development road? If yes, has the unique development road been formed in China? Which development road shall be selected by China in the future? What are the problems that hinder China's current development road and how can they be adjusted? These subjects shall be further discussed.

1. Urban and Rural Structure: The Correct Road of Urbanization

In the book *China's Way-Out,* the author discusses about the differences of the four roads of urbanization adopted by East Asia, Latin America, India, and China, respectively.

What type of urbanization or development road shall be applied to China? No detailed research or plans have been made on the key strategies, systems, and policies, in the three decades after the reform and opening up.

Since the reform and opening up, China's road of urbanization has accumulated huge social risks for the future. The road of urbanization practiced in the last 30 years can be summarized as follows: (1) The system of temporary residence instead of the open household registration system, was adopted, so the rural population transferring to cities could not enjoy government's public services, such as urban education, medical care, social security, and minimum living security. Instead, they are discriminated in employment and vehicle purchase; (2) The population transferring to cities could not permanently stay in cities because they couldn't afford houses owing to the prohibition of slums, the prices of legal houses in urban areas were too high, the incapability of liquidating houses in rural areas, and the slow increase in salaries based on the oversupply of urban labors; (3) A large-scale floating population was formed between the rural and urban areas, leading to a large population with no regular jobs and houses in cities which resulted in the appearance of low-cost living methods, such as small villages within cities, makeshift houses, and capsule houses; (4) As rural youths have constantly moved to cities, and because of the inability of the old to move with them, and the fact that some peasant workers may return to villages at middle or old age, the population aging issue is more serious in villages. Particularly, in the following two and three decades, many villages will become depressing places where only the elderly would live. In comparison, China's road to urbanization in the previous three decades is no better than the method of "slum" adopted in Latin America and India. Without adjustments in the development road, social unrest and disaster are likely to occur.

The road of urbanization, as mentioned in the chapter, refers to the method of transferring the rural population to urban areas. Which road of urbanization should we choose which is more scientific and optimized for the future of China? First, the household and population management system should be reformed to realize free residence and migration of the population. Second, all people working and living in cities for a certain period of time shall enjoy the same and fair public service as other urban residents without any institutional discrimination between the identities of existing original residents and new residents. Third, the land, local, fiscal, and housing systems shall be reformed to realize appropriate housing for the population migrating from rural to urban areas.

Regarding China's road to urbanization, the following methods should be adopted in order to enable the population migrating to cities to "permanently stay" in urban areas: (1) Cities shall encourage business startups, develop small enterprises, expand services trade, reduce unemployed and impoverished population and increase the proportion of medium-income population, implement a wage hike policy that will be commensurate with the increase in demand for labor, and enable most people who migrate to cities to rent long-term or purchase appropriate houses; (2) The government shall regulate the price of land and houses to control their growth rate in accordance with the growth rate of peasant workers incomes; (3) For the peasants leaving rural areas, their interests in their rural assets would be protected, including their farmland, woodland, grassland, and house lots, by providing rational compensation for the farmland and housing lots in suburbs and rural areas for traffic, water conservancy, industrial mining and city construction; (4) In addition to the control of land and housing prices, the central government shall invest in low-rental housing for people that cannot afford to buy houses; and (5) Governments at all levels can purchase the house lots of peasants who move to and buy houses in cities, and provide subsidies on their purchase.

Different solutions shall be applied to the housing demands of urban residents and new immigrants according to different income levels. First, the allocation between rental and the purchase of houses shall be rational. Second, the housing problem shall be solved by both — government support and the efforts put in by the inhabitants. However, solutions shall be in accordance with the economic development level of China and the fiscal capacity of governments at all levels in order to avoid heavy burden on government expenditure, its failure to follow policies, and to prevent premature welfare which may lose the trust of people and lead to high deficit and financial risks.

The government would play following roles in solving the housing problem: First, it shall encourage cooperative housing. For example, many European countries encourage residents to establish the housing construction cooperative. The Chinese government may provide the land at lower prices and reduce or exempt some taxes. People who are in need of houses will establish housing construction in terms of cooperative consumption and build houses by themselves to avoid unwanted housing cost. Second, the government shall build economically affordable housing for families of medium and low-income groups. To create affordable housing, the government will lower the land price and reduce or exempt some taxes to adapt to the purchase capacity of medium and low-income groups. Third, the government shall build low-rent housing for low-income groups and for families who undergo critical financial conditions and cannot afford to buy houses; meanwhile providing housing subsidies for them.

In the road to urbanization, China shall balance the role of government regulation and market, while dealing with the differences in public service and social security in rural and urban areas and the goal to realizing the long-term fair welfare for every citizen, and handle the relations between the increasing demands of residents and fiscal capacity of governments. The realization of urbanization in the above three aspects is closely related to China's value and the correct selection of the road to urbanization.

2. Industrial Structure: Expanding the Third Industry

As required by urbanization, urban industries shall absorb the labor flowing into cities. How well can the industrial structure accord to the various methods of urbanization at different development stages? The development of the third industry is an important contributing factor in economic growth and development, and enables the transfer and allocation of labor among the primary, secondary, and tertiary industries to transform the structure of rural and urban areas.

2.1. *Backward development of china's third industry*

In the first three decades after the foundation of New China, the theory that the service trade does not create values had dominated. The theory actually opposed urbanization and advocated to building cities of production, but opposed cities favorable for living and consumption, leading to the extreme slow development of the Chinese services trade.

Owing to the slow development of service trade and the low proportion of added value, labor serving the third industry also account for low proportion. In the first 30 years after the foundation of New China, the labor percentage working in agriculture had dropped from 83.5% in 1952 to 70.5% in 1978, with a decline of only 13%; labor percentage in the industry grew from 7.4% to 17.3%, with a growth of only 10%; and the labor percentage in the third industry only developed from 9.1% to 12.2%, with a small growth of 2.1% (Table 3.1). In comparison to other countries of low incomes, such as Sudan, Yemen, Nigeria, Angola, Congo, and Korea, China had seen a growth in the proportion of labor in the third industry from 11% to 16%; while the countries of low and medium incomes had raised the proportion from 18% to 28% (World Bank, 1984).

Table 3.1. The Variation of GDP Productive Pattern in the First and Second Three Decades.

Year	GDP	%	Primary Industry	Secondary Industry	Industry	Building Industry	Third Industry
1952	679.0	100.0	50.5	20.9	17.6	3.2	28.6
1978	3548.2	100.0	28.2	47.9	44.1	3.8	23.9
2008	300670.0	100.0	11.3	48.6	42.9	5.7	40.1

Data source: The website of the Statistics Bureau of the People's Republic of China.

Table 3.2. Variation of the Labor Employment Structure in the First Three Decades After Foundation.

Year	Employed People Million People	Composition (100%) Primary Industry	Secondary Industry	Third Industry
1952	207.29	83.5	7.4	9.1
1957	237.71	81.2	9.0	9.8
1962	259.10	82.1	8.0	9.9
1965	286.70	81.6	8.4	10.0
1970	344.32	80.8	10.2	9.0
1975	381.68	77.2	13.5	9.3
1978	401.52	70.5	17.3	12.2

Data source: The website of the Statistics Bureau of the People's Republic of China.

Several discussions have taken place about the three decades after the reformation and opening up. China gradually became aware of the mistakes made in its theory that the services sector, including commerce, only transfers and reallocates value and has come to realize that the services sector, in reality, also creates value. The third industry has been incorporated into the calculation of the added value of national economy. China has also promoted urbanization, changed the production-centered structure that ignores living levels and cultural consumption, and significantly increased the proportion of employment in services industry.

China's GDP per capita reached 3,200 USD in 2008. The added value of the primary industry amounted to 3.4 trillion yuan, accounting for 11.3% of GDP; the secondary industry reached 14.6183 trillion yuan, accounting for 48.6%; and the third industry reached 12.0487 trillion yuan, taking up 40.1%. Obviously, the proportion of the added value of the third industry was even 10% lower than the proportion of 50% when the world's GDP per capita reached 1,000 USD. The structural deviation is even greater in terms of urbanization, production structure, and employment structure. See Table 3.4.

If the proportion of employment in China's third industry in 2008 could reach the global average level of 60%, the labor in the third industry would amount to 464.88 million people. If the

Table 3.3. The Variation of the Employment Structure in the 30 Years after Reformation and Opening Up.

Year	Employed People Million People	Composition (100%)		
		Primary Industry	Secondary Industry	Third Industry
1978	401.52	70.5	17.3	12.2
1980	423.61	68.7	18.2	13.1
1985	498.73	62.4	20.8	16.8
1990	647.49	60.1	21.4	18.5
1995	680.65	52.2	23.0	24.8
2000	720.85	50.0	22.5	27.5
2005	758.25	44.8	23.8	31.4
2008	774.80	39.6	27.2	33.2

Data source: The website of the Statistics Bureau of the People's Republic of China.

proportion of employment in industry is assumed to be the same, the third industry will create 207.65 million jobs, i.e., the labor in agricultural industry will decrease by 207.65 million, so the labor productivity of GDP in agricultural industry will be increased from 34,285 yuan when compared to the actual 11,081 yuan and the gap with the

Table 3.4. The Structural Deviation of China When GDP Per Capita Reached 3,000 USD.

Item	China (2008)	General Global Level	Deviation
Urbanization level	45.7	60–65	14.3–19.3
Proportion of employment in service industry	33.2	60–65	26.8–31.8
Proportion of added value of service industry	40.1	55–60	14.9–19.9
Proportion of employment in agriculture	39.6	10–15	29.6–24.6
Proportion of added value of agriculture	11.3	10	1.3

Note: unit: %. The data of China comes from the Statistical Yearbook of China 2008 and the Statistical Communiqué of the People's Republic of China on the 2009 National Economic and Social Development published and issued by the Statistic Bureau, while the data of general global level comes from the development report and calculation of the World Bank.

average productivity of "GDP/labor" of 38,806 yuan in 2008 will be narrowed. Therefore, the key to transferring the excessive labor in agriculture, lowering the unemployment rate, and narrowing the gap between the rural and urban areas, is by expanding the proportion of the third industry and facilitating the transfer of labor from agriculture to services sector (under the circumstances of improving the composition of industrial capital), through progressive technologies. It is important to note that only general laws exist in various industrial structures in different development stages in absorbing labor transferred from rural areas. Developing agriculture and industry with a unique law that emphasizes on "China's development road" alone can solve the problem of labor transfer and employment.

2.2. Strategies and plans for the development of the third industry

How to alter the backward development of the third industry? The problem shall be discussed based on ideas, thoughts, strategies, systems, and policies.

First, China should actively promote the transfer of rural population to the cities, facilitate urbanization, and propel the development of the third industry. The insufficient development of the third industry inhibits the transfer of rural labor and population to urban areas which leads to excessive population and a large amount of labor in rural areas; therefore, hindering urbanization, which in turn obstructs the development of the third industry.

Population shall be concentrated geographically to facilitate the development of cities and towns, in order to expand the third industry; to transfer excessive population; and to decrease the actual unemployment rate; and to save energies and reduce emission.

Second, due to the significance of finding a solution to the unemployment problem, medium and long term plans shall be developed and implemented for the third industry. Both central and local governments, especially the municipal and district government, have listed the infrastructure development, such as industry development and traffic construction, in the annual five-year and ten-year plans.

Local leaders have emphasized on the industry and its infrastructure and have established a whole set of methods in proposals, reporting for approval. These include planning, absorbing investment, expropriating land, environment evaluation, coordination in financing, and taxation support because these industry projects could facilitate the development of GDP and tax income as the highlights of their political performances. However, governments did not pay much attention to the third industry due to its size and slow effect in GDP.

2.3. *Systems and policies for the development of the third industry*

In addition to the backward urbanization, unregulated systems and improper policies also significantly contribute to the backward development of the third industry, i.e., the service industry. Therefore, China needs to promote the system reform and issue effective policies to facilitate the development of the third industry. The following cites the research of Professor Xia Changjie (2008).

First, the system foundation shall be laid in the market access for the rapid development of the service industry. The open, fair, and standardized access system of the service industry shall be established and the threshold shall be lowered.

Second, taxation policies shall be adjusted and improved to create a favorable external environment for the service industry's development.

Third, the prices of the means of production and the administration fees for the third industry shall be reformed. The price of land, water, electricity, and gas for the service sector are generally higher than any other industry.

Fourth, the service industry shall be further specialized and socialized by the following: (1) The enterprise service and the production of the manufacturing industry shall be further separated; (2) The enterprises shall be reorganized and the "large and all-inclusive" or "small and all-inclusive" structure shall be changed; (3) The state organizations, enterprises, institutions, and social societies shall be encouraged to accord priority to the needs of service industries.

3. Business Structure: Small Enterprises Closely Related to the Prosperity of People and Social Stability

Should business startups be encouraged? Should China attach importance to the development of small enterprises? These are major concerns in the selection of China's development road based on the large population and excessive labor.

3.1. *Wrong thinking set and correct theories*

In terms of the absorption of labor: (1) The number of employees of state-owned enterprises has reduced from more than 80 million in the mid-1990s to less than 30 million today, while the labor serving in collective enterprises reduced from more than 56 million to the current 5 million, leading to a total loss of 100 million jobs. In the 21st century, more than 90% of new employees and the labor transferring from rural to urban areas work in individual and private enterprises and in micro-enterprises as well; (2) Along with the rise in labor costs and prices of agricultural production, as well as the mechanization, electrization, and chemization of agriculture, only fewer labor are needed, while more and more jobs and opportunities are provided along with the development of industry and service trade in cities and towns; (3) The production capacity and market are concentrated increasingly in East China, as 70% of GDP and 85% of foreign investment are placed in the East. The East has provided numerous employment opportunities for the West. However, the West has a smaller employment scale owing to its slower industry and commercial development. In Western China, many students that graduate from local schools are unemployed; (4) More jobs are provided in very large cities, especially in the capital, provincial capitals, and district capitals, but finding employment is more difficult in smaller towns. It was only after the presentation of strategies for business startups at the 17th Session of the General Assembly of CPC, that changes began to be implemented. Business startups will increase the number of enterprises, especially small-sized ones, which in turn will create jobs for several people, thereby; solving the unemployment problem of China.

What are the comparative advantages of developing countries — capital, technologies, labor, or market? The capital accumulation and technical progress are crucial for the extraordinary development of the developing countries to catch up with the developed countries. However, cheap labor is still the competitive edge of developing countries, while some developing countries are also featured with the advantages of a large population and market capacity. Therefore, these countries shall develop small labor intensive enterprises, compete in the global market based on the low labor costs and intensive human resources, and turn the disadvantage of idle labor resources into real economic advantages. Regarding the relations between supply and demand, the slow development of small enterprises will lead to inactive productivity, inactive labor resources, and slow increase of residents' income, limited market demands, and overproduction. The best solution is to encourage residents to invest in the establishment of small enterprises, which increases the employment rate of these enterprises, and form the virtuous cycle of savings, investment, employment, income, and consumption. In a country with such a large population, only the rise of the employment rate and income level can form the market capacity, create enough conditions for the large-scale development and upgrading of industries, and also obtain the advantages of low transport cost.

Large and small enterprises play different roles in the economic development of a country. Large enterprises mainly aim to create and allocate wealth based on capital, with revenues mainly distributed to capital owners and government taxes. Meanwhile, small enterprises create and allocate wealth based on labor, with revenues mainly distributed among entrepreneurs, labor, and residents. When special attention is paid to the development of large-scale enterprises, the proportion of allocation to capital owners, senior officials, and department managers will be comparatively higher, a small number of people own a large amount of income, and the wealth is more concentrated. However, owing to fewer number of micro and small enterprises for each thousand people, owners of micro, medium, and small enterprises, have low incomes. In addition, the high unemployment rate will lead to absolute poverty with low or extremely low incomes. The final result is the serious polarization between the rich and the poor. Therefore, establishing more numbers of small and medium enterprises will result in more people with adequate incomes, more labor, and fewer people in poverty. This would be the foundation to avoid social polarization and realize fair distribution of wealth.

3.2. *Development of small enterprises as the national strategy of highest level*

Employment is the source of people's livelihood. Excess labor and unemployment will lead to problems in the living conditions of a large amount of rural and urban residents, resulting in difficulties in acquiring medical care, education, and housing based on residents' low payment capacity. This deepens the dependence on exports owing to insufficient internal consumption, resulting in an economic crisis. Insufficient participation of labor in the creation and allocation of wealth and failure to export further escalates the gap between the rich and the poor, generates a negative feeling among residents' toward society, and reveals hidden dangers of social unrest and instability. In the face of this unprecedented problem, it will be a regret if the state and the nation does not pay high attention to decision-making to evolve appropriate policies to develop the economy.

The fundamental method to promote urbanization is to narrow the gap between the rural and urban areas. Private, micro, and small enterprises are not in high demand in transferring and absorbing labor. The new rural construction and agricultural modernization is the base for China's food security, while the construction of an innovation-oriented country is the foundation for the competitiveness of the national economy. The new rural construction shall be combined with urbanization and the development of small enterprises, and it is expected that such a movement will guarantee employment and longevity of a large amount of labor. The current outflow of peasant workers can be prevented, slums can be prevented from forming in cities similar to such formations in Latin America and India, the food security can be ensured, and the Chinese labor can be given full play for better competitiveness. The four strategies, new rural construction, urbanization, development of small enterprises, and construction of an innovation-oriented country are closely linked and all indispensable. Based on the transfer and employment of huge labor in China, the construction of an innovation-oriented country and development of small enterprises shall prevail.

Therefore, the author believes that the party and the country shall accord high priority to its national strategy of upgrading the construction of an innovation-oriented country and the development of small enterprises. The logic lies in the following: encourage business start-ups; increase the number of private, micro, and small enterprises leading to an increase in the demand for labor and jobs; expand the service trade; give full play to abundant labor; increase the income of labor; improve the living standards of residents and narrow down the income gap among the residents of rural and urban areas; improve the consumptive capacity; and realize the virtuous cycle of production and consumption.

The most important task the State Development and Reform Commission (SDRC) is to macro-control in lowering the unemployment rate and promoting employment. Without practical systems and steps for implementation, the major strategies issued by the central government have not been well implemented. In order to carry out the major strategy of "business startups to increase employment," the SDRC has formulated the 10-year action plan for the development of small enterprises (2011–2020), in view of the lack of business startups and small enterprises. The state department required the SDRC to organize relevant institutes and departments to research on the promotion plan of small enterprises in South Korea, Japan, Taiwan, Italy, and Germany; learn from the implementation of their systems and policies for the development of small enterprises and form a practical and operable action plan for the development of the same back home. The author believes that this action plan is much more important than

China's earlier plan to revitalize ten major industries in 2009 for the sake of the long-term development of the nation, under a pressing need to improve its employment generation capacity.

In addition, the author believes that the state department and its relevant departments would attach more importance to employment, give up the department divergences and interests for the state and national safety and recommends that the Department of Industry and Information should move the division of small enterprises back to SDRC as it enables them to control the unemployment rate and coordinate with other departments to promote the development of small enterprises.

The author suggests reforming statistical indicators. The labor and statistical department shall objectively and factually calculate the unemployment rate, in order to provide a reliable basis for macro-control by the central government and relevant departments. According to the published statistics, the registered urban employment rate in 2008 was 4.2%. In fact, scholars, foreign research institutes, people, and even statistical and labor departments do not believe this false indicator, which reads far from the actual economic and social development situation. Even though it will not make any difference if the indicator is completely indifferent to the state and nation, however, the indicator is very important to assess economic development. A false indication of the unemployment rate may not help leaders at various levels to gauge people's living situation, thereby misleading the decision making of the central government and state department in the control of commodity prices and employment promotion. "Seeking the truth out of facts" is one of the ideologies of CPC, so the unbelievable statistical indicator shall be completely reformed now. The author suggests that the state department should ask the Labor and Statistical Department to abolish the registered urban unemployment rate indicator, study the statistical indicator and its methods, ask the Vertical Statistical Department or Independent Social Investigation Institute to conduct an overall or sample investigation on the unemployment rate of the whole country to form a more objective unemployment rate of the macro economy, and issue the results each month.

3.3. *System reform and policy formulation for the development of small enterprises*

Why is there an unfavorable proportion of service trade production and employment, as China had already proposed to develop the service industry since the 1990s? Why is the environment for startups and development of small enterprises in China so poor?

3.3.1. *Relaxing the access of small enterprises*

Actually, it is difficult to start businesses in China. The insufficient development of private, micro, and small enterprises results from the discrimination and restrictions imposed on the industry and commerce system by the earlier ideology that placed emphasis on control instead of service, restrictions instead of development, charges instead of aid, fines instead of tolerance, and suspending businesses instead of providing education and guidance. Of course, the reform has been vigorously forging ahead in the industry and commerce department in recent years, under the leadership of director Zhou Bohua, and its economic support has turned from charges to finance, showing great progress. However, the author believes that further reform and innovation in the administration of trade and industry is needed to encourage people to start businesses and solve the country's employment issue, therefore, certain steps must be taken in order to achieve this goal. First, a non-registration enterprise system should be established where privately or individually-owned businesses only need to be taken down in record, but do not need formal registration; and the informal methods of business startups, such as temporary stalls, street vendor, small stores and flexible employment forms shall be allowed; and training, education, and guidance shall be conducted on food safety. Second, China shall lower restrictions over the capital, allow the utilization of real properties and intangible assets as the registered capital, and relax the restrictions on enterprises with considerable real properties and science and technology-oriented enterprises. Third, restrictions on the location of the registered office should be relaxed, so that some enterprises such as the design companies shall be allowed to register their homes as place of work, and for residents applying to work from their houses, the industrial and commercial bureau shall lower the bar of the approval of the residential committee. Meanwhile, the enterprises that are not suitable for working from houses shall be restricted according to the relevant rules, which shall be formulated at the earliest in view of the great employment pressure. Fourth, the annual inspection conducted by the industrial and commercial department, including other government departments and administration institutes on companies and enterprises, shall be cancelled. When the annual inspection is indeed necessary, the industrial and commercial department and other relevant departments shall report to the financial departments and necessitate them to bear the fee for an annual inspection, which is now assumed by the enterprises. In addition, it is prohibited for the industrial and commercial department to order newspapers and magazines through an annual inspection. Fifth, the association of private businesses and private enterprises shall be separated from the industrial and commercial department and instead they would be addressed as non-governmental organizations, or, based on the current status the fee for the above associations shall be supported by the financial departments instead of the individual and private enterprises. Sixth, the finance departments and governments at various levels are recommended to conduct careful investigations on the personnel of the industrial and commercial system and their economic status, and provide enough financial support to prohibit them from replenishing the finance based on charges and fines on individual and private enterprises. Seventh, the industrial and commercial department shall attach importance to education, training, and service in administration and try their best to avoid seizure and heavy punishment. The industrial and commercial department shall facilitate the development of private and individual economy rather than trying to control such a development.

3.3.2. *Cleaning up the charges and fines on small enterprises*

The central organizations, including the National People's Congress, Central Commission for Discipline Inspection of the CPC, Supreme Procuratorate and state department, are recommended to undertake pricing, financing, and auditing; and the supervision division of the SDRC to jointly check and cancel all unreasonable charges and fines on individual, micro, and small enterprises collected by all government departments and administration institutes. Currently, according to conservative estimates, fees and fines on various societal groups collected by government departments and administration organizations have amounted to 2000 billion yuan. Since budget, price and finance departments do not allocate all or part of funds to government departments and administration organizations or some of their personnel, leading to different lines for income and expenses, and some local financial departments adopt latent rules, such as bonuses for overcharging and sharing the fines. These relevant units, therefore, concoct various pretexts to charge fees. The charges collected by government departments and administration organizations from citizens and enterprises that have already paid taxes have aroused many problems. First, without any budgetary control of governmental administration organizations and personnel, such organizations will expand based on charges and fines, and such expanding organizations will collect more fees and fines, forming a vicious cycle between fees and charges and increase in organizations and personnel. Second, many private, micro, and small enterprises are suffering difficulties in operation, and some are even going bankrupt, due to the fees and fines. From 1999 to 2004, about 8.1 million private enterprises have gone bankrupt due to fees and fines collected by the government departments and administration organizations, resulting in a loss of 16 million jobs, and many people who want to start businesses resign due to these fees and fines. The following suggestions may be implemented. First, the National People's Congress, relevant departments of the government and party, and people's representatives shall establish a fees and fines clearance group to thoroughly check the fees and fines collected by the government departments and administration organizations. In addition, the National People's Congress shall propose, vote for, and issue an emergency act to announce the cleared items, fees and fines, and penalize, according to the criminal law, the relevant departments, unit leaders and civil servants that are illegally collecting fees and fines. Second, state department's right to formulate the taxes shall be withdrawn by the National

People's Congress and the NPC Fund-Raising Committee shall be formed. All government taxes, fees, and fines shall be approved by NPC, and major taxes and fees shall be set up as special items for discussion with the society through hearings. Third, financial departments shall provide a certain sum of money including various financial and industrial control commissions, to specific major departments collecting fees and fines, such as quality supervision, health epidemic prevention, traffic administration, environmental protection, and municipal administration. This will enable in altering the current system of departments self-supporting themselves by collecting fees to a system of unidirectional fund appropriation from financial departments without collecting fees from others. Of course, the budget for environmental protection can be balanced by increasing the effluent charges, but they shall be collected by tax departments and not related to the departments of environmental protection. The same principle can also be applied to traffic, security, and police systems. It shall be noted that the random inspection by quality control and other departments is a kind of public action, so the charges shall not be paid by the inspected units, but shall be acquired from financial departments. The quality inspection department shall abandon the work without financial aid, because the department may inspect some items that do not need inspections, conduct more inspections on some items which are not necessary, and repeat inspections in different regions in order to regulate the charges. Fourth, some administration departments entrust agencies to act on their behalf to collect fees to jointly make money, an action that shall be checked and prohibited. Projects where the government provides service are prohibited to transfer to agencies and charge the regulated. Fifth, the self-financing system for the construction of administration departments and administrative undertakings shall be abolished, including the construction of office buildings, training centers, vehicles, etc., which shall be assumed by financial departments. The SDRC and financial departments shall not approve any self-financed construction project, in order to avoid "building of the governmental department or administrative organization at the cost of the bankruptcy of millions of private and small enterprises." Sixth, preparation departments shall consult with financial departments to strictly control the internal divisions and personnel of governmental departments and administrative organizations. The number of organizations and personnel cannot increase without the financial allocation. In addition, the relations of obligations and fiscal taxation between central and local authorities shall be adjusted to reduce the levels of government. The incomes shall be allocated according to central government (50%), provincial government (15%), and local government (35%) and the transfer payment from central to local authorities shall be regulated, to change the current situation where the central government mainly depends on taxes, and local government mainly relies on fees and sales of land. Seventh, the NPC or the state department shall approve a law or emergency ordinance that governmental departments shall not ask for financial aid from private, micro, small, large, and medium-sized enterprises, otherwise the behavior shall be regarded as a major offense and the officials in charge shall be held accountable according to the laws. According to some cases in our investigation, many enterprises in middle and East China with financial difficulties have gone bankrupt due to governments and their departments' requirements on financial aid.

3.3.3. *Regulating the method of tax collection and tax abatement*

The reality for new businesses in China is harsh and unpromising. In fact, 99% of business startups in China are expected to fail and most enterprises are expected to go bankrupt if they pay all the taxes and fees, including the VAT of 17%, business tax of 5.5%, two additional taxes, income tax of 25%, workers' insurance expenses, graduated personal income for high bonus at the end of the year, and the fees and fines by governmental departments and administration organizations. Therefore, the author proposes the following suggestions. First, three items in tax system and action shall be abolished, i.e., to abolish the annual plan target and task system that requires a high growth rate of taxes by financial departments, regardless of the current economic development level and performances of enterprises; abolish local governments' act of collecting taxes from private, micro, and small enterprises at a tax rate higher than the actual rate regulated by tax laws; and abolish the rewards for tax staff for fulfilling their targets which may provoke them to collect advance taxes. The tax departments lay heavier burdens on private, micro, and small enterprises in many regions through high tax rates, informal acts, and interest-oriented acts. Second, the fiscal policy that can promote employment shall be issued. The author believes that a mistake in the fiscal policy of 2009 was the transformation of value added tax, which cost 125 billion yuan, but only benefited capital intensive enterprises that contribute little to employment. It will be better to invest a large amount of fiscal cost in tax abatement for private, micro, and small enterprises that can absorb a large amount of labors. For small-scale taxpayers, the VAT shall be reduced to 2%, business taxes shall be reduced to 4%, income taxes shall be reduced to 15%, and the graduated rate of personal income taxes for enterprise investors, executives, medium and senior managers, and technicians shall be controlled under 20%. For general taxpayers whose labor cost has accounted for 50% of the VAT, the VAT shall be decreased to 10%.

3.3.4. *Strictly standardizing the behaviors of the government and administrative organizations*

It is suggested that the State Department, Central Commission for Discipline Inspection of the CPC, and inspection and supervision departments strictly standardize the method and act of the administration, approval, permission, supervision, and law enforcement of government departments and administrative organizations. The fees and fines as mentioned above are closely related to the administration, approval, permission, supervision, and law enforcement of government departments and administrative organizations, so these departments and organizations always try to collect fees and fines, leading to adulterated products making their way into the market, since these departments let the products pass inspection after they get money. Therefore, the author proposes two suggestions. The first is to urgently formulate relevant laws to check and resolve the fees and fines collected by government departments, or separate from legal collections and submit to the state treasury for those that were not cancelled recently, which shall have no relations with the benefits of organizations and personnel collecting fees and fines, otherwise there are chances of committing offenses. The administration hall and one-stop service of local governments shall be checked to prevent them from becoming the centralized charging system or the third "tax bureau". The second is to merge and centralize the repeated and crossing administration, approval, permission, supervision, and law enforcement affairs and give priority to the act of training and guiding these enterprises, instead of enacting strict punishment to shut them down. Third, the finishing time and level for administration, approval, and permission shall be regulated, and the procedures and regulations of officials' supervision and law enforcement shall be standardized and open, in order to save the time for private, micro, and small enterprises to come into contact with government departments and administrative organizations and their fees on public relations. According to an investigation, the fees for private, micro, and small enterprises to handle with these affairs are too high. In some regions, the fees have accounted for 30% to 50% of the total taxes, expenses, fines, and fees to contact with the government.

3.3.5. Developing small banks to solve the financing problem of small enterprises

The author suggests that the Banking Regulatory Commission give consideration to business startups, employment and people's livelihood, release the monetary control, vigorously develop small banks in cities , treat them differently, and delegate the monitoring of small banks to local authorities. The banking sector shall be monitored respectively by central and local levels. Small enterprises all over the world have difficulties in securing finance, but difficulties are even greater in China. There are different ideas, systems, and policies in place to solve this difficulty. The current method is to allocate a certain proportion of the credit of major banks to micro and small enterprises as the central government and the state department, including the Banking Regulatory Commission, will inform major banks of the political task. These major banks will inform their branches, offices, and basic banks of this task, in order to solve the difficulties of private, micro, and small enterprises in financing.

However, according to our investigations in many regions in 2009, the number of credits given to medium and small-sized enterprises in the report submitted by major banks may be false, because many small-sized private and micro enterprises assert that they had not or could not obtain loans from the bank, an assertion also expressed by owners of small enterprises. As stated by some small enterprises that had once obtained loans from banks, the banks said that the central government required them to issue loans to small enterprises, so they had asked the small enterprises to return their old loans and promised to provide new loans, but new loans were not issued after the old loans had been returned.

The author again suggests that it is impossible for the state department and the Banking Regulatory Commission to necessitate major banks to provide loans to small enterprises and private companies and the method cannot actually solve the financing problem of private, micro, and small enterprises. According to economic laws and actual practices, the following have been asserted: (1) Information asymmetry between major banks and their branches and the private, micro, and small enterprises costs the banks a lot of time and a large amount of fees to search for the information of private, micro, and small enterprises and select the borrowers, which makes it difficult to guarantee the truth of information; (2) It is very unremunerative for major banks and their branches to provide loans to private, micro, and small enterprises, when compared to the huge loans granted to large-scale enterprises with apportioned costs in staff, branches, and operation taken into consideration; (3) Major banks and their branches cannot control the risks of loans to private, micro, and small enterprises owing to their short operational period, rapid changes, high mobility of owners, little or no mortgages, and difficulties in finding security; and (4) The loan officers find it easier to regain loans from large state-owned or state holding enterprises and share fewer responsibilities if they fail to get the loans back, when compared to the responsibilities involved if the private, micro, and small enterprises fail to repay their loans. Therefore, although the Central Government and state department, including the Banking Regulatory Commission, require banks to provide loans to private, micro, and small enterprises, the banks may act in another way; the higher authorities of banks may follow the requirements, while loan officers and the branches at the grass root level may act in a different manner; the data and promotion on loans to private, micro, and small enterprises may be well set up, while banks actually only release a few loans to private, micro, and small enterprises. This method will not yield any good result.

In addition, the current small-loan companies cannot take deposits, as they are restricted in the capital source, short-term loan from major banks or other organizations, leading to the rise in capital and corruption.

The current financial system of high hegemony should be reformed and small banks should be vigorously promoted. In addition, large banks shall not become the shareholders of the small banks to prevent the small banks from becoming branches of major banks, which will also refuse to provide loans to private, micro, and small enterprises. The comparatively profound way of reform is to develop small banks exclusively for private, micro, and small enterprises based on social capital and restrict their scale, legalize underground creditor–debtor organizations and allow them to develop into small banks, and encourage some bonding companies to form into small banks. In brief, the property rights shall be distinct, small-scale community banks shall be developed, and the guarantee system on assets or others shall be designed. The relevant government departments shall actively promote the reformation of the financial system and form the financial system of current and future financing for private, micro, and small enterprises.

It will be better for the government to provide a guarantee for business startups by peasants, although this seems impossible. Since the government cannot provide a guarantee, peasants assets, including immovable properties such as house, land, and collectively constructed buildings, shall be allowed for collateral financing, otherwise peasants have no way to start businesses without mortgages.

3.3.6. *Other policies to encourage the development of small enterprises*

The author also puts forward the following suggestions in addition to the above system reform and policy design. First, the land administrative department shall allocate land to entrepreneurs and small enterprises. Under the current land allocation, lands are predominantly allocated to large enterprises, to projects with investments by foreign capitals, and to governments and real estate projects, while small enterprises cannot gain land resources owing to their low status and weak industrial structure. Therefore, the land administrative department, especially governments at various levels, shall consider the land requirements of labor intensive enterprises that can absorb employment, adjust the proportion of land allocation, and establish some pioneer parks for small enterprises to guarantee the land resources for the start-ups and investment of small enterprises. The second is to reform the secondary and higher education system in accordance with the demands of business startups and employment. There are a lot of complaints on the current education system under which the university graduates can neither run their own businesses nor serve well in enterprises. I believe the following reforms should be made: (1) To reform the enrollment proportion of ordinary schools and vocational education to 50% of higher education and 50% of vocational education after their graduation from middle school; (2) To adjust the curriculum structure of institutions of higher education and vocational schools. In particular, the knowledge on working as the cadre in the government should be significantly reduced. It shall be noted that in the current university curriculum there is too much information taught to students that does not necessarily pertain to their careers, however, which consumes a great deal of the students' time and energy, and has nearly no use in business startups and employment; and (3) To train students on business startups and employment, especially the former, which includes teaching them the procedures of registering a business, selecting the area of startups, managing finance, controlling risks, and conducting market investigation and marketing in order to cultivate more entrepreneurs. Third, the labor, finance, and civil administration departments shall provide all-bearing support to business startups. The finance department shall allocate a certain amount of budget to the labor department to mobilize employment training programs for peasant workers, university graduates, and social youths, as well as training those who want to run their own businesses. The civil administration and labor department shall advocate and approve the establishment of a nationwide promotion campaign for startups and employment and set up non-governmental organizations, which would establish the funds and mobilize training programs, facilitate exchanges, and contact the government to reflect their requirements. The fourth is to redraft and issue the Law on Promotion of Business Startups and Small Enterprises as soon as possible. The Law on Promotion of Small Enterprises, previously approved by the National People's Congress, was too rigid when compared to Korea's laws, and the specific obligations and responsibilities of government and governmental departments and the ways to promote small enterprises could not be found in this law. It was mainly because, in the process of making the law, no department is willing to give up any interest or right or assume their own obligations and responsibilities. Then, the law of firm principles has to be approved as these relevant departments minimize their obligations and responsibilities in their enforcement regulations, but add some clauses about fees, fines, and law enforcement, not to promote, but to hinder small enterprises. Therefore, the author strongly advocates NPC to be discreet in making laws. It will be better not to establish or approve laws with rigid principles which are difficult to adhere. The author suggests that NPC abolish the current Law on Promotion of Small Enterprises and advises relevant commissions to organize experts and committee members to go to South Korea, Chinese Taiwan, and Japan, etc., to learn their laws on promoting business startups and development of small enterprises. It is hoped that a useful Law on Promotion of Business Start-ups and Small Enterprises can be formulated and implemented based on China's actual conditions.

In short, Chinese people do not lack entrepreneurial spirit and ability. Many Chinese have created successful careers overseas, so why can they not establish a successful career in China? The author believes that their inability back home results from the problems and disadvantages in the strategies, ideas, systems, mechanisms, and policies in the transfer and employment of surplus labor. The author hopes that governmental departments, academic circles, members of CPPCC National Committee, and NPC members can carefully consider the state and national security and abandon the department benefits. The government may invest some costs to reform relevant systems, issue practical policies, formulate and implement useful laws, and create a favorable system and policy system for entrepreneurship, thus promoting employment, overcoming the difficulties in transfer and employment of several hundreds of millions of people, and enabling Chinese people to lead a satisfying lifestyle.

3.4. *Improving competitiveness: establishing an innovation-oriented country*

In the early 21st century, China ranked second in world wealth, however, China should develop its technological and economic competitiveness to sustain its economic performance. How will China improve its competitiveness in the coming three decades? In addition to the three above-mentioned structural adjustments, it is equally important to maintain the ability to innovate in science and technology that would change the current phrase "made in China" to "created in China". However, this needs serious discussions on how to improvise on the innovation ability in sciences and technologies.

3.4.1. *Strategy of modernization and technology catching-up model*

Professor He Chuanqi divided modernization into two phases: the first phase based on traditional industrialization, and the second phase based on knowledge economy.[1] The author has assessed China's first

---

[1] According to He Chuanqi, the first modernization refers to the transformation process and changes from the age of agriculture to the age of industry, from agricultural to industrial economy, from agricultural to industrial society, and from agricultural to industrial civilization and is featured with characteristics such as

phase of modernization in 2008 in the book *China's Way Out* and reached the conclusion that China had completed 68.5% of the process and arrived at the second stage (Zhou Tianyong, 2010). At present, China's modernization combines both the first and second modernization phases. China shall improve the quality of the first modernization and accelerate the second modernization, which will be realized by implementing the strategy of establishing an innovation-oriented country.

It should be pointed out that the rapid economic growth of China mainly resulted from the investment of its resources and general labor. Experts calculate that the income factor contributes to 54.38% of the economic growth, while the technological progress contributes to 45.62% of the economic growth (Zhou Shaosen and Hu Delong, 2009), much lower than the proportion of developed countries (60% to 70%). In the next three decades, if the world's average annual economic growth rate (excluding China) is 4% and China's annual GDP growth rate is 7%, the Chinese economy will occupy one-fourth of the total world economy by 2040, considering the appreciation of RMB, and will take up one-third of the world by 2050 (Zhou Tianyong, 2009).

However, despite its healthy prospects, China cannot resume its path of development based on the consumption of resources and environment, owing to the large population and comparative lack of resources such as land, minerals, and fresh water. Then, how would China promote its economic growth? In addition to the development of the service industry and full use of labor resources, another

---

industrialization, urbanization, welfare, democratization, and secularization. Ten evaluating indicators for the modernization include GNP per capita, proportion of the add value of agriculture, proportion of the add value of service industry, proportion of the agricultural workforce, proportion of urban population, medical service, infant survival rate, life expectancy, adult literacy rate, and rate of population receiving a university education. The second modernization refers to the transformation process and changes from the age of industry to the age of knowledge, from industrial to knowledge economy, from industrial to knowledge society, and from industrial to knowledge civilization and is featured with characteristics such as knowledge, decentralization, networking, globalization, innovation, individualization, ecologicalization and informationization.

important factor is the constant progress in science and technology. In the next 30 years, the progress in science and technology shall promote economic growth, preserve ecology and environment, enable the development of social undertakings, and the progress and modernization of the whole nation.

Next, how is the competitive strength of China compared to the rest of the world? As indicated in the 2010 Report on Global Competitiveness released by the Lausanne International Institute for Management Development, China ranked 18th (20th in the previous year) among 58 most representative economies, two ranks higher than the previous year and three ranks lower than in 2008, while India, Brazil, and Russia respectively ranked 31st, 38th, and 51st (Zhangsi, 2010). The Lausanne Report's assessment is mainly based on four major indicators (economic performance, government efficiency, enterprise efficiency, and infrastructure) and 329 secondary indicators. Regarding China's rank in the 2009 Lausanne Report, Rodman an expert from the Institute of World Economics of Germany considered that despite the outstanding economic performance of China that ranked first in the economic evaluation and prospect, the continuity of China's growth rate is hard to maintain. A special report indicated that: "First, China encounters many bottlenecks during economic development, such as in the areas of science, information technology, engineering technology, finance, education, population, etc. Second, many problems lie in the management of Chinese enterprises, such as the low efficiency of large enterprises, insufficient executives, and incompetence to adapt to market changes. In addition, shortcomings can be found in China's financial system, environmental protection of enterprises, and supervision by the government and enterprises" (Qing Mu *et al.*, 2009). China has to rank at least in the top five of the Lausanne International Institute Rank by 2040 if it aims to become a competitive world power.

What is the strategy for boosting the progress in science and technology? Based on the science and technology level, countries of the world can be categorized into three types: countries and regions of advanced science and technology, such as the U.S., developed Western countries, Singapore, and Chinese Taiwan etc.; countries and regions of medium-level development in science and technology like the inland of China; and countries and regions of low-level development in science and technology like Afghanistan. Three types of strategic thinking can be employed in the science and technological progress, including the inaction strategy, the follow-up strategy, and the catching-up strategy. Inaction strategy refers to conditions when countries or regions cannot promote science and technology restrained by the productivity, financial strength, education, and human resources, but can only accept the influence of science and technologies from developed countries instead. The second is the following-up strategy, which refers to relying on the introduction and absorbption of external science and technologies through studies and imitation instead of self-innovation, without the goal to own the most advanced science and technology. Catching-up strategy refers to countries of medium and low-levels of development in science and technology that are trying to "catch up" with others based on self-innovation or re-innovation in addition to the introduction and absorption of external science and technologies with the sole aim of catching up with developed countries and seek their unique advantages in some aspects.

Key points for the catching-up strategy are summarized as follows: (1) It is important to define the scientific and technological goal. The goal shall be set for a long period, which shall be divided into several stages, with a specific goal for each stage. Goals can be categorized into 'keeping-up goals', which refers to reaching the top level based on the development of a mature technology in a certain period; 'surpassing goals', i.e., to achieve their own intellectual property rights based on self-innovation; and 'preparatory goal', which means to implement a preliminary plan when developed countries make some progresses in certain fields; (2) It is very crucial to accelerate the scientific and technological progress within a defined time period and achieve a leap-style progress. China has been left behind by the global scientific and technological progress while advanced countries have been constantly promoting their scientific and technological progress, therefore, when the catching-up strategy is adopted in China, China must accumulate the explosive forces to accelerate the progress within a scheduled time and promote the scientific and technological progress rapidly than other countries, in order to realize the catching-up strategy.

The "Matthew trap" exists in the scientific and technological progress of developing countries in their global economic and social development competition. The trap refers to when developing countries accumulate and gather scientific and technological resources from developed countries based on their leading edge. Comparatively, the education cost of the developing countries which are in an inferior position, may become the resources for the scientific and technological progress of developed countries along with the talent outflow, so the achievements made by developing countries based on their own scientific and technological strengths under the block of developed countries in science and technologies are relatively backward, which may have already been washed out or replaced by more advanced technologies. Therefore, developing countries become continually weaker in science and technology, while developed countries become more and more advanced. This is the "Matthew trap" of the scientific and technological progresses of developing countries.

It is obviously impossible for China to adopt the inaction strategy in the scientific and technological progress in the future. Has China stepped over the "Matthew trap" stage? Should China adopt the following-up strategy or catching-up strategy? Chinese economists believe that China should select the catching-up strategy. When technological innovation is mentioned, the same question emerges: Are China's technologies satisfactory? The government and residents always believe that foreign technologies are more mature than China's in procurement. However, China actually owns some advantages against developed countries in future technological innovation: (1) The research, development, and manufacturing costs in China are relatively lower than in developed countries. In addition, the salaries for research staff and the cost of materials in China are much lower than in developed countries. For example, an investment less than 400 million RMB was contributed to the research and development of 3G mobile communication technology, compared to the investment of 30 to 40 billion USD in developed countries. The research and development cost of other technologies in developing countries is 1/50 to 1/500 of the cost in developed countries, which is China's most important advantage when compared to developed countries; (2) Chinese researchers have an unyielding spirit toward their career. Researchers in many developed countries will never work overtime (past the 8-hour work day) or work on holidays, no matter how urgent the project is, but Chinese researchers will constantly work overtime and abandon holidays to complete tasks on time; (3) Talents for science, technologies, and special industries have been cultivated and accumulated for 30 years. Owing to the 30 years of education and cultivation of talents since the reform and opening up and the return of many talents from overseas, the human capital and innovation talents have increased thus producing a large amount of domestic technological innovations. Many Chinese talents studying abroad are involved in the research and development of energy technologies in many developed countries; (4) The 30-year reform and opening up, including introducing and absorbing technologies from abroad, has narrowed China's gap with developed countries in some important fields and in the overall technology level, and even enabled China to catch up with world's leaders in some aspects; (5) China has a large population and land area, so it is rich in human resources to promote scientific and technological progress and attract large scale applications of science and technology; (6) Chinese economy is developing at a rapid speed, and the progress of science and technology is also contributing to the rapid growth of the economy. Therefore, a harmonious cycle can be formed between economic growth and scientific and technological progress. Of course, if not cautious, China may also fall in the "Matthew trap." However, it currently seems that China has overcome the "Matthew trap" and has accumulated strength in accelerating the scientific and technological progress and implementing the catching-up strategy.

Take the energy strategy for example. The technological catching-up strategy is very significant for China. The new energy technologies can be divided into three types. The first is the traditional technological energy, such as coals, oil, and natural gas, based on which the secondary energy, electricity, is generated. The second type is the transitional technological energy, such as dynamic coal-to-oil, the previous energy for internal-combustion engine, the dynamic oil-to-electricity, the current energy for automobile batteries, and nuclear energy. The third type is the ultimate technological energy, solar energy, wind energy, biological energy, and biohydrogen production, the inexhaustible and zero-emission energy.

The traditional technology evolution is the gradual replacement of energies. For example, the traditional energies, such as the secondary energy, electricity, generated from coal, oil, and gas, replace oil and gas which acts as fuel for automobiles; then the solar, wind, nuclear, and hydraulic powers replace the traditional energy; and, by the end, the ultimate hydrogen energies are applied.

China's main development may be in hydraulic energy. China will research and develop electricity based on coal to replace oil and natural gas, industrialize the energies and recoup the investment; then research, develop, and industrialize nuclear and other energies and recoup the investment; and finally, industrialize the ultimate energies of solar, wind, and hydrogen energies, replace transitional energies, recoup the investment, and utilize these energies continuously. Therefore, in terms of the time schedule, China will mainly employ traditional energies and develop transitional energies from 2010 to 2020 and form the combined energy structure by 2020; develop the transitional energies to replace the traditional energies and develop the combined energies, such as hydrogen, from 2020 to 2040 or 2050; and then vigorously develop and industrialize the combined energies, such as hydrogen, to replace the transitional energies from 2040 or 2050. This is the proper sequence of the energy development strategy.

The current problem is whether or not China would adopt the traditional technology evolution, i.e., the following-up strategy of energy development. China has to keep a time gap between the developed countries in energy technology and industry evolution if the following-up strategy for energy development is employed, which means that these developed countries will take the lead in researching, developing, and industrializing the transitional energies, transferring these technologies and industries to China, and then further research-ing, developing, and industrializing the ultimate energies. In this way, China is mainly utilizing transitional energies when developed coun-tries are replacing the transitional energies with ultimate energy tech-nologies and industries. This indicates that after developed countries have replaced transitional energies with ultimate energies, China has to temporarily use transitional energies before ultimate energies are accepted.

Both advantages and disadvantages exist in the following-up strat-egy relating to energy. Regarding the advantages, China can intro-duce and absorb the mature technologies developed by others or utilize the current technologies, in order to lower the initial invest-ment and industrialization cost. As for the disadvantages, it is difficult to handle the relationship between hydrogen and other new energies, because similar to LC (liquid crystal) replacing the picture tube and digital information replacing magnetic tapes, coal power replacing oil and other restrained new energies are called as transitional technolo-gies. If hydrogen technologies can be matured soon, it will be a huge loss and waste to invest in transitional energy technologies.

The following strategic problem is whether it is possible for China to employ the catch-up strategy in energy technologies and industrial upgrading, which refers to whether China can step over the transi-tional energy technologies and directly enter the ultimate energy technologies. China shares the same starting line in the research and development of hydrogen energies, and some domestic researches are even more advanced and practical (have lower costs) than foreign researchers. Is it necessary to follow the path of "elimination, replace-ment, re-elimination, and re-replacement" in energy technologies and industries to solve key technologies and develop the energy industry in China? First, why did China not select the step-over development or the catching-up strategy for energy technologies and industries? Second, why did China introduce black-and-white TV, color TV, picture-tube TV, video recorder, and filmstrips and follow the path of "elimination, replacement, re-elimination, and re-replacement?" Third, why does China have to be the industry base for foreign tran-sitional energy technologies and allow them to earn profits from their original investments in transitional energy technology? The author suggests China should ignore the stage of transitional energy technology and apply the catching-up strategy for energy industry, i.e., mainly focusing on solar energy, wind energy, and the combination of hydrogen energies.

The U.S., Japan, and Europe have hugely invested in the development of hydrogen energies and vigorously promote the development process and planning of transitional energies. Some technologies have already been applied.

Under the circumstances of energy competition, China shall pay special attention to the following: (1) China should prevent itself from becoming a base for foreign countries where they could recoup their research and development cost in transitional energy technologies, transfer their eliminated technologies and equipment, and earn huge profits. The transitional energy technology will finally be replaced by ultimate energies, such as digital replacing filmstrips, semi-conductors replacing the electron tube, LCD replacing kinescope, and digital recording replacing magnetic tapes. Some research and development institutions of developed countries have invested large amounts of money in the transitional energy technologies, and they are hopeful of recovering their investment and earn profits from China's large market; (2) China shall pay close attention to developed countries who tempt them into employing the following-up strategy in the energy technologies and development and thus leaving China far behind. Some developed countries outwardly promote transitional energy technologies, but secretly develop ultimate energy technologies and mislead China to put more efforts in the introduction, research, development, and industrialization of transitional energies and leave it far behind in the competition; (3) China shall avoid being misled in national defense thereby falling behind developed countries. In some European and American countries, hydrogen fuels have started to replace nuclear submarines and are used in the navy because they are devoid of heat and are hard to detect. The hydrogen fuel battery has been applied in land forces for new battle measures, such as communications, navigation, surveying, and mapping and electric driving motion, owing to its light weight and long endurance time. It has also been utilized in scouting aeroplanes, surveying and mapping planes and aerial photography planes due to its long time of incurrence. It has been also employed in mobile hydrogen generation stations and modular hydrogen power generator in the replacement of battleground diesel engine generators and battery jars as required by the field war owing to its source from water, silence, and long endurance time. The author is not familiar with the progress in military electron technology. However, if traditional or transitional energies are utilized in energy supply for national defense, China may lose in energy technology and supply equipment when war occurs.

According to research, the Chinese government has shown great support for relevant research institutes, academies, and enterprises for hydrogen energies. For example, the hydrogen energy research institutes established by the Department of Science and Technologies and the Chongqing municipal government have been transformed into the current LN High-Tech Company greatly supported by the "863" project of the state during the 9th, 10th, and 11th five-year plans. Based on the outcomes of the independent intellectual property rights obtained by domestic organizations, some key Chinese technologies show little difference with foreign technologies, while some technologies are leading the world. Meanwhile, the basis of industrialization has been well founded.

The current technology related research and development in relevant domestic enterprises has solved some key problems: (1) The hydrogen fuel batteries are developed in varying sizes — large, small, modular, and integrated — enabling a wider and more convenient application; (2) The technologies including the direct combustion of hydrogen internal combustion machine, single button control of oil and hydrogen, on-vehicle high-pressure hydrogen supply, and rapid cylinder filling-up have been evolved; (3) Innovations and replacements have taken place in materials, arts, and technologies, which greatly lower the cost. The industrialization of many technologies has met the cost line and can lower the cost of some current energy utilizations; (4) Pollutions from the production and disposal of materials are much lower than in the current technology or products, like the batteries; (5) Both hydrogen fuel batteries and hydrogen internal combustion machines have a longer endurance time than any other new energy technology; (6) Technologies and applications of hydrogen production, hydrogen storage, filling-up, utilization of hydrogen, and on-vehicle high-pressure hydrogen have passed the safety test of relevant departments.

Therefore, hydrogen energies can be applied in the following industries and sectors: (1) Hydrogen fuel batteries for mobile phones, laptops, etc; (2) Reserve power supplies for networks of banks, taxes, finance, government, insurance and population management, mobile communication stations and lighting guard of high voltage wires; (3) Supply hydrogen-based power that combines wind, solar, and nuclear energies thereby solving the problems of unstable power supply of other new energies, the incapability to integrate into one network, and the high cost; (4) Disposal of garbage, since hydrogen, except brine electrolysis, can be produced from many sources, including garbage and refining residues, which can increase energies, reduce emissions, and absorb current pollutions, in addition to the zero emission of hydrogen energies; and (5) National defense, including military clothing for soldiers, mobile energy stations, scouting airplanes, and mobile communications to improve the capability of national defense and combat. This means that China's has the capability to produce mature and practical hydrogen energy technology which however, has not yet aroused the attention of governmental departments and the military.

3.4.2. *Significant relations to establish an innovation-oriented country*

China shall take the catching-up path in science and technology and implement the strategy of an innovation-oriented country, in order to build a modern power in the future. Therefore, some significant relations shall be theoretically and practically rationalized. The adjustment and reform of the system and mechanism shall be conducted accordingly.

First, the relation between the theory and application of scientific innovation shall be correctly recognized and handled. Science can be divided into fundamental science and applied science. The innovation of fundamental science and applied science is different to the innovation of technologies. Fundamental science is science that describes the natural phenomena and mode of the motion of matter and explores the law of development of the natural world.[2] Applied science is science that turns basic theories into practical use, which includes application of science in the technologies and techniques of material production, and the research on the applications of horizontal science, such as applied economics, sociology, science management, the study of science policy, policy methodology and the study of value analysis. Economics divides commodities and services into public-oriented products, semi-public oriented products, and private products.[3] In terms of the theory for establishing an innovation-oriented country, science and technology shall also be divided into public-oriented products, semi-public oriented products, and private products, as the important basis for the division of the government support or market adjustment. It shall be noted that innovation in fundamental and applied science is the basis for a country's independent technological innovation. Fundamental and applied science share common characters, but are different. Regarding the innovations in fundamental science, the research findings will become public knowledge, but cannot be applied directly and the research and investment cannot bring direct benefits for researchers or even may obtain negative profits. Comparatively, most studies on applied science are common

---

[2] Fundamental science includes six basic subjects: mathematics, physics, chemistry, astronomy, geography, and biology and their sub-disciplines and interdisciplinary subjects. The research results of these subjects constitute the theoretical basis of the whole science and technology and play the guiding role in the field. Refer to Baidu Baike entry "fundamental science."

[3] In economics, public products refer to products owned by the public, which can be used by everyone without returns and paid for by the public, such as street lamps. Semi-public products refer to products of certain public character and certain exclusiveness, such as public traffic, which may be owned by the public, such as the running-water company, or owned by individuals but used by the public, but users shall pay for it. However, the government often provides some subsidies to public traffic and running water supply, so some of their costs are assumed by the public. Private products refer to products of obvious exclusiveness. For example, the ownership of a car purchased by a family belongs to the family. It can only be used by the family members and the cost shall be borne by the family who owns and uses the car.

knowledge, but the studies and publication of applied science have a bigger market than fundamental science and its returns may be greater than the innovation in fundamental science. Though under some circumstances, applied science can be regarded as semi-public oriented products to some extent, innovations in fundamental and applied science are private products in economics.

Theoretically, scientific studies belong to public-oriented and semi-public oriented products, which require public investments from the government and society. It needs to distinguish between the studies on fundamental science and the studies on applied science, and further differentiate the studies on nature, technologies, and engineering and human society in applied science. China shall attach importance to applied science on nature, technologies, and engineering, and also increase the investment in and rationalize the system of strategic studies, management system, scientific polices, and policy making owing to their importance in state governance and control.

The second is the relation between innovations in technologies that benefit the public, and commercial technologies. Technologies can also be divided into public-oriented, semi-public oriented, and private products. If the inventor cannot directly apply the technology on a large-scale and earn profits, the products may be considered as belonging to public-oriented products; when the technical products are sold and profits are earned, but the inventor requires governmental subsidies, the technology is considered as belonging to semi-public oriented products; and if the inventor can recover investment and obtain profits through the transfer and transaction of technologies, such products are said to belong to private products and are the commercial technologies that do not need governmental subsidies.

The theoretical difference in the essence and policies of these technologies can be summarized as follows: (1) It needs to recognize the innovations in technologies that are beneficial to the public and necessary for economic and social development, especially the ones which are in urgent demand. The central and local government should be prodded to invest; (2) The above-mentioned innovations in semi-public-benefit technologies shall also be recognized by the central and local governments according to the demands of social and economic development. The list shall be made based on the order of priority and the degree of public interests with the technology, based on which the proportion and scale of the investment shall be confirmed. Since such technologies are often applied in the semi-public oriented service fields, such as ecological environment, the government shall audit, hear, and rationalize the cost and profits of the semi-public-benefit technologies; (3) The innovations in the technology in essence of the private products that have no relation to the national economy, people's livelihood, and national strategies shall be subjected to market supply and demand and market price. However, the government shall provide support by taxation, government procurement, and subsidies to encourage technological innovation.

The participation of the government, market, and society in technological innovation shall be rationalized to theoretically distinguish among public-benefit, semi-public-benefit, and commercial benefits.

The third is the relation between short-term technological innovation and long-term technological innovation. Short-term technologies need less investment and can earn profits quicker while long-term technologies seek large investment, lengthy development period, great uncertainties, high risks, and slow efficiency. While the relation between benefits in the long-term, short-term and current benefits are understood by governments, but practically, people will hesitate to contribute to great fiscal, human, and physical resources in the development of major technologies that will play their fundamental and strategic roles in the long-term, because it takes a longer time to research and develop major and fundamental science with slower efficiency. Since leaders of regions and departments will change upon the completion of their terms in office, the long-term technologies cannot be counted in their performance of the current performance assessment criteria of cadres.

For the sewage disposal and ecological restoration, some technologies need long-term comparison, filtration, and studies and large investments, so the time value is too big (such as the loss of opportunity profits and financial cost of interests for loans). Even though the main aim of the the Chinese government is to render public service, long-term technologies cannot be counted in the political performance of a cadre, since the term of office of a local secretary and municipal leader is only five years, in addition to the frequent transfer and promotion of these positions. Thus, the innovations in long-term technologies actually end up promoting the profits and performance of the next cadre. Therefore, under such a system, it would be difficult to secure investment of financial and human resources in long-term public-benefit or semi-public-benefit technologies.

Moreover, many enterprises are not willing to invest in innovations in major strategic long-term commercial technologies, such as mobile 3G, 4G, and large aircrafts, though they accumulate enough strength, owing to their large investments and slow efficiency. Innovations in major strategic long-term commercial technologies can only succeed after many trials and require huge investments. Enterprises can obtain considerable profits if they invest in short-term commercial innovations, but face high uncertainties and risks, lose the opportunity to earn profits, or even pay the financial cost for loans if they invest in long-term technological innovation.

Therefore, institutional guarantee is necessary for long-term public-benefit, semi-public-benefit, and major commercial technologies related to the catch-up strategy of science and technologies. For long-term public-benefit and semi-public-benefit technologies, the relevant appraisal system for leaders should be changed so that the special assessment indicators shall be added for the work in ecological environment, energy-saving, and emission reduction that may only show performance afterwards. For long-term technologies that common enterprises are not willing to invest in, such as mobile 4G, the government shall list them as public or semi-public products at the prior stage of development and satisfy the research and development requirements under strict supervision of fund utilization and audit.

The fourth is the relation between the introduction of technologies and independent innovation. Two methods can be employed to implement the scientific and technological catching-up strategy and build an innovation-oriented country. Introduction of technologies and independent innovation are often combined in modernization. Generally, the introduction of technologies will take up a higher proportion initially, while independent innovation occupies more proportion at the later stage. Two points shall be considered in China's strategy of independent innovation: (1) Should China apply independent innovation in all fields, or only independent innovation in select important fields? As a developing country, China is still low in productivity and limited in economic strength, so it does not have enough financial resources to conduct an overall and large-scale scientific and technological independent innovation. Therefore, independent innovations shall be implemented in some major scientific and technological projects that relate to the nation's economy and people's livelihood and are in urgent need for the safety, resources, and development of China; (2) For some technologies, is it more beneficial to introduce, learn, and absorb technologies or to independently innovate? The cost of independent innovation of some scientific and technological projects, regardless of whether they are short-term or long-term, could be higher than the cost of the introduction and absorption of technologies, so China can obtain these technologies through introduction, and conversely the independent innovation can be applied if at a lower cost. For some scientific and technological projects that may take a longer time than other competing countries conducting similar innovations, China shall select to introduce such technologies (developed by competing countries) at home; the other option is to develop and implement technologies through independent innovation before others do. If, according to the risk assessment, independent innovation may probably fail owing to the lack of talents, conditions, and knowledge, which need a long accumulation time, the introduction of technologies shall be applied; otherwise, independent innovation shall be employed with lower risks.

On the one hand, in terms of global competition, China needs to secure a place at the top in the development of science and technologies, so it shall strike at leading world scientific and technological projects where China has foundations, advantages, and conditions in order to improve their scientific and technological competitiveness. On the other hand, some technologies that are not directly favorable for global competitiveness, but are in urgent need by the country, still require independent innovation. For example, based on China's basic conditions of large population and limited resources, the technological innovation in saving oil, fresh water, minerals, and forest resources in production and living and increasing agricultural yield is critical. Therefore, China shall conduct independent innovation in technologies related to national safety and in the improvement of industrial technologies in order to secure a place in the leading world technologies, as well as in the technologies of urgent need by the country.

The fifth is the relation between technological innovation and the availability of skilled and cheap labor resources. Generally, the innovation and progress of industrial technology will facilitate the improvement of the organic composition of industrial capital, so the technological innovation in industries replaces and rejects labor. Therefore, the very rapid progress made in the capital-intensive technologies may lead to the availability of large amounts of surplus labor and unemployment. In terms of the global trade, China will lose more than it gains if it participates in the global market competition with its disadvantages in technologies, instead of the advantages of possessing rich and cheap labor.

Then, how will China deal with the relationship between technological innovation and the employment opportunities? First, China shall develop labor intensive, knowledge intensive, and technology intensive industries, such as software industry and industrial design industry. High-tech, high-knowledge, and labor intensive industries can meanwhile promote innovation and increase employment. Second, China shall promote the professional division of industries based on technological progress, in order to extend the industrial chain and increase the number of chains, therefore increasing the employment rate. Third, new industries, products, and services shall be developed based on technological innovation, so as to increase employment. Fourth, China shall pay attention to the spillover effect of the technological and knowledge innovation among universities and research institutions, develop the knowledge economy and increase employment.

China's lost-cost technological innovation and manufacture features a unique competitive edge in global innovations in science and technology in the future. Developed countries suffer high labor costs in manufacturing and in the innovations in science and technology. China can conduct research and development with low-cost scientific and technological talents and combine it with the low-cost manufacturing to form stronger competitiveness in innovation. It shall be noted that, first, China shall adhere to its low cost of skilled labor and accelerate the research and development in science and technology; second, China shall make full use of the growing period of China's economy and attract more skilled labor to China with its great development opportunities; and third, China shall combine the low-cost manufacturing and low-cost scientific and technological research to establish its comparative edge.

Of course, the increasing organic composition of capital and technological progress in agriculture and industry will extrude labors. Therefore, based on rich labor resources, China shall develop those agriculture that require intensive cultivation by employing labor intensive technological progress (i.e., greater proportion of labor in the ratio of labor to capitals along with the technological progress) or neutral technological progress (stable ratio of capital to labor). In addition, China shall attach importance to the development of the service sector, especially the service industry of high technical content.

The sixth is to correctly handle the relationship between innovation in military technologies and civilian technologies. Military technology innovation benefits the public, and many confidential technologies are owned by the government and are used in national defense and safety. Therefore, common enterprises will not invest in or industrialize these projects without capital resources. However, military and civilian technology innovations can also transform into or promote each other in many developed and emerging countries and regions.

Some technology innovations can be first applied in military use and then civilian use. The restraints in the research and development of major technologies in the catching-up strategy include unsatisfying fields for experiment and improvements and commercial companies' unwillingness to assume huge costs for initial studies. Therefore, if some major technologies can be initially applied into military use, it can transfer the technological innovation to technological applications and guarantee the financial support to the innovation, as the initial cost for the research and development can be assumed by the national defense budget. Some other technologies can be initially applied into civilian use and then transferred to military use. In addition, some mature technologies in civilian use can be directly purchased by the military for national defense and safety. For technologies researched and applied first into civilian use can lower the cost of technologies for national defense and reduce the risks of technological research and development.

To handle the relationship between the military and civilian technological innovation, the relation between s-oriented products and commercial products shall be well handled and an economic checking system for cost, value, and transaction and market adjustment system shall be introduced. For example, the general relationship between both parties related to technological research and development on the general delivery of goods, time, quality, specifications, performance, and prices, as well as the confidential relation, can be agreed upon by signing a confidential and general contract on technology research and development. For example, the military can invite public bidding for technologies among civilian institutions, so as to ensure the low cost, best researcher, and timely completion.

The seventh is the relationship among scientific and technological talents, enterprises, society, and the government. The positions of innovators (scientists, engineers, and technicians, etc.), enterprises (including the enterprises of technological development), society (social organizations related to science and technology), and government (administration sectors of science and technology and relevant departments) shall be clarified and their relations shall be well handled, in order to implement the scientific and technological catching-up strategy and building an innovation-oriented country. (1) The scientific and technological talent is the critical factor for innovation and progress. All scientific findings, technological inventions, and technological transfers originate from intellectual work such as researches, inventions, and creation of scientists, engineers, technicians, and other scientific and technological personnel, i.e., the innovative labor factor. Labor factors can be divided into general and innovative labor factors, where the latter refers to scientific and technological talents including scientists, engineers, and technicians, i.e., the human capital for innovative capability and skills in economics. In terms of the innovative labor factor, China shall first form a force of top fundamental and applied scientists; second, cultivate talents such as senior and medium engineers of high quality in research, development, and applications, as well as a great number of talents to implement technologies, who are also known as technicians; and third, own professional work of high quality. (2) Enterprises are the subjects of innovation. In the previous planned economy system, it was the government that conducted innovations in select projects, preparing budgets, transmitting orders to lower level, allocating funds, and examining and checking before acceptance. Many innovative results are not needed by the market and thus cannot be transformed to products and industries. In the market economy system, enterprises act as the subjects of innovation. Enterprises can integrate various factors and relations, such as the market demand, innovative talents, capital, and land and national policies, organize scientific and technological talents, and establish a research and development center; or they can cooperate and transact with research institutions, develop new technologies based on market demand, apply new technologies into products, expand the scale, form the industry and industry cluster, and thus improve the technological level and competitiveness of all enterprises and the whole industry. (3) Non-governmental organizations behave as the coordinator of innovation. Social organizations related to innovation play the role of coordinating scientific and technological talents, enterprises, and activities, which cannot be fully coordinated by the government or market. (4) The government is the promoter and the server of scientific and technological innovation. The government shall not go against laws of scientific studies and technological research and development, nor separate itself from the environment of market economy and conduct scientific studies and independent innovation by itself; nor do anything but wait for the success or failure of scientific and technological researches and development. The functions and tasks of the government include formulating the strategy for the scientific and technological development of counties, provinces and municipals and plan for some key breakthroughs; investing in scientific study projects beneficial either wholly or partially to public, research institutions for fundamental science and for the benefit either wholly or partially of public; proposing the research plan, transmitting research tasks, organizing forces to conduct studies, or entrust social research organizations or even scientific and technological enterprises to conduct studies; and providing an environment of favorable systems, polices and services for scientific studies and technological research and development. In conclusion, the resources can only be integrated to form a force to promote innovation when the tasks and functions of scientific and technological talents, enterprises, social institutions, and governments in implementing the catching-up strategy and building the innovation-oriented country are complete.

The eighth is the relation between the government and the market in scientific and technological innovation. What is the role of the government and the market in scientific and technological innovation and what is the relation between the two? The author believes that the main functions of the government include: researching and releasing the strategy for long-term independent innovation in science and technology; ensuring the financial investment in public-benefit and semi-public-benefit scientific study and technological research and development; guaranteeing and increasing the investment in fundamental science and major projects of scientific and technological progress; organizing the national study system for key fundamental science and technological innovation projects; formulating the fiscal, tax, talent, and industrial policies for various scientific and technological independent innovations; integrating and coordinating the promotional policies issued by various governmental departments; organizing joint attacks against some major projects; guiding and supervising industrial associations to draw up technical specifications; formulating laws and regulations to protect intellectual property rights and controlling patent and technology market, etc. The government can neither replace enterprises to conduct independent innovations in some technologies, nor replace the market for adjustment.

In the market system, the most efficient market adjustment mechanism to transfer technologies to the production and service capability is formed by enterprises, social organizations, mediators, supply and demand markets, the price of intellectual property rights, salaries of talents, and estimated profits of application technologies. The driving force generated upon this mechanism is to promote innovation, which includes the mechanism of the price of intellectual property rights and estimated profits, salary mechanism for human capital; transaction mechanism between scientific and technological talents and technologies; risk and investment mechanism for technological transfer, interest distribution, and professional division; coordination mechanism, etc.

The ninth is the relation between the guiding position of the department of science and technology and the cooperation of other departments. An overall perspective is needed for scientific and technological innovation. It is an extremely comprehensive strategy for building an innovation-oriented country, involving a unified plan covering education, personnel, finance, public finance, scientific and technological research, development and application, and legislation of science and technology. Therefore, innovations in science and technology need both the guidance of the science and technology department and the cooperation of other departments. The overall scientific and technological perspective can be divided into six aspects: (1) The catching-up strategy and construction of an innovation-oriented country shall coordinate with the overall economic and social development strategy of the country, the department of science and technology shall cooperate with comprehensive governmental departments at all levels, and, in particular, the department of science and technology shall cooperate with the Development and Reform Commission of China; (2) In terms of the human factor of the scientific and technological innovation, the department of science and technology shall cooperate with departments of education and personnel; (3) In terms of the public- and semi-public-oriented products that need governmental support, the department of science and technology shall cooperate with the financial and tax department; (4) In terms of the technologies transferring to products and industries, the department of science and technology shall cooperate with risk investments, credit capital, and capital market, i.e., the China Banking Regulatory Commission, China Security Regulatory Commission, and China Insurance Regulatory Commission; (5) In terms of the applications of science and technologies, the department of science and technology shall cooperate with industry and information, state-owned assets, agriculture and forestry, environmental protection and national defense etc.; and (6) In terms of the encouragement of scientific and technological progress and protection of intellectual property rights, the department of science and technology shall cooperate with the legislation department. In conclusion, this is the overall perspective for the development of science and technology in China that would materialize with active cooperation between the department of science and technology and other relevant departments.

In general, China shall promote the quality of the first phase of modernization, facilitate the process of the second phase of modernization, employ the catching-up scientific and technological innovation plan, handle some major relations, carry out reform, establish the mechanism and system for scientific and technological innovation, and finally build a power of competitive scientific and technological force.

Bibliography

Cao Jing (2006). Strategic thinking on the development of the tertiary industry of China. *Studies on Productivity*, 3.

Special report from Germany and Hong Kong, Qing Mu, Dai Ping and Zhong Yuhua (2009). China dropping by three ranks in global competitiveness. *Global Times*, 20 May 2009.

World Bank (1984). *World Development Report of 1984*. Beijing: China Financial & Economic Publishing House.

Xia Jiechang (2008). Thirty-year development process, experiences, and reform measures of Chinese service industry. *Journal of the Capital University of Economics and Business*, 6.

Zhou Tianyong (2006). *New Development Economics*. Beijing: Renmin University Press.

Zhou Tianyong (2009). *China's Way Out*. Beijing: People's Daily Press. Edited by Zhangsi, Xinhua Net, 18 May 2010.

Zhou Shaosen and Hu Delong (2009). Study on the contribution of scientific and technological progress to economic growth. *Soft Science Journal.*

Zhou Tianyong (2010). *China's Way Out.* Beijing: People's Daily Press.

Note: Relevant data from the website of the State Statistics Bureau.

Chapter 4

Without the Transformation of the Development Mode, China Has No Way Out in Resources and Environment

Economic development is the process where people significantly increase wealth and constantly improve their living standards. However, people's increasing demand for wealth depends on natural resources and the capacity of earth's ecology and environment. If people go beyond the capacity of resources, ecology, and environment, it will lead to resource exhaustion, land desertification, species reduction and extinction, water deterioration, garbage buildup, stale air, rising temperatures, melting glaciers, and unsafe food.

1. Over Population and the Dilemma in Adjusting the Family Planning Policy

What is the acceptable population size of China based on the availability of its land, fresh water, minerals, and other resources? Which is better for China: large or small population? What are the advantages and disadvantages of the family planning policy and will it lead to high dependency ratio, continuous decrease in population, long-term economic recession, and national decay?

1.1. *Various theories on population size*

Different theories on the size of population are introduced here. Various discussions, over many years, have taken place on the future of humanity in terms of economics, society, ecology, and environment. Some religions preach about the "end of the world," perpetuating a pessimistic idea of the future of the human race. Malthusian theory of population has discussed the prospect of the human race in an economic perspective, believing that the world population grows geometrically and grains grow by arithmetic progression, so the unlimited growth of population will incur catastrophic results. On the contrary, the optimistic school of thought believes that the future of the human race is bright. American economist Shultz is the most representative among those who conduct systematic research and demonstration on the bright future of the human race in terms of economics. In his theory of investment in human capital, he believes that people will find new materials, energies and technological progress along with an improvement in their knowledge and abilities, so as to satisfy the increasing demand for grains, solve ecological and environmental problems, and overcome nature's restraints on human beings. Therefore, economic development will not be inhibited along with the accumulation and increase in the value of human capital.

An appropriate population range is defined in the theory of population. The definition of a static population refers to the property of a population that can be assessed with a measurement or estimate at a single point in time (a "snapshot") for e.g., population size according to certain economic standards, based on presumptions of existing production technologies, economic structure, material resources, product allocation, age structure and employment patterns, and without consideration of external factors such as international trade or immigration. The dynamic population refers to the property of a population that can only be assessed with measurements or estimates taken at two or more points in time as confirmed by relevant economic standards related to economic growth, based on changing production technologies, economic structure, material resources, and product allocation (Sauvy, 1982).

1.2. Arguments about acceptable population size of China

The first population census in Chinese history was conducted in 1953 in mainland China, which showed that the total Chinese population amounted to 601,938,035 as of 30 June 1953. At that time, the population was estimated to grow by 12 to 13 million each year with a growth rate of 20%. The population census had aroused the attention of Ma Yinchu, the famous economist and the president of Beijing University. He questioned the validity of the result. According to his knowledge, the net growth rate of Shanghai had reached 39%. He had researched this for three years and found that the annual growth rate of Chinese population should be 22%, even 30% in some places. This was considered too high a figure (Wang Yong, 2007).

What, then, is the acceptable population size of China? Tian Xueyuan and Chen Yuguang from Chinese Academy of Social Sciences had studied the acceptable population size of China between 1979 and 1989 from the perspective of economic development. According to their findings, based on the proportion of workforces in modern industry, agriculture, and tertiary industry and stable age structure of unchanged population, the total Chinese population between 650 million and 700 million is the most favorable for economic development (Tian Xueyuan and Chen Yuguang, 1981). Hu Angang had explored the goal of acceptable population size in terms of economics, resources, environment, and population structure: (1) Regarding economically acceptable population levels as calculated based on population in terms of employment, the population shall be approximately 1 billion in 2000, 1.15 billion in 2020, and 1.38 billion in 2050. To further improvise on the income per capita, the economically acceptable population size of China shall be 809 million in 2000 and 2 billion in 2100 with the low-income level of poor countries as the standard; 485 million in 2000 and 800 million in 2100 with medium-income level as the standard; 250 million in 2000 and 400 million in 2100 with upper-income level as the standard; and 60 million in 2000 and 170 million in 2100 with the income of developed countries as the standard; (2) Regarding the resources capacity, the agricultural resource capacity of China can at best serve a population size of 1.5 to 1.6 billion, according to the Comprehensive Expedition Committee for Natural Resources of the Chinese Academy of Sciences; (3) The population of environmental capacity shall refer to the research findings of Song Jian and Yu Jingyuan (1985) etc.; (4) In order to prevent serious population aging Phenomenon, the total population size shall be controlled between 1.3 and 1.6 billion by 2050 and between 1 and 1.7 billion by 2100. It will be more beneficial to aim for the lower limit; (5) Taking the above-mentioned into consideration, the population goal of different stages of China can be put forward thus: 1.25 to 1.27 billion by 2000, 1.38 to 1.46 billion by 2020, 1.31 to 1.51 billion by 2050, and 1.02 to 1.44 billion by 2100 (Hu Angang, 1989).

Yi Fuxian (2007) is the representative of scholars who opposes controlling population and does not consider limiting population in China. His opinions include the following: (1) Excessive Chinese population is just a widespread falsehood; (2) The population shall be no less or no more than the previous generation (for generation replacement); (3) A healthy population structure is the necessary condition, instead of sufficient condition for economic take-off, rise of the country, and the foundation of rational pension system, but a distorted population structure is a sufficient condition for economic regression.

1.3. *The dilemma in adjusting the family planning policy*

From the perspective of the existing relationship among population, resources, environment, and development in mainland China, some dilemmas exist in planning future economic and social development. On the one hand, three devastating scenarios will emerge if the family planning policy is not strictly implemented in the 9.6 million km² land and 1.3 to 1.55 billion people who live in 36% of that land. First, the pressure on resources, environment, and ecology may exceed its capacity, leading to considerable damages to ecological environment. Second, the population will obviously go beyond the resource supply and environmental capacity if it continues to grow at an annual rate of 8% for three decades and no change occurs in the production mode and consumption method. The third would be the huge pressure on gaining employment. There are more than 200 million excessive labor in rural areas and more than 20 million people face the employment problem each year. Unemployment and the widening gap between income and wealth will result in severe social problems.

On the other hand, various policies, such as only one child per family in urban area, two children allowed in rural area, and more than one child allowed for minority nationalities, may lead to a series of problems. First, the population aging will be facilitated. In the future economic and social activities, the proportion of youth desiring to engage in startups and employment will decrease and the elderly population will need to be taken care of, thus increasing the cost of social care and reducing economic competitiveness. Second, the constant population decline may be unstoppable and the minority nationalities living in areas not suitable for living or development may face population expansion of unbalanced proportion. Third, pollution in industrialization and genetically modified food may lower people's fertility in different degrees. The population transferring from rural to urban areas, the rising cost of living in cities, and competition in urban business startups and employment would significantly decrease peasant workers' willingness to bear children and thus decrease their fertility. Young peasant workers born after the 1980s, 1990s, or even the 21st century are unlikely to move back to villages with their children. However, owing to the employment pressure, income and housing in cities, and high temporal and cost restraints on childbearing, they may significantly change their ideas on family planning comparatively to previous generation. The challenge of finding and retaining employment and living standards in the cities may lower women's fertility. The significantly increasing number of single-child families, imbalanced gender proportion, and death of the only child from disease, suicide, or accidents, may lead to a rapid decline in the population after 2040. It is difficult to change the habit of single-child family planning.

Will China follow Japan's way of negative population growth and slow economic growth and decline after 2040? I think it is possible. Therefore, I consider it is the right time to change China's family planning policy from the current single-child policy to the policy that strictly controls up to three children, but releasing the control over two children in a family, in order to maintain continuous reproduction and prosperity in the Chinese nation.

2. Overstrained Water and Soil and Unfavorable Ecological Environment

By the end of 2008, the Chinese population had reached 1.32802 billion, accounting for 19.53% of the entire world population (about 6.8 billion people). Economic development unavoidably consumes land, fresh water, energies, metallic minerals, non-metallic minerals, and other resources. A comparison between Chinese per capita natural resources and the world average level provided in Sec 2.1.

2.1. *Low level of per-capita resources*

China has a very small per-capita land area, with the arable land, forestland, and grassland area respectively accounting for only 27%, 12%, and 50% of the world average level. The area of desert and potential desertification of land takes up 20% of China's land. China is also very short in water resources, since the water per capita only equals one-fourth of the average world level and the resources are unevenly distributed. The per capita resources of coal, oil, and natural gas are also very low. Coal is the main energy resource of China. In addition to the lack of per-capita metallic resources, China's per capita non-metallic resources only equal 58% of the average world level. As a country with a large population and relative lack of resources, China is lower in the per capita resources of land, fresh water, energy, and other minerals than the world average level. Moreover, in view of the demand for increased per capita GDP growth in the future, and the resource consumption of developed countries, China will see a wider gap in the resources.

2.2. *Overstrained water and soil*

According to population economics, every country has an acceptable population size based on its environmental capacity, and available resources of arable land, grassland, minerals, and fresh water. A series of problems, such as resource shortage and ecological and environmental deterioration, will emerge when the country goes beyond the population limit, meaning the population exceeds the capacity of the country.

2.2.1. Overstrained and deteriorated land

Chinese people, accounting for 20% of world population, are living in a land area covering 6.44% of the world. Such a large population living in a relatively small place, particularly with mostly living in East China, will definitely place huge pressure and damages to land, fresh water, resources, ecology, and environment, as well as a series of economic and social problems, such as unemployment, insufficient housing, traffic congestion, and heavy burden of care for the elderly.

(1) The quality of an arable land is generally low. As stated in the *Investigation and Assessment on the Quality and Grade of Nationwide Arable Land* published by the Ministry of Land and Resources on 24 December 2009, the fundamental characteristic of the quality and grade of the arable land in China is generally low. The main reasons include the serious erosion of the land and severe pollution of limited arable land during industrialization.

(2) Grassland deterioration and desertification. Desertified grassland has covered approximately 90 million hectares, taking up one-third of the total area of Chinese grassland, due to the increasing scale of animal husbandry, over-grazing in limited grassland, over-exploitation of water resources of the grassland, and the conversion of grassland to arable and forestry land. At the end of the 20th century and in the beginning of the 21st century, about 1.33 million hectares of grassland are deteriorating and soil erosion in livestock zones is worsening.

Based on the view of various countries and regions, compared to the green hills and clear water of other countries and regions, China has a larger area of desertified area, lower forest coverage, deteriorated grassland, dense distribution of villages, and yellow land.

2.2.2. *Approaching the limit of fresh water supply*

Due to the population exceeding the capacity and the great pressure to augment China's agricultural, industrial and urban development, the current supply of water resources is depleting and conversely leading to serious pollution of fresh water resources.

The water resources are in very short supply, which is mainly manifested by the lack of water for agricultural, industrial, and urban use. More than 33 million hectares of land in China are suffering from drought, leading to a 5% reduction in grain production. Economic and social development has meant that existing water sources have been diverted for irrigation and placed greater pressure on the agricultural water supply. In normal years, the nationwide shortage of agricultural water supply reaches about 30 billion m^3. For industrial water supply, the shortage amounts to at least 6 billion m^3 in normal years, reducing the industrial output by 200 billion yuan. According to the nationwide water supply investigation in 667 cities, more than 420 cities are suffering from water shortage including 46% of these cities lacking water due to resource problems, 8% due to water quality, and 26% due to engineering. The total water shortage of these cities reaches approximately 10.5 billion m^3 (CCTV.com, 2010).

Water shortage leads to over exploitation of ground water. In 2008, relevant departments conducted an incomplete survey on the ground water depression funnel "funnel" in 21 provinces and found 81 funnels with a total area of 70,000 km^2. Among the 38 shallow (diving) funnels, 11 had a total area of funnel over 500 km^2, while 24 had a buried depth of ground water over 20 m at the center of the funnel. Among the 43 deep (confined water) funnels, 25 had a total area of funnel over 500 km^2, while 13 have a buried depth of ground water over 50 m at the center of the funnel. Based on the comparison between the beginning and the end of 2008, the area of shallow funnels has increased in 21 places of ground water and the water level at the center has lowered in 21 places; while the area of deep funnels has increased in nine places and water level at the center has lowered in 10 places (Ministry of Water Resources of the People's Republic of China, 2004, 2006, 2008).

2.3. *Severe environmental pollution*

Tremendous pressure is exerted on ecological environment along with the increasing population and modernization in agriculture, industrialization, and urbanization.

2.3.1. *Serious pollution of water bodies*

Regarding the surface water of China, seven river systems, including the Changjiang river, Yellow river, Pearl river, Songhua river, Huai river, Hai river and Liao river, are moderately polluted. Hai river suffers from severe pollution when compared to the pollution levels in the Yellow, Huai, and Liao rivers. According to the examination of 409 sections of 200 main and branch waterways, 45% of them belong to grade IV water quality, which is applicable for general industrial water supply. The major pollution indicators include ammonia nitrogen, petroleum, biochemical oxygen demand, (BOD) and permanganate. In addition, 78.6% of water in key state-controlled lakes (reservoirs) belongs to grade IV water quality or lower, with total nitrogen and total phosphorus as the major pollution indicators. Meanwhile, the water quality in 11 urban lakes, such as Taihu lake, Chao lake, Baiyangdian lake, and the West lake, is worse than the grade IV (The Ministry of Environment Protection, 2008).

Rural water faces a more and more serious pollution problem. As shown in relevant data, 700 million Chinese people living in rural areas are drinking unqualified water, and the content of hazardous substances in drinking water for 190 million people exceeds the stipulated standards, with Escherichia coli exceeding 86%. Eighty eight percent of diseases and 33% of deaths in China are related to contaminated domestic water. Factors contributing to the increasingly severe pollution problems of rural water include: (1) The agricultural area pollution; (2) Pollution of industrial waste; (3) Pollution of irrigation with dirty water; (4) Pollution of agricultural breeding; and (5) Pollution of domestic sewage and wastes.

It is economically impossible to treat the pollution of rural water owing to the high cost caused by dispersed villages. According to the second nationwide agriculture census, only 19.4% of China's urban domestic sewage has undergone centralized treatment. As shown in the investigation *Report of Conditions and Problems of Residential Environment in Rural Areas* by the Ministry of Construction, 96% villages have no drainage channels or sewage treatment systems (Chinese Urban Water Net, 2008).

2.3.2. Trend of rural and urban waste pollution

Various types of waste pollutions in rural and urban areas are increasing along with the urbanization, industrialization, and agricultural modernization of China, with more and more secondary pollutions of fresh water, food, and air. However, waste disposal has been gradually controlled owing to the improvement of public services in urban areas, but the waste pollution in rural areas is becoming more and more serious due to the high cost of treatment in scattered villages and limited financial investment in rural public service.

2.3.2.1. Urban waste pollution is gradually taken under control

Currently, 600 million people are living in urban areas of China. At a conservative estimate, every person living in urban areas produces 200 kg of domestic waste each year, so the domestic waste of urban areas reaches 120 million tons every year, which will increase along with the increase in urban population. The treating capacity and comprehensive utilization of industrial waste are increasing, while the waste discharge is declining.

2.3.2.2. The increasingly serious problem of waste pollution in rural areas

The categories and number of rural consumer goods have significantly grown along with the rapid economic growth in rural areas, which made it difficult to classify and treat solid waste in rural areas. In previous years, China had placed the focus of environmental protection on medium and large-sized cities, but ignored the environmental pollution of rural areas. Presently, the rural environment continues to deteriorate.

Urban areas transfer the waste pollution to rural areas. Owing to financial difficulties and lagging equipment for waste disposal, many domestic wastes have been transferred from urban to rural areas without pollution-free disposal systems, and some suburbs and villages have become cities domestic waste dump, which occupy and damage a large number of roads and land and pollute the air and water sources. This is one of the biggest sources of pollution in the rural environment.

Pollution by human and livestock bodily waste in rural areas. Most human and livestock bodily waste is directly discharged to the environment, resulting in great pollution to water, soil, and air.

The pollution of domestic waste of peasants. The domestic wastes of peasants mainly include kitchen residues, packaging residues, disposable products, and old clothes.

Pollution of straw in villages. The annual output of straw amounts to 600 million tons, including 180 million tons of rice straw, 220 million tons of corn straw, and 110 million tons of wheat straw. The straw produced from rapeseed plants, soybeans, sugarcanes, sorghums, and peanuts, etc. exceed 10 million tons every year.

Pollution of plastic films for agricultural tents. More than 1.8 million tons of plastic films were used in 2005.

2.3.3. Greenhouse gases and air pollution

Atmospheric problems mainly include two difficulties: First, CO_2 emission generated from energy consumption will lead to a "greenhouse effect" of the earth and a warming of the climate; second, sulfur dioxide, dust, carbon monoxide, and other harmful substances will affect people's living environment. Unlike solid waste pollution, air is flowing among different countries, so this problem needs global concern and solution.

Huge pressure on China to reduce its carbon emissions. In the 2009 Copenhagen Climate Meeting, some experts believed that even though China promised to lower the CO_2 emission for unit GDP by 40% (to 45% by 2020), China's total emission would still be doubled owing to its 8% economic growth rate.

The atmospheric environment is improving along with the actions of energy conservation and emission reduction, despite the serious pollution by acid rain. In terms of the structure of nationwide air pollution, in 2008, the emission of sulfur dioxide reached 23.212 million tons, smoke emissions reached 9.016 million tons, and industrial dust emissions came to 5.849 million tons, which were respectively 5.9%, 8.6%, and 16.3% lower than the previous year. The air quality in cities is improving, owing to the efforts taken at the end of the 10th five-year plan and beginning of the 11th five-year plan. The overall air quality in China since 2008 has improved, although some parts of cities still suffer from severe pollution. The acid rain pollution problem is severe and the nationwide distribution of acid rain remains unchanged, mainly concentrated in Chengdu and Chongqing and in the middle reaches of Changjiang river, Changjiang river delta, and Pearl river delta.

In conclusion, in the recent three decades, especially in the latter 20 years after industrialization, the population exceeding land's capacity and the increasing pressure on economic and social development has led to deteriorated soil. Water resources are severely polluted, where significant improvements can be seen in the control of pollution, but no fundamental long-term plans have been made. Cities lack water treatment facilities, water and sewage drainage pipelines, and sufficient funds for sewage treatment factories. Water pollution in rural areas, without proper treatment, is becoming more and more serious. Urban and rural wastes have increased. Garbage dumps are surrounding cities and polluting water, and the waste pollution in small cities and towns are worsening. Waste pollution in rural areas is increasingly serious, including waste from production, plastic, packaging materials, constructions, and feces of humans and livestock, since no sufficient funds or proper systems can be provided for the waste

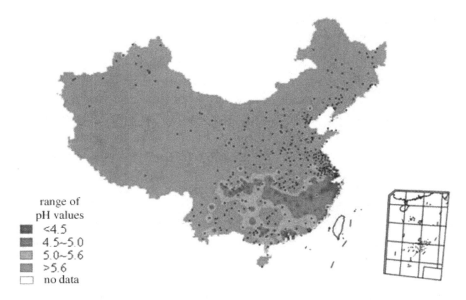

range of
pH values
■ <4.5
■ 4.5~5.0
■ 5.0~5.6
■ >5.6
☐ no data

Fig. 4.1. Nationwide Distribution of Acid Rain Pollution.

transfer and treatment. Air emissions and pollutions have been improved in both rural and urban areas, but the whole situation is not optimistic. Automobile emissions are still increasing, acid rain pollution is still severe in some regions and pressure to discharge pollutants and greenhouse gases such as CO_2, sulfur, and dust is urgent, due to the energy structure and development demands on coal.

3. Land Supply Far from the Future Demands

From the perspective of supply and demand of resources such as land, fresh water, energy, minerals, environmental capacity, and other resources, the most crucial aspect of the development mode is the investment and output method to be applied for various combinations of factors. This aspect is presented by the investment proportion, consumption, output level, and dynamic growth, and change of investment and production level. Here, the author discusses the future situation without any change in the development mode in terms of land, fresh water, oil, and iron resources.

3.1. *Comparison of land resources between China and other countries*

The supply and demand of land resources is summarized here. The land of a country can be classified into forests, grasslands, arable land, wetland, water land, traffic land, village land, independent industrial and mineral land, and land for urban construction use. Some countries also own desert, gobi, and semi-desertified land, also known as inefficient or low-efficient land since these lands cannot be utilized.

Based on the comparison and analysis of the above Table 4.1: (1) The population density of the Chinese mainland is 138 people/km², ranking 11th in the world. However, if calculated based on efficient land area, China's population density is 364 people/km², ranking third in the world, only after Bangladesh and India; (2) The arable land of China covers 1.82 billion mu (a Chinese unit, a mu equals to 0.165 acres). Since the actual area is slightly different than the statistical area, we suppose here that the arable land of China is 2.42 billion mu, so the per capita arable land of China only equals to 55% of the world level, ranking sixth from the bottom after the United Kingdom, Japan, Italy, Bangladesh, and Vietnam. The arable land per agricultural labor of China ranges between 0.36 and 0.49 hectares, the third from the bottom after Bangladesh and Vietnam.

A careful study should be conducted on how much land is needed for future economic and social development and where it is needed. The land can be used to build residences and offices, roads, hydropower plants, independent factories and mines in the development zone, and large processing and resource-oriented enterprises. The land can be further classified as ecological land to protect and restore ecological environment, arable land for the production of agricultural products, grassland for animal husbandry, and forest land to improve the green coverage. Four types of lands, including land for urban construction; rural construction land; land for traffic, water control, and independent factories and mines; and arable land for agricultural use are analyzed here.

Table 4.1. Comparisons of Land and Arable Land of Some Countries.

Country	Population	Land Area	Population Density	Arable Land	Per-Capita Arable Land	Agricultural Labors	Arable Land per Labor
World	667,172	14,900.00	45	14.9	0.22	266,868	0.56
Russia	14,425	1,707.50	8	1.26	0.88	840	15.0
Canada	3,359	997.10	3	0.68	2.02	39	174.0
China	132,256	960.10	138	1.21	0.09	33,000	0.36
China (actual arable land area)	132,256	960.10	138	1.61	0.12	33,000	0.49
America	30,195	936.40	31	1.97	0.65	225	87.5
Brazil	18,808	854.70	22	2.80	1.49	470	59.6
Australia	2,170	774.10	3	0.51	2.35	34	150.0
India	116,902	297.47	393	1.70	0.15	23,000	0.73
Argentina	3,874	278.00	14	0.27	0.70	155	17.4
Kazakhstan	1,676	271.70	6	0.35	2.10	190	18.4
Sudan	3,811	250.60	15	0.84	2.20	1,295	6.48
Algeria	3,282	238.20	14	0.08	0.24	100	8.00
South Africa	4,869	121.90	40	0.15	0.31	165	9.10
Saudi Arabia	2,429	215.00	11	0.036	0.15	100	3.60
Mexico	10,745	195.80	55	0.23	0.21	1,200	1.92
Indonesia	24,545	190.50	128	0.34	0.14	4,909	0.69
Bangladesh	15,867	14.40	1102	0.09	0.06	5,950	0.15
Japan	12,772	37.78	338	0.05	0.04	300	1.66
Philippines	8,947	30.00	298	0.14	0.16	1,232	1.14
Vietnam	8,738	32.96	265	0.10	0.11	3,200	0.31
UK	6,060	24.48	248	0.06	0.01	50	2.00
Germany	8,245	35.70	231	0.12	0.22	65	18.5
Pakistan	16,580	80.39	206	0.80	0.48	4,560	1.75
Italy	5,813	30.12	193	0.03	0.05	95	3.16
Nigeria	13,388	92.38	145	0.60	0.45	5,154	1.16
France	6,018	55.10	109	0.18	0.29	100	18.0

Source: Data of population, land area, arable land and agricultural labors comes from relevant websites. The population mainly adopts the data of 2008, and only a few employ the data of 2007 and 2009. Other data ranges from 2005 to 2009. The area of arable land of a few countries equals to the area of cultivable land.

3.2. *Demand for land for urban construction in the future*

Land for construction covered 495.87 million mu in China in 2008, which approximately included 78 million mu of land for urban construction, 64.5 million of land for independent factories and mines, 261.35 million mu of land for rural use, 37.35 million mu of land for traffic, and 54.67 million mu of land for water conservancy construction, though it is difficult to extract a precise figure.

By 2040, China will see a per capita GDP of more than 25,000 USD and an urbanization level above 90%. Urbanization needs land. We assume that China would control its population at 1.55 billion and reach an urbanization level of 90% in 2040; further assuming that when the urban population is 1.395 billion, the built-up area in cities would cover 140,000 km^2 based on the standard of 10,000 people for every km^2. This means that 210 million mu of land would be required. China's urban built-up area was 50,868 km^2 in 2007. In 2009, China's urban population was 622 million, so the built-up area was estimated to be around 52,000 km^2. Based on the standard of 10,000 people for every km^2, it was 10,200 km^2 smaller than the predicted urbanization level; 15.3 million mu more of land should have been provided in the past 28 years.

In the next 32 years (including 2009), 132 million mu more land is needed solely for urban construction, so 4.13 mu of land should be supplied annually on average. The demand of urbanization and compensation for the current lack of land, 88,000 km^2, i.e., 132 million mu of land, should be increased for future urban construction for the next 32 years. Therefore, 285.5 km^2, or 4.13 million mu of land would be required to satisfy the demand of urbanization.

The current urban residential area reaches approximately 12.5 billion m^2. It should be clarified that for the standard of 10,000 urban people for every km^2, the residential area is calculated based on 40 m^2 for each person and the nationwide average level is calculated based on the floor area ratio of two. Therefore, the residential area is 56 billion m^2, so a land area of 45 million mu would be required that would include supporting facilities, such as schools and community hospitals, which cover 22.96% of the urban built-up area. However, in the next 32 years, if every family owns two, three, four, or five houses, another land area of respectively 45 million mu, 90 million mu, 135 million mu, and 180 million mu may be needed. The number of houses owned by urban residents is the key factor for the area of land needed in future urbanization.

3.3. *Land for traffic, water conservancy, and independent factories and mines in the future*

As mentioned above, as a country of large population and area, China ranks third in the world, in the population density based on efficient land area. The traffic volume of China will grow rapidly along with an increase in production and and enhancement in people's lifestyles. When China attains the level of developed countries in 2040, the infrastructure requirements would definitely be greater than the needs of the current developed countries, so a large amount of railways, highways, ports, and airports should be built.

In the next 32 years, including 2009, supposing the ports can be built based on reclamation, 107.18 million mu of land would be required to be supplied to railways, highways, airports, water conservancy construction, and independent factories and mines, with the reclamation of factories and mines of 30.32 million mu of land deducted.

Land for infrastructure also includes ports and airports. It can be assumed that most ports will be built by reclaiming from the sea. According to developed countries, one airport is built per 10,000 km^2, and each airport covers 5,000 mu on average. Therefore, 5 million mu of land is necessary for the construction of 960 airports. Currently, the Chinese mainland possesses 150 airports, so 810 more are needed, which will cover 4 million mu of land. A total of 110 million mu is necessary for the future construction of railways, highways, and airports. Supposing that four-fifths of the traffic facilities gets completed in the first 22 years (including 2009), hence 4 million mu of land should be supplied each year. Then 2.2 million mu of land shall be provided each year in the last 10 years.

Currently, the land for independent factories and mines covers 27.5% of the land for construction, excluding the land for village use. How much land is needed for independent factories and mines? The author estimates based on the method proposed by Liu Wensheng from the College of Civil Engineering and Architecture of Hubei University of Technology. The author concludes that 34.18 million mu of land is needed for independent factories and mines, according to the annual GDP growth rate of 7%, 30.32 million mu lesser than the 64.5 million mu in 2008 (Liu Wensheng, 2007), which is mainly because some development zones are combined with urban construction and are no longer independent factories and mines, while some mines are reclaimed after exploitation.

3.4. *Land for village use in the future depending on government guide*

The data regarding the amount of land that the Chinese rural areas cover is unclear. The author collected data from relevant governmental departments. In 2004, China had 3.27 million natural villages. Since every natural village has 58 families and 232 people and covers 135 mu (Zhou Tianyong, 2010, p. 238), the national village coverage amounts to 445 million mu. This can be calculated via another method based on the per capita residential area of rural residents. The rural population in 2007 reached 727.5 million and per capita residential area was 31.6 km², so the land for village use covered 272 million mu in total (Zhou Tianyong, 2010, pp. 198, 199). About 261.35 million mu is needed, according to the statistical yearbook of 2009 (National Bureau of Statistics of China, 2009).

How much land will villages occupy in the future? We assume that rural population would account for 10% of total population by 2040, which is 150 million people. Different situations under different models can be predicted.

Model 1: 171.35 million mu of land can be revived in 2040 from the current land used for villages and be reclaimed as arable land and land for urban construction.

Model 2: If rural inhabitants who have transferred to cities do not abandon their houses in rural areas, but live in both rural and urban houses, the land for village use will reach 412 million mu by 2040, 150.65 million mu more than the current coverage with the improvement of rural houses taken into consideration.

Model 3: If urban residents are allowed to buy houses in rural areas, the land for village use will expand to 620 million mu, so 358.65 million mu more is needed.

3.5. Amount of arable land needed to feed the Chinese population

China's grain output in 2008 amounted to 528.5 million kg. The planting area for grains reached 1.602 billion mu, with a production of 330 kg per mu. The rapeseed output is 12.1 million kg, with a planting area of 192 million mu, and a production of 630 kg per mu. Currently, 550 million mu of arable land is needed for cotton, vegetables, tea, flax, tobacco leaf, sugar, and natural rubber planting. According to statistics, arable land covers an area of 1.82 billion mu, the planting area covers 2.34 billion mu, and the multiple cropping rate is approximately 29%. As shown in the study below, the imported agricultural products of China need a planting area of around 580 million mu. In summary, the planting area of agricultural products shall be 2.92 billion mu, which is 580 million mu more than the current planting area. The problem is now actually solved by the import of grains and oil.[1]

Considering the population increase and upgrading consumption structure, 2.51 billion mu of arable land would be required by 2040. Even if the current arable land of 1.82 billion mu does not reduce, 700 million mu of land would be required. Chinese population would reach 1.55 billion by 2040, including 1.395 billion urban population

---

[1] China only introduced 42.55 million tons of soybeans in 2009, only taking up 7.8% of total output of grains and rapeseeds in 2009. The output per mu of soybeans is approximately 115 kg; 370 million mu of land will be needed if China produces the imported soybeans in 2009 by itself.

and 155 million rural population. According to the research made by Liang Shumin and Sun Qingzhen, the per capita grains and oil amounts to 498 kg in urban areas and 482 kg in rural areas, considering changes in the dietary consumption structure. Therefore, the demand of urban residents on grains and oil would reach 672.3 billion kg and the demand of rural residents on grains and oil would reach 74.7 billion kg, amounting to 747 billion kg. If the output remains unchanged, the planting area required for grains and oil would be 2.479 billion mu. If the demand for other agricultural products including grains and oil grows by 38.2%, then the agricultural products excluding grains and oil would need 760 million mu. The total demand for planting area would reach 3.239 billion mu (according to the current multiple cropping rate, 2.51 billion mu of arable land is needed), which is 900 million mu higher than the current 2.34 billion mu of planting area. Even though 1.82 billion mu of arable land will not be occupied, lack of 700 million mu of the agricultural arable land will be evident by 2040, based on the current multiple cropping rates.

3.6. *Newly increasing demand of land ranges from 856 million mu to 1.556 Billion mu in the future*

According to the above analysis, three possibilities of the supply and demand of land in 2040 are stated below:

Possibility 1: The total demand on the land for construction would be 157.66 million mu, the gap in the agricultural land is estimated to be 700 million mu, and the total gap in land supply is estimated to be 857.66 million mu.

Possibility 2: The total demand on the land for construction would be 563.66 million mu, the gap in the agricultural land is estimated to be 700 million mu, and the total gap in land supply is estimated to be 1.26366 billion mu.

Possibility 3: The total demand on the land for construction would be 855.66 million mu, the gap in the agricultural land is estimated to be 700 million mu, and the total gap in land supply is estimated to be 1.55566 billion mu.

4. Restraints on the Supply of Fresh Water Resources

Water resources can be categorized into four categories, based on their application: water for agricultural irrigation, industrial use, service industry, and urban domestic use. Some statistics regard water for service industry as part of urban domestic water. Water supply in China, from surface water, ground water, and other sources, amounted to respectively 479.64 billion m^3, 108.48 billion m^3, and 2.87 billion m^3 in 2008, a total of 591 billion m^3. The demand for agricultural water is 366.35 billion m^3, the demand for industrial water is 139.71 billion m^3, domestic water is 72.93 billion m^3, and ecological water is 12.02 billion m^3, respectively accounting for 62%, 24%, 12%, and 2%. The total demand reaches 591 billion m^3. Many experts have already analyzed the future supply and demand of water resources.

4.1. Increase in the demand for water resources

The author reaches the following predictions based on analysis.

Agricultural water: Chinese population is estimated to reach 1.55 billion by 2040. As analyzed above, the per capita consumption of grains and oil would be 482 kg every year, so a total of 747 billion kg of grains and oil are needed. According to the calculation of Professor Liu Changming (Liu Changmin and He Xiwu, 1998), 1.23 m^3 of water is currently needed in the production of 1 kg of grains. Supposing if water conservation reaches by 40% in 2040, 0.74 m^3 of water would be needed in the production of one kg of grains and the demand for agricultural water would, therefore, be 552.8 billion m^3.

Domestic water: The urbanization level of China would amount to 90% by 2040, so nearly 1.4 billion people would be living in cities. The demand for domestic water will mainly increase for two reasons. First, the water consumption will increase due to urbanization and change of residents' lifestyle. Second, the proportion of tertiary industry may grow to 65% in the industrial structure, so the water for urban service industry will significantly grow. As the medium level of per capita water consumption in developed countries is 0.5 m^3 each day, the per capita water consumption will amount to 182 m^3 each year. By 2040, the domestic water consumption for the 1.55 billion population of China will equal 282.1 billion m^3 according to the current average standard of developed countries.

Industrial water: Based on the annual growth rate of 7%, industry is expected to maintain a proportion of 25% in the industrial structure by 2040, about 50% lower than the current proportion. However, the total industrial added value would reach 7.05 billion yuan, which is 4.5 times the amount of 1.57 billion in 2009. If no water-saving technology is employed, 627.45 billion m^3 of water resources will be consumed by the industries if the consumption of water resources for each 10,000 yuan of added value remains unchanged. Even if the consumption of each 10,000 yuan of added value decreases by half, i.e., 45 m^3 of water for each 10,000 yuan, 317.25 billion m^3 of water is needed.

Calculated based on the proportion of 2%, ecological water consumption is 23.6 billion m^3.

By 2040, the total demand for water, including agricultural, industrial, domestic, and ecological water is expected to rise to to 1181.1 billion m^3. According to Lester R. Brown (Brown, 1998), the total water consumption would reach 1068.5 billion m^3 by 2030, 112.6 billion m^3 more than the figure of 2030.

4.2. *Supply possibility of water resources and the gap between supply and demand*

Based on an current estimates, the actual available water resources may only amount to 800 to 900 billion m^3 by 2030 and the exploitation of water resources may approach the limit.[2] The total supply of a country's

---

[2]According to the report of Xinhua News Agency from Hefei on 5 November 2006, Hu Siyi, the vice minister of water resources proposed the research and estimation on the 2006 annual conference of China Society of Hydraulic Engineering.

water resource is generally fixed. Even if a new water source is found in 2040, which can supply 10% more water and increase the total amount of water resource supply from 880 to 990 billion m³, the gap between the supply and demand still ranges from 301.1 to 191.1 billion m³.

5. An Import of 10 to 18 Billion Tons of Ferrous Metals is Needed in the Next Three Decades

China is growing into a developed country, so large quantities of iron and steel, as the most important resources for economic and social development, are required in (a) urbanization including construction of residences, office buildings, and hotels; (b) industrialization including construction of factories and manufacturing of equipment, construction of power grid, railways, highways, and pipelines in traffic and transportation, automobiles, and development of shipbuilding industry. Then, what would be the amount of iron needed by 2040, and what would be the condition of supply and demand?

— 300 to 600 kg/person/year of steel are consumed after industrialization by the developed countries.

The change in steel consumption in developed countries can be categorized into two types. In the case of gradual industrialization, the consumption of steel grows slowly, reaches the peak, declines, and maintains consumption at a fixed level. In rapid industrialization, the steel consumption increases sharply, reaches maximum, and then declines, and maintains at a fixed level.

China has been in the process of rapid industrialization and urbanization since reform and opening up. The current per capita steel consumption has reached 350 kg/year. Since the Chinese population is estimated to reach 1.55 billion by 2040, the demand for steel in the future can be calculated, which is described below.

Low demand for steel: Between 2011 and 2020, the per capita steel consumption will reach 400 kg and the demand for steel will amount to 5.467 billion tons due to urbanization. Between 2021 and 2030 when China attains peaks in urbanization, the per capita steel

Table 4.2.   Maximum and Per-Capita Steel Consumption of Top Six Countries.

Country	Maximum Consumption	Per-Capita Consumption in 2003
America	711 (1973)	349
Japan	802 (1973)	603
South Korea	985 (2003)	985
Germany	660 (1970)	454
France	485 (1973)	280
UK	473 (1964)	238

Data source: Statistics on Domestic and Foreign Steel Consumption from 1949 to 1979 and Statistics on Chinese Steel in 2005.

consumption would be 450 kgs and the demand for steel would amount to 6.548 billion tons. Finally, between 2031 and 2040 when urbanization is basically completed, the per capita steel consumption would drop to 350 kgs and the demand for steel would be 5.298 billion tons. A total of 17.5 billion tons of steel would be needed in the next 30 years, with 583 million tons each year.

Medium demand for steel: Between 2011 and 2020, in order to satisfy the housing demands of all rural and urban residents, the per capita steel consumption is estimated to reach 500 kg and the demand for steel would amount to 6.833 billion tons due to urbanization, because many peasant workers would desire to own a house in the city. Between 2021 and 2030 when China's urbanization peaks, the per capita steel consumption would be 550 kg and the demand for steel would amount to 7.919 billion tons due to an increase in the demand for houses and automobiles. Finally, between 2031 and 2040 when it is expected for complete urbanization to be achieved, the per-capita steel consumption would decline to 450 kg and the demand for steel would be 6.81 billion tons. A total of 21.6 billion tons of steel are needed in the next 30 years with 743 million tons each year.

High demand for steel, considering shock-resistant requirements of houses, safety factors of automobiles, and most families possessing two houses: Between 2011 and 2020, the per capita steel consumption is expected to reach 600 kg and the demand for steel would amount to 8.199 billion tons due to urbanization. Between

2021 and 2030 when China achieves peaks in urbanization, the per capita steel consumption would reach 650 kg and the demand for steel would amount to 9.359 billion tons. Finally, between 2031 and 2040 when urbanization is basically completed, the per capita steel consumption would drop to 550 kg and the demand for steel would be 8.323 billion tons. A total of 25.9 billion tons of steel are needed in the next 30 years with 863 million tons each year.

According to the statistical yearbook of 2008 issued by the National Bureau of Statistics, the fundamental iron ore reserves are 22.64 billion tons. The Chinese reserves of ferrous metals of 35% grade are about 8 billion tons. The gaps between the current supply of ferrous metal reserves and the demands of the three versions are respectively 9.6 billion, 13.6 billion, and 17.9 billion tons. The main problem of Chinese iron ore lies in the low grade between 25% and 35%. Based on current technologies and investment, the Chinese iron ore is low in exploitation value and high in cost, while the geological conditions and the traffic for exploitation are comparatively poor. Of course, the quantity of the import of iron ore in the future depends on the new iron ore reserves, as well as progress in the smelting technologies of low-grade iron ore and decline of the exploitation cost if no breakthrough is made in the exploration of high-grade iron ore.

China will step into the levels of developed countries by 2040. According to the above estimation, Chinese iron metals consumption in 2040 would account for 22% to 33% of the world iron metal reserves discovered in 2004. If no progress is made in the exploration of new minerals, especially in high-grade iron ore, and no breakthroughs are made in the technologies and cost of low-grade iron ore, by 2040, China will use all iron metal reserves of 2008 and would need to import 9.5 billion tons, 13.6 billion tons, or 17.9 billion tons of iron, i.e., 17.3 billion tons, 24.8 billion tons, and 32.6 billion tons of ores at the grade of 55%, respectively, according to the low, medium, and high-level version. As predicted by Morgan Stanley, China may need to import 685–864 million tons of iron ores each year between 2011 and 2015, much higher than the author's estimation.

6. China Consumes 50% of the Global Energies, Mainly Oil and Natural Gas

Developed countries can be divided into three models according to the per capita energy consumption of 2007. The countries of high per capita energy consumption, higher than 5 tons/person, include America, Canada, Norway, Australia, Iceland, Holland, and Finland; the countries of medium per capita energy consumption, between 3.5 and 5 tons/person, include New Zealand, France, South Korea, Japan, Austria, Germany, UK, Switzerland, and Ireland; and the countries of low per capita energy consumption, lower than 3.5 tons/person, include Italy, Portugal, Greece, and Spain (Yu Wenjia and Wang Anjian, 2009).

The future energy supply of China will mainly come from both domestic production and imports. Main energy resources produced in China include coal, oil, natural gas, hydropower, nuclear power, and wind power. Hydropower, nuclear power, and wind power belong to renewable resources, while the other three resources greatly depend on the current domestic reserves. Insufficient supply will be solved by import. The import structure is decided by the structure of domestic demand on energy consumption. For example, the change in residents' lifestyles after urbanization, such as the ownership of cars, will require an increased import of oil and natural gas if no breakthrough is achieved in technologies that can solve automobile energy consumption of urban families, industries, and commercial sectors.

According to the 2009 Statistical Yearbook of China, the current oil reserves amount to 2.89043 billion tons, natural gas is 3.4049 trillion m^3 and coal is 326.1 billion tons. The per capita reserve of China's oil and natural gas is one-tenth of the world average level. Coal resources are relatively richer in China, but the per capita reserve only amounts to 40% of the world level. China had consumed 375.82 million tons of oil in 2008 and 408.375 million tons in 2009, only second to America in the world. The consumption of natural gas was 78 billion m^3 in 2008 and 87.5 m^3 in 2009. The coal consumption reached 2.74 billion tons in 2008 and 3.02 tons in 2009.

The per capita consumption of oil in China amounted to 284 kgs in 2009, while the per-capita consumption of natural gas was 66 m^3 and coal consumption was 2.28 tons. If China were to curtail its economic development now, and if all consumptions were to be supported by domestic reserves, the available oil, natural gas, and coal can only support the Chinese economy for 7.08 years, 39 years, and 108 years, respectively. Based on the annual consumption of oil and natural gas in the next 31 years as calculated with the following three versions, the domestic oil reserves can support for 1.88 years, 1.46 years, and 1.18 years, respectively, while the domestic natural gas reserves can support for 7.49 years, 4.16 years, and 2.14 years, respectively.

In the future, energy consumption by increasing numbers of cars and traffic volumes will lead to an increasing demand for energies for the motor vehicles. Second, the demand for natural gas among residents and urban service industries will significantly grow along with urbanization. Since China is relatively rich in coals, only the demand for oil and natural gas is analyzed here.

Low consumption of oil and natural gas: If no progress is made in the vehicles driven by other energies, such as electric cars, the per capita consumption of oil and natural gas in China may respectively reach 1.74 tons and 530 m^3, the same level as Japan, along with the development of urbanization and increase in natural gas consumption.[3] By 2040, the demand for oil consumption would amount to 2.697 billion tons, while the demand for natural gas consumption should reach 821.5 billion m^3. The accumulated demand for oil would be 59.577 billion tons and the demand for natural gas would be 14,089.5 billion m^3 by 2040. Based on the reserves in 2008, if no breakthrough is made in the exploration, the gap between domestic oil reserves and the total consumption demand would be 44.7 billion tons and the gap of natural gas would be 10,684.6 billion m^3.

---

[3] In 2008, the per-capita oil consumption of China was 283 kgs, compared to the world average level of 587 kgs, America with 2.91 tons, and Japan with 1.74 tons. In 2006, the per-capita natural gas consumption in America was 2,000 m^3, 530 m^3 in Japan and 400 m^3 of average world level.

Medium consumption of oil and natural gas: the per capita consumption of oil would reach 2.32 tons, the same level as America and Japan, and per capita natural gas consumption may reach 1,000 m³, the same level as Germany. By 2040, the demand on oil consumption would amount to 3.596 billion tons, while the demand on natural gas consumption would reach 1.550 trillion m³. The accumulated demand for oil would be 61.563 billion tons and the demand for natural gas would be 25,381.2 billion m³ from the present to 2040. Based on the reserves in 2008, if no breakthrough is made in exploration, the gap between domestic oil reserves and the total consumption demand would be 58.7 billion tons and the gap of natural gas would be 21,976.3 billion m³.

High consumption of oil and natural gas: the per capita consumption of oil is estimated to reach 2.91 tons, the same as America and per capita natural gas consumption may reach 2,000 m³, the same level as America. By 2040, the demand on oil consumption would amount to 4.511 billion tons, while the demand on natural gas consumption would reach 3.100 trillion m³. The accumulated demand for oil would be 75.745 billion tons and the demand for natural gas is 50.7624 trillion m³ from the present to 2040. Based on the reserves in 2008, if no breakthrough is made in the exploration, the gap between domestic oil reserves and the total consumption demand would be 72.9 billion tons and the gap of natural gas would be 4.7358 trillion m³.

The proven global oil reserves in 2009 amounted to 1.3331 trillion barrels. Based on the conversion rate of 7.33 barrels to 1 ton, the reserves reached 181.87 billion tons, with an annual output of 3.98 billion tons. The current reserves/exploitation ratio is 45.7 years. In the next 31 years, without the increase in oil reserves, 40.08%, 33.8%, and 26.2% of global oil reserves will be consumed by China based on the high, medium, and low consumption versions, respectively. The annual oil consumption of China equaled 61.42%, 49.89%, and 38.6% of global oil output in 2009. If the output remains unchanged, then it can be said that China's consumption of oil in 2040 will be 5.31 tons more than the total oil output of the whole world in 2009, based on the high consumption version. Even based on the low consumption version, China's oil consumption in 2040 will take up to 67.76% of global output in 2009.

By the end of 2008, the global natural gas reserves amounted to approximately 6.254 trillion cubic feet, 177.09 trillion m³, with an annual output of 2.82 trillion m³ and a ratio of reserve to exploitation of 62.8 years. In the next 31 years, without the increase in global natural gas reserves, China will consume 8% of global reserves. The annual natural gas consumption of China takes up to 56.52%, 29.03%, and 16.11% of global natural gas output in 2009 based on the high, medium and low consumption versions, respectively. Even the natural gas output of the whole world in 2009 will be 280 billion m³ lower than China's consumption in 2040, based on the high consumption version. Even based on the low consumption version, Chinese oil consumption in 2040 will take up to 29.13% of global output in 2009.

It is clear that the domestic oil and natural gas reserves are far from sufficient over the next 31 years, even according to the lowest consumption level of current developed countries. The gap of oil is 15.5 times of domestic reserve in 2008, while the gap of natural gas is 3.14 times. If no fundamental change occurs in the development mode, and living and consumption method, or no major and widespread breakthrough is made in energy technologies and applications, the economic and social development of China in the future will basically depend on global energy reserves and production, so the national economy and geopolitics are placed in an extremely unsafe relations with foreign resources.

Then, what should China do when faced with resource and environment problems in the future? Though China has made great efforts in energy conservation and emission reduction in the 11th five-year plan, it continues to be at the economic development mode of "high energy consumption, high pollution, and exportation of resource products" compared to the advanced levels of the world. The living and consumption method is premature and attempts to unrealistically compare with developed countries of high consumption. If China continues to develop with a higher resource and environment consumption than developed countries, China will lack 2 billion mu of land and 400 billion m³ of fresh water in the future three decades and use 80%, or even all, oil, natural gas, metallic minerals, and other mineral resources. Therefore, its foreign economic and political relations will become rather intense. In addition, several hundred thousand km² of land will be desertified; the water quality of inland rivers and lakes will generally turn to grade IV or V; the seawater pollution at the coastal area will deteriorate; the emission of CO_2 and other harmful gases will increase by one or several times; and solid waste will surround cities and cover the rural areas. The global complaints will increase, and China will become hot, dirty, and desertified.

Based on the above analysis, even though China can adopt lowest consumption level of developed countries in land, fresh water, minerals, and energies, huge gaps still lie between supply and demand in various fields. Therefore, China cannot go on with the development mode of "high energy consumption, high pollution, and exportation of resource products" or develop with the low consumption mode of developed countries in the future due to constraints of large population, resources, and environment. Solving the resource and environment problems now is very critical. The waste development and people's consumption modes must be changed immediately. In order to change the development and consumption modes and establish an energy-efficient and environment-friendly society, a comprehensive study should be conducted on the idea, strategy, route, system, mechanism, and policies, in order to form the scientific mode, strategy, system, and policies suitable for China's reality, which must be practically implemented.

Bibliography

Alfred Sauvy (1982). *General Theory of Population*. France: Commercial Press.

Bai Xu (2006). Desertified Land Accounting for 18.12% of Total Area of China. *Xinhua Net*, Beijing. Accessed on 17 June 2006.

Hu Angang (1989). *Population and Development: Systematic Study on Chinese Population Economics*, 12th edition. Zhejiang: Renmin Press.

Hu Baosheng and Wang Huanchen (1981). Research on China's goal of total population based on possibility degree and satisfaction degree. *Collected Papers of the 3rd Scientific Symposium on the National Population.*

Increasingly severe aridity of grassland in China (2004). *Science and Technology Daily*, 26 October 2004.

Lester R Brown (1998). China's Water Shortage could shake would food security *World Watch*, 11(4).

Liang Yaodong and Xie Jinsen (1994). On Mao Zedong's idea of population. *Journal of Fuqing Branch of Fujian Normal University*, 2.

Liu Wensheng (2007). Study on the model of land for independent factories and mines. *Journal of Hubei University of Technology*, 4.

Liu Yuxin (2010). China's potential ferrous mineral resources exceed 200 billion tons. *Beijing Daily*, 2 April 2010.

Lu Changmin and He Xiwu (1998). *Scheme on China's Water Problem in 21st Century*. China: Science Press.

Lu Weidong, Zhou Shaoqi, and Lu Jiangtao (2007). Current situation and prevention measures on solid waste in chinese rural areas. *Sanitation Science and Technology Net*. Accessed on 2 January 2007.

Ministry of Water Resources of the People's Republic of China. Communique on water resources of 2004, 2006, and 2008.

More than 60% cities lose 200 billion yuan in the year of water shortage, *CCTV.com*, 22 March 2010.

National Bureau of Statistics of China (2009). *Statistical Yearbook of 2009.* China: Statistics Press.

Pollutions of arable land entering people's bodies through food (2007). *Chongqing Evening News*, 23 April 2007.

Song Jian and Yu Jingyuan (1985). *Theory on Population Control*. Beijing: Science Press.

The current situation of water pollution in Chinese rural areas. *Chinese Urban Water Net*, Accessed on 24 June 2008.

The Ministry of Environment Protection. Report on China's environment conditions in 2008.

Tian Xueyuan and Chen Yuguang (1981). Discussion on proper population in terms of economic development. *Collected Papers of the 3rd Scientific Symposium on the National Population.*

Topic Group on Water Resources Allocation and Territorial Control. The preliminary analysis on the supply amount and structure of water resources of China, No. 99-3 of the Survey Research Communications of Economic and Cultural Research Center of Chinese Academy of Social Sciences, 20 March 1999.

Wang Wei and Chen Peng (2009). 3/4 growth of global energy consumption comes from China in 2008. *Energy Review*, 8.

Wang Jiansheng (2009). China's arable land quality is generally low. *China Reform Daily*, 25 December 2009.

Wang Xinxiao. *Current Situation About Chinese Waste Pollution*. Available at eblog.cersp.com/userlog21/136502/archives.

Wang Yong (2007). The whole story of criticism on Ma Yinchu's theory of population. *Historical Monthly*, 12.

Wei Yu and Su Yang (2007). Types, current situation, and results of Chinese agricultural environmental pollution. *Chinese Agricultural Information Net*. Accessed on 27 November 2007.

Wu Shukang (2002). Current situation and development trend of livestock feces. *Shanghai Agricultural Science and Technology*, 1.

Yao Runfeng (2009). Comprehensive scientific investigation on the erosion of land and ecological safety in China. *Xinhua Newspaper Net*. Accessed on 29 January 2009.

Yi Fuxian (2007). *A Big Country in an Empty Nest: Chinese Family Planning Heading a Wrong Way*. Hong Kong: Strong Wind Press.

Yu Wenjia and Wang Anjian (2009). Analysis on the zero growth of per-capita energy consumption of developed countries. *Commercial Times*, 12.

Zhang Zhiwei (2009). On the water pollution in rural areas. *Collected Papers of the Environment and Resources Law Society of China Law Society in 2008*, Environmental Law Institute of Wuhan University.

Zhou Rui (2010). Increase of quarterly emission of sulfur dioxide for the first time in three years. *China News Service*, Beijing, 13 May 2010.

Zhou Tianyong (2006). *New Development Economics*. China: Renmin University Press.

Zhou Tianyong (2010). *China's Way Out*. Beijing: People's Daily Press.

Zhu Lei (2007). Domestic and foreign problems in pollution of China's electric waste. *China Quality Newspaper*, 17 May 2007.

Chapter 5

Resources and Environmental Constraints: What China Should Do in the Future

By 2040, when China reaches the level of developed countries, based on the lowest resource and environmental consumption of industrialized countries, China will consume approximately 50% of global oil, natural gas, and iron resources and produce more than 50% of the world's emissions. In the face of the formidable challenges in the future, which development path should China choose in terms of the relationship between China's development and living methods, and resources and environment?

1. The Path of Sustainable Development

China, with a current population of 1.33 billion and a future population of 1.55 billion, is unrealistically comparing itself to the consumption method of developed countries and adapting to high consumerism. However, is the high consumerism pattern of an affluent country like America suitable for China, a country of relatively small per-capita land and resources?

The prices of China's resources and resource products are only half, or even less, when compared to other countries, while its limited environment is used for free or at low cost, because, in many people's opinion, China is a developing country where residents of low income cannot afford resources and environmental products of high prices and taxes. Therefore, the prices of necessities should be affordable that includes electricity, fresh water, grains, natural gas, while prices for oil, channels, and space should be tax free or with a negligible tax. Pollution discharge shall be charged at a low price, or even free of cost at many instances. However, in a country where resources and land (in proportion to the growing population) are in shorter supply than many other countries, these opinions only consider the immediate interests of the current generation, but ignore the interests of future generations. As the Communist Party of China (CPC) and the government assumes power over its people, should they only give consideration to the current generation, or to the sustainable interests of future generations?

Should China give priority to energy saving during urbanization and relieve ecology, or place its focus on saving land in rural areas, protect ecology, and reduce pollution, in that order? Should China only adjust technology, techniques, and product structure within industries to save resources and reduce emissions, or adjust the structure of primary, secondary, and tertiary industries to save resources and control pollution? Should China develop large enterprises and big projects and utilize capitals to promote economic growth in order to save resources and reduce pollution, or should China promote the development of small enterprises, make full use of labors to facilitate economic growth and thus save resources and reduce emissions? Most people do not have a clear idea about these issues and therefore practice incorrect methods.

In the past three decades, China has formed technological systems, and in particular, introduced a series of technologies into automobiles, lighting, power generation for heating, refrigeration, television etc. and information sought after developed countries and conducted re-innovation. However, most of these technologies can be applied in large-scale production, generated with traditional resource supply in European and American resource environment.

Europe and America are thinking about the advantages and disadvantages of these traditional technologies and promoting their progresses in terms of resources and environment. In this aspect, China should actively research, develop, and apply new technologies, vigorously adjust the urban and rural as well as the industrial and enterprise scale structures, establish a clearer property right system, set higher prices according to the degree of scarcity, and increase tax to control pollution and wastage for the welfare of future generations and formulate a living and consumption method that meets the resource and environmental constraints of high prices and taxes.

Which development road should China choose in terms of resources, ecology, and environment? This is a vital question related to the survival and development of the nation.

2. Technical Progress is the Key to Balancing the Resource Supply and Demand and Reduction of Emissions

The previous idea of China's resource strategy was to open up the source and regulate the flow of resources. This may lead to the exhaustion of domestic resources or tense relations with the foreign world by over-opening up sources. Without a possible alternative, regulation of the flow will necessarily lead to slower development. Therefore, only technological progress can save China's future based on basic conditions of China and future demands for resources and ecological environment. This technological progress for the expansion of resources and environment is more urgent to sustain the growth of Chinathan the strategic implementation of the technology to succeed in the global development competition.

According to the above analysis, the technologies would be directed towards the resource bottleneck and small environment capacity, which mainly includes technologies on saving land, increasing and saving fresh water, replacing materials such as iron, saving and replacing traditional energies, reducing pollution, and restoring ecology.

2.1. *Technological renovation of unused land is the key to raising land supply*

After 30 years, China will face a lack of about 1 billion mu of land owing to the rapid urbanization and the conflict between the protection of arable land and construction land. However, the unused land, including desert, saline and alkaline land, and mudflats covers 3.1 billion mu in China, taking up 21.52% of the land mass. In recent years, China is attempting to increase the area of land and has supplemented the arable land of more than 450 million mu through land improvements between 1997 and 2009 (Zhu Liuhua, 2010). In addition to the village improvement, an important and practical measure to protect arable land and meet the requirements of rural and urban construction is to make full use of current mature biotechnological methods and incorporate desert, saline and alkaline land, and mudflats into the comprehensive improvement of land, which can renovate at least 900 million mu and rapidly replenish land in a much lower cost.

Currently, China's comprehensive improvement of land does not include the unused land such as desert, saline and alkaline land, and mudflats. Two assumptions now exist in the data of the saline and alkaline land of China. The first conclusion is that "the total area of saline and alkaline land in China covers 99.133 million hectares," "the saline and alkaline land of China covers about 1.5 billion mu," or "the area of saline land in China reaches 80 million hectares" (Guangming Daily, 2002). The second assumption comes from a second nationwide general survey of soil organized by the Ministry of Agriculture, who claimed that China's saline and alkaline land covered about 35 million hectares. Consequently, the area of saline and alkaline land in China ranges from 600 million to 1.5 billion mu. Mudflats and desert cover an area of about 3.1 billion mu. According to the statistics of maritime sector, the area of mudflats reaches more than 30 million mu, while saline and alkaline land covers 560 million mu. As shown by the statistics of the third desertification monitoring of the Forestry Bureau, the desertified land covers 1.7397 million km² (2.60955 billion mu).

Scientific development should be used to finding solutions to treat saline and alkaline land as they would become precious land resources soon. Based on research, scientists find that with the active BPA (a microorganism technology), it is possible to filter bacterial strains suitable for the transformation of saline and alkaline land by producing a microorganism organic fertilizer. The fertilizer will be applied to saline and alkaline land, where it will absorb the saline and alkaline content with several types of active acid-producing bacteria and lower the pH value and salt content to satisfy the requirements of planting. Then the land can be used for planting pasture grass in the first year and crops in the third year. In addition, the technology can also be applied to transform the hardening arable land formed due to the long-term use of fertilizers, as well as in the mudflats and the deserts. In view of the mature technologies for improving saline and alkaline land with biotechnologies, the government is suggested to release policies on land, science, and technologies in order to meet the requirements of grain safety and land for urban and rural construction with lower cost, which is further explained in the following paragraphs.

(1) The policy is suggested to incorporate the improvement and planning of saline and alkaline land in national strategy. (2) It is suggested to establish a lead group that will monitor the improvement of saline and alkaline land, mudflats, and deserts, with the prime minister as the direct leader, considering the special significance of land increase for China's future development. (3) The government is suggested to supply the funds for land improvement. (4) Relevant preferential policies shall be released to lead social forces to participate. By absorbing social funds for land improvement, it is expected that the availability of land supply would increase, thereby inhibiting social funds from speculating on houses, land, and other properties, which in turn would stabilize housing prices and price levels of other consumer goods.

2.2. *Technologies for saving land and achieving external balance*

Technologies for saving land mainly refer to improving the output per mu of agricultural products such as grains, as seen from the perspective of agriculture and the technology of improving transportation efficiency in traffic construction. If the progress of technologies for improving the output of agricultural products cannot catch up with the speed of the increasing demands for agricultural products, it needs to improvise more on marine fishing, rely on the import of agricultural products, or execute the idea of building farms into foreign lands to achieve balance.

The progress in technologies for improving the output per mu of agricultural products such as grains. As of 2009, China has a grain planting area of 1.635 billion mu, a total grain output of 530.82 billion kg, and an output per mu of 325 kg. In terms of the grain import, the net import of cereal after deduction of export reached 1.742 million tons in 2009. In terms of oil-bearing crops, the import of soybeans has reached 42.552 million tons, edible oil seeds of 45.237 million tons, and edible oil of 9.386 million tons (soybean of 55.21 million tons according to the oil yield of 17% and 37.54 million tons based on the oil yield of 25%). The total net import of grains (mainly soybeans and oil seeds) amounts to 144.741 billion kg. With a higher output of rapeseed plants and lower output of soybeans, the import of grains accounts for a small proportion. On average, the domestic output per mu of imported grains is about 250 kg, so it means that grains covering 578.964 million mu were imported in 2009.

Supposing the sown area of grains remains unchanged by 2040 with the same 1.635 billion mu of land in 2009, and supposing that China achieves self-sufficiency in grains production, the average output per mu shall increase from 325 kg in 2009 to 457 kg in 2040, with a growth rate of 41%.

According to the plan for land use, 157.66 million mu of land is necessary for construction after the land reclamation from villages, independent factories, mines, and houses of rural population. Considering multiple cropping, if the arable land is occupied for construction, another 204.96 mu of land shall be deducted from the above planting area. By 2040, the output per mu shall be raised to 522 kg, 61% higher than the average output per mu in 2009. Of course, this also depends on the progress of grain production technology of China.

The technology for saving land for traffic and construction use is mainly to improve the transportation efficiency. The demand on land for road development will be lower if the road per unit area can transport goods quicker in a certain time. If the speed per hour of a high-speed railway can rise to 360 km, only one-third of land is needed compared to the railway of 120 km/hour, while if the high-way raises its speed per hour from 100 km to 140 km, the land covered by highways will be reduced by 40%.

Half of the land for railway construction will be saved if the railway speed is improved to 250–350 km/hour from the current 120 km/hour. The greatest significance of raising the railway speed in recent years, particularly the development of a high-speed railway system lies in the conservation of land for the construction of railways. China has become the leader in high-speed railway technologies through self-innovation and introduction, absorption, and re-innovation of foreign technologies. The high-speed railway transportation only consumes 1/40 of the energies consumed by air transportation. In addition, the development of a high-speed railway system also contributes to the balance of resources, which lowers the proportion of demands on oil in the increasing transportation. The development and popularization of high-speed railway plays a very strategic role in adjusting the structure of transportation energy, saving oil, and overcoming the oil bottleneck in China, a country with a large and dense population.

There is no obstacle in developing the technology for construction of high-speed highway and improving the speed of vehicles. In order to save 25% of land for highway construction, the main task is to improve the running speed, guarantee the construction quality, build fewer highways, and keep the highways smooth. Currently, two problems lie ahead. The first is the low speed restriction of freeway, which is 100 to 120 km/hour. The author considers due to the restriction in the speed, the vehicles will occupy 27.23% more land than the speed limit of 140 km/hour. More land will be needed for vehicles if the speed limit of classified highways is too low. Therefore, the second task of saving the land for road construction is to increase the speed of freeways and classified highways.

Based on the above analysis, the biggest gap in the future land supply of China is the scarcity of lands for agricultural usages, which will be replenished by external factors. The author believes this is the set future of China, independent of man's will. If the diet consumption structure of Chinese residents is upgraded, especially if meat accounts for a greater proportion of their daily diet, a large number of agricultural products will be consumed, leading to a greater demand for land. Imports will be necessary if the domestic output per mu cannot be increased by 60%. First, import of agricultural products can replenish the sufficient supply of grains in China. In particular, the import of agricultural products of low output per mu and large water consumption is acceptable for saving the land and fresh water resources of China. Second, Chinese entrepreneurs are encouraged to develop and build farms abroad to plant agricultural products, especially those that consume great water resources, and deliver products back to China to narrow the gap between the supply and demand of grains.

2.3. *Technologies and methods to save and increase fresh water resources*

The most serious problem in China's future resource supply is the shortage of water resources. Without the seawater desalination technology, the maximum supply of fresh water resources is nearly fixed, since no technology can be applied to significantly increase the fresh water production and supply in inland China. If China cuts off the river flowing to other countries and regions, it is possible to incur disputes between the countries. In general, water resources cannot be balanced based on trade due to the high cost. Third, despite the lower value of fresh water compared to minerals, grains, and energies, it is the most fundamental necessity for living and survival. People can live without mineral resources for a day, but can never survive without fresh water resources. Therefore, there is a hard gap between supply and demand of water resources.

The most significant water saving techniques comes from the promotion and application of water-saving agricultural technologies. Other than underdeveloped technology, the three restraining factors for the promotion of water-saving technologies are summarized as below. The first is the excessively low price of grains, which cannot afford the cost brought up by the water-saving technologies. The second is the small scale agricultural production as they cannot afford the cost of the water-saving technologies. The third is the excessive labor and high living labor costs in agricultural production cannot afford to the high price of the technologies. The fourth is the low price of water, so pressure is exerted on the no-cost water saving system in agricultural production. The cost of technologies and equipment will be higher if they cannot be promoted and applied. Conversely, the higher cost makes it more difficult to promote and apply these technologies. Therefore, the key to the promotion and popularization of agricultural water-saving technology is to raise the prices of water and grains, transfer excessive labors in agriculture, and encourage the operation of a fairly large-scale agricultural production.

A huge potential exists in industrial water-saving technologies. Industrial water saving can be divided into technological and administrative types. There are two technological measures: The first is to establish and improve the water circulation system for the repetitive usage of industrial water. The higher repetitive rate will lower the water consumption, reduce the industrial wastewater, and thus significantly reduce the pollutions to water environment and release the pressure on water resources supply. The second is to reform the production technique and water-usage technique, including the applications of new water-saving techniques, technologies of no or low pollution, and new water economizer (Baidu Baike). If China reinforces the momentum to save industrial water and lower the water consumption of each 10,000 yuan of industrial add value to 25 m^3, the total industrial water consumption will decrease by 176.3 billion m^3.

Various technologies on domestic water have been formulated. In addition, the consumption of domestic water is mainly decided by the lifestyle habits of rural and urban residents, and, more importantly, the price of water. As stated above, the consumption of domestic water for the 1.55 billion population of China by 2040 will amount to 282.1 billion m³ according to the average standard of current developed countries, which is three times the 73.93 billion m³ in 2008. The pressure on future domestic water supply lies in the increasing urban population, whose living habits vary from the rural population because of the more convenient water supply and usage, and high water consumption in their day-to-day lives. Therefore, it is important to raise the price of water resources and collect the sewage fee along with the water provision fee to restrain people's consumption method of water resources. China shall control the per capita domestic water consumption under 400 m³ and try to control the total domestic water consumption in both rural and urban areas under 223.2 billion m³.

As promoted by technological progress, the agricultural, industrial, domestic, and ecological water consumption will amount to 744.3 billion m³ in total by 2040, which is within the limit of China's usable water resources.

In addition to the increase in water prices, China shall also promote the technological innovation of marine fresh water by forming an industrial chain to obtain water from the sea. Though basic conditions of the industrialization have been satisfied for the seawater desalination of China, China is still far behind other countries in the research levels, innovation and development abilities, manufacture of equipment, and system design and integration. The priority shall be given to the foundation of a complete industrial chain for the seawater desalination equipment. With the the cost of seawater desalination as the key problem, China shall develop core technologies, such as membrane materials and crucial equipment, research and develop new technologies, techniques, equipment, and products of seawater desalination with intellectual property rights, improve the localization of key materials and equipment, and develop the ability to independently build large-scale seawater desalination projects (Baidu Baike).

According to the special planning of national seawater utilization, China's seawater desalination ability shall reach 2.5 to 3 million tons per day by 2020. The author believes that the suggested scale is not suitable for China's supply and demand of water resources. Along with the rise in water prices, the seawater desalination technology can regain its cost. By 2040, China shall attempt to provide one-tenth of total fresh water consumption by seawater desalination, i.e., 74.4 billion m^3. Therefore, the daily production capacity of seawater desalination shall reach 203.83 million m^3 in order to release the pressure on the supply of water resources.

2.4. *Technologies for saving and replacing steel resources and the import and export of steel*

According to the plans for the short-, medium- and long-term, China will use up all ferrous metal reserves of 2008 and would require import of 9.5 billion tons, 13.6 billion tons, or 17.9 billion tons of metallic iron, i.e., 17.3 billion tons, 24.8 billion tons, and 3.26 billion tons of iron ore at the grade of 55% by 2040. According to the above calculation, China will use 22% to 33% of the 80 billion tons of global ferrous metal reserves discovered by 2004.

Steel replacement technology. Many types of materials can replace steel, but it mainly depends on its relative price. Plastics, aluminum, and wood are often used in the replacement of steel. However, the new alternative materials are subject to many restraints. Take the technology of steel replacement in automobiles as an example. The 2007 Twingo and 2008 Kangoo, the latest models of Renault, adopted light, durable, and hard Noryl GTX resin for the wing instead of the steel. Compared to the steel, the high-performance technology has reduced the weight of the wing by about half and improved its performance to withstand collision at a low speed (Xiaoyi).

In particular, the export of products with relatively high steel value shall be restrained, especially the export of steel and pig iron. The export value of high steel and iron is extremely unremunerative because it enlarges the scale of import of iron ore, reduces the domestic supply of ferrous metals, and increases domestic energy and fresh water consumption, pollutions, and CO_2 emission.

2.5. *Energy strategy and technology of new energies*

As stated above, based on the estimation of the 1.55 billion population in 2040 and the three plans for the per-capita consumption of five, four, and three tons of energies, the total energy consumption of China in 2040 would respectively reach 7.75 billion, 6.2 billion, and 4.65 billion tons, while the accumulated energy demand would be respectively 169.6 billion, 144.8 billion, and 120 billion tons.

The crucial way to cope with the significant growth of oil and natural gas consumption in the industrialization and urbanization of China is to develop new energies, and promote and popularize the technology of new energies. It is believed that two main factors contributing to the structure alteration and rapid growth of energy consumption include the following: The first is the energy consumption by families toward electricity for the operation of refrigerators, televisions, washing machines, air-conditioners, fuel gas, and heaters. The second is the power energy used in material transportation, including oil, biologic oil-bearing products, natural gas, and electricity. China must consider which among these new energies would be selected and what would be the ultimate strategy.

(1) Should China open sources in China or foreign countries? The author believes that it is inadvisable to open sources in foreign countries owing to the limited oil and natural gas reserves globally, and China's demand based on the consumption method in the future. (2) Should the revolution be conducted for all energies, or follow the process with coal and electricity, and finally combine the energy of solar, wind, and hydrogen? Energy is used as an example in the above discussion on the strategy of technological progress. The energy combination of solar, wind, and hydrogen is always deemed as the ultimate plan to solve the energy crisis. (3) How will China transform the coal energy for use in transportation? In terms of the transformation of energy forms, is it better to transform coals to oil, or to electricity, as the transportation force? The author believes that the government should carefully consider solving the demands on the transportation of energies in the future by transforming coals to electricity or oil and by comparing the two in terms

of technical feasibility, cost, risks, transportation, safe utilization, and pollution treatment. (4) How will China deal with the structure of energy supply? According to China's actual conditions, the author believes that energy consumption will still depend on coal in the long term, aided with the development of other new energies. In a longer period, coal will be gradually replaced by inexhaustible and renewable energies, including nuclear, solar, wind, ocean, geothermal, and hydrogen energy. In view of the relatively small land mass compared to the large population, as well as the sensitive ecology, the biomass energy that consumes land and water resources is not suggested. (5). What would be the distribution of the power and oil energy transformed from coals? Currently, many power stations are located at key places, leading to the pattern of transferring coal from the West to the East and transporting coal from the North to the South by railways and highways, which increases the cost. Therefore, the investment in and construction of coal power plants should be strictly controlled, and the investment in and construction of mine power plants at resource locations should be vigorously developed.

2.6. Technology of reducing pollution and restoring ecology

As discussed above, the capacity of Chinese ecological environment is limited. Though the governance of environmental pollution has been strengthened in recent years, China continues to face a seriously damaged ecology. Technological innovation, promotion, and large-scale application are necessary to control pollution and restore ecology.

The technologies for controlling pollutants include using petroleum chemistry to reduce agricultural pollutions caused by, fertilizers, farm chemicals, plastics, and feces through industrial cultivation; technologies to dispose or to recycle urban sewages; technologies to deal with grain straws and garbage; and technologies to eradicate the formation of pollutants caused by the production of raw materials for solar-grade silicon. The technologies to restore ecology include planting trees and grass to control desertification and the technology of culturing seedlings. Owing to China's small investment and high cost, the current environmental and ecological technologies cannot be promoted and applied. The investment needed to facilitate the promotion of environmental protection and ecological restoration is also insufficient.

In addition to the technological innovation in pollution governance and ecological restoration, relevant systems should also be established in education, property rights, prices, and taxes. Otherwise, the pollutants cannot be completely controlled, and the ecology cannot be ideally restored. It will be further discussed in the following research.

3. Significance of the Urban, Rural, and Industrial Structure and Their Living and Consumption Habits

In addition to the technological progresses, the structures and living habits shall be adjusted to save resources and solve the environmental and ecological problems of China.

3.1. *Adjustment direction of the industrial structure*

China's GDP reached 30.07 trillion yuan in 2008, and therefore, the per-capita GDP was 3,268 USD, according to the exchange rate. The structure of the primary, secondary, and tertiary industriesof GDP is 11.3:48.6:40.1. According to the development report from the World Bank, countries or regions of per-capita GPD of about 3,500 USD often own the primary, secondary, and tertiary industries' structure within 8:30:62.

Unlike the low levels of energy consumed by services industry in other countries, China consumes higher rate of energies and other resources under the same development level for each 10,000 yuan of GDP. Conversely, the low proportion of add value of the service industry in GDP is actually the structural and fundamental factor contributing to the high consumption of energies and other resources. For statistical reasons, only the energy consumptions of all industries

Table 5.1. Energy Consumptions of Different Industries in 2008.

	Add Value of the Industry	Energy Consumption of Production	Energy Consumption of the Industry
Total and average	300,670.00	259,550	0.8632
Primary industry	34,000.00	6,013	0.1769
Secondary industry	146,183.40	213,115	1.4579
Tertiary industry	120,486.60	40,422	0.3355

Note: The unit for the add value is 100 million RMB. The unit for the energy consumption is 10,000 tons. The unit for industrial energy consumption is ton of standard coal/GDP of 10,000 yuan. Data comes from the State Statistics Bureau: *2010 Statistical Yearbook of China*, published by the Statistics Bureau Press of People's Republic of China.

are analyzed here. The year of 2008 is taken as an example in the table below (Table 5.1).

Seen from the coefficient of energy consumption in the secondary and tertiary industries, the secondary industry consumed 1.4579 tons of standard coals for each 10,000 yuan added value, while the tertiary industry only consumed 0.3355 in 2008. The effect of increasing the proportion of the tertiary industry in the industrial structure is much more significant than saving energy by reducing consumptions within the secondary industry.

As discussed above, slow urbanization leads to the slow development in the tertiary industry. The economic structure mainly relying on industrialization, especially heavy industry is the main reason for bringing about high emissions. Supposing that China has a rational industrial structure of 10:30:60 in 2007, the emissions and pollutions under this structure are shown as below (Table 5.2).

As seen from the table, under rational industrial structure, the discharge of CO_2, SO_2, smoke, dust, and emission only accounts to respectively 67.38%, 60.63%, 61.65%, 61.67%, and 3.65% of actual remission and pollution in 2007. The sewage and solid waste generated by the industries including the tertiary industry only take up 89.65% and 64.21% of the actual figure of 2007. The discharge generated by China's national economy is relatively greater than any other country under the same development level. Environmental pollution

Table 5.2.   Distribution of pollutions in different industries and contamination coefficient.

		Primary Industry		Secondary Industry		Tertiary Industry		Rational Emission and Pollution
	Actual Pollution	Distorted Structure	Rational Structure	Distorted Structure	Rational Structure	Distorted Structure	Rational Structure	
Domestic GDP	249,529	28,095	24,953	121,381	74,859	100,053	149,718	
CO_2 – 100 million tons	67.39	2.09	1.92	48.25	29.72	9.22	13.77	45.41
Ton/10,000 yuan	2.7	0.77		3.97	0.92	0.92		1.82
SO_2 – 10,000 tons	2,468.1	—	—	2,140.00	1,319.79	118.12	176.74	1,496.53
g/10,000 yuan	989.0	—		1,763.04		118.05		599.74
Smoke emission – 10,000 tons	986.6	—		771.10	488.97	79.74	119.31	608.28
g/10,000 yuan	395.4	—		635.27		79.69		
Dust emission – 10,000 tons	698.70-	—		698.70	430.90	—		430.90
g/10,000 yuan	575.62-	—		575.62		—		
Sewage discharge – 10,000 tons	361.37	—		246.6	151.96	114.77	172.18	324.14
ton/10,000 yuan	1.45	—		2.03		1.15		
Solid waste – 100 million tons	—	28.6		17.6	10.85	0.53	0.7920	
Kg/10,000 yuan	—	—		144.99		5.29		

Note: GDP of 2007 is used here, in a unit of 100 million yuan. The data of the solid waste from the tertiary industry and the residents adopts the amount of waste cleared and delivered in cities in 2007. The urban domestic sewage is excluded.

is, therefore, a serious issue now due to the irrational industrial structure that lays particular stress on the secondary industry; lagging urbanization; and the slow development of the tertiary industry. Therefore, the adjustment of the industrial structure, especially the development of the tertiary industry is very important to show significant effect on saving energies and reducing discharge.

3.2. Significance of the adjustment of the urban and rural structure to resources and environment

As modern production and lifestyle infiltrated into the rural society, the dispersed population and the development method incurred great wastage of land and resources and damages to ecological environment which is difficult to control and protect.

3.2.1. Great wastage of land resources due to dispersed population and development

Lagging urbanization and dispersed population and development have actually consumed a great amount of land. Urbanization spatially concentrates on the population, enterprises, factors and infrastructure, intensively utilizes the land area and significantly reduces the occupation of land. Moreover, wastage of arable land is caused by the development of rural industry, instead of the enterprises in urban areas. In view of land for traffic, a city of one million people saves much more land than 1,000 villages of 1,000 people, since highways shall be built to connect villages.

Economically, agriculture belongs to the arable land-intensive economy, and the decentralized economy covers more area than a centralized economy. In terms of the input–output of the land, the sequence from the largest to the smallest would be information and finance, commerce, industry, and agriculture, while the input–output of a decentralized economy is lower than the intensive economy. For the sake of land resources, the decentralized economy shall be transformed into a centralized economy in terms of the changes in the economic growth and development method. If these theories are ignored, the arable land can never be transformed into enterprises and cities, it will inhibit economic development and pave way to more wastage of lands.

3.2.2. *Villages of scattered population exert greatest damages to ecological environment*

The scattered population and development, and slow urbanization also contribute to the deterioration of ecological environment. Over several decades, China has experienced water loss and soil erosion, deforestation, vegetation deterioration, desertification, and deterioration of grassland and pollution in the township enterprises in the plains. Many beautiful grasslands and villages have disappeared. Due to low levels of industrialization, more than half of Chinese people are living in rural areas, therefore, according to previous ideas, China's ecological environment should be better than Euro–American countries. However, why is the ecological environment of China's farming and pastoral area worse than other countries and continuing to deteriorate?

3.2.2.1. Pressure on and damage to ecological environment due to scattered population

First, the deterioration of ecological environment of China's farming and pastoral area resulted from the overgrowth and overexpansion of population that the land and grass cannot bear. The increasing population in the farming and pastoral area proposes more demands on natural energies, leading to a large amount of trees being cut down, grass being mown, and plants being seriously damaged. Energies are required for cooking, heating, and to light fire for the production in rural areas, where the firewood is used as the natural energy resource. The author was once asked if coals, electricity, or fuel gas be applied in rural areas in the place of firewood. Unfortunately, the transportation fee to get coals from cities is too high for peasants. In comparison to coals, the cost of firewood is much cheaper. Why is it so? Economically, the choice between firewood and industrial energy largely depends upon the comparison of the costs and the opportunity sought out to obtain these energies.

3.2.2.2. Industrialization of rural areas incurs environmental pollution that is difficult to control

The main factor contributing to the serious environmental pollution of China's rural areas is the rural industrialization and spatial integration of rural and urban areas, which leads to fire and smoke in every village, sewage from scattered factories, and garbage all around the villages. The cost of pollution reduction shall be paid, which is affected by the scale and distance. For scattered sewage, waste, and dust, the fixed cost of facilities for pollution reduction is too large because of the small scale of pollution sources, and the marginal cost is higher when the scale of pollution sources is smaller. Economically, it is impossible to solve the problem of pollution incurred by rural industrialization and spatial integration of rural and urban areas.

3.3. *Adjustment directions of living and consumption habits*

The adjustment of living and consumption habits may share the same significance with the change of development method in coping with resource shortage, limited capacity of ecological environment, and the possibility of continuous deterioration.

The living habits often refer to people's method and form of consuming material goods, intellectual goods, and labors include in two basic forms: individual consumption and public consumption. The ecological environment where people conduct living and consumption activities is known, in an economic sense, as the living and consumption environment. The living and consumption environment has a great influence on people's consumption activities, quality, subject, and object of consumption, while it directly restrains the macro living and consumption mode, including rationalization of the consumption structure and method. Therefore, the living and consumption method is based on the consumption environment of the country or region which considers the capacity of the ecological environment.

Select the living and consumption method suitable for China's actual conditions. In the three decades after reform and opening up, Chinese residents' living and consumption habits have changed greatly in line with economic development, such as increasing proportion of meat consumption in diet structure, popularization of durable consumer goods in daily consumption, increasing one-time consumption of drink cans and plastic bottles, growing residential areas, widespread appearance of cottages and other residential forms, and widespread usage of own cars. In the next 30 years, what will be the direction of the change of Chinese residents' living and consumption method? The answer is: (1)Avoiding wasteful consumption; (2) Attaching importance to rational diet consumption structure; and (3) Rational residential and travel mode.

In short, only by adopting economic living and consumption methods, the economic development can be achieved.

4. Market System and Governance System for Rational Utilization of Resources and Environment

The system arrangement and supply shall be guaranteed if the following problems can be solved: how to save resources and realize continuous utilization; how to protect and restore ecological environment; how to apply, promote, and popularize technologies and ideas of saving resources and restoring ecological technologies; and how to win the identity from public.

4.1. *Clear definition of property rights and resource saving and environmental protection*

The market system on the rationality of resource utilization, the controllability of environmental pollution, the protection and restoration of ecology, property rights and prices plays the most fundamental regulating role.

4.1.1. Mechanism of the function of property rights of resources and environment

The theory of property rights in ecological and environmental economics is constituted with research achievements in the "tragedy of the commons," externality of economy, and external sources and property rights.

To demonstrate the significance of property rights boundary definition in environmental protection, the research on the protection of common land shall be conducted first. The concept of the "tragedy of the commons" comes from the paper of the same name written by Garrett Hardin. His descriptive model is a piece of pasture land open to all herdsmen. In the ecological system, the pasture is "public owned." There is no clear definition on its property rights, but the herds are privately owned. Individual interests drive all herdsmen to do all they can to increase their livestock. They will gain more profits based on every increase of an animal. On the other hand, since the capacity of the pasture can hardly support more livestock, every increase of two animals may damage the pasture. However, the damage is jointly borne by all herdsmen. Therefore, as driven by immediate interests, everyone strives to increase the number of livestock, finally leading to the deterioration and even ruining of the pasture.

The concept of externality of economy was put forward by A. Marshall and A. C. Pigou of Cambridge University in the early 1900s. The externality of economy, relative to market system, refers to the by-products or side-effects of economic activities that are not reflected in the product price, and these by-products and side effects may be beneficial or harmful. The pollution without emission restraints is the most typical example. In a market economy, even if a few enterpreneurs are environmentally conscience, they will also be forced to follow the path of free pollution if they cannot find a way to reduce pollution without increasing the product cost, the same as other enterprises, owing to the fierce market competition. Only two choices are given to the society: The first is to leave the environmental deterioration to nature, and the second is to control pollutions if the funds are available. Obviously, the latter choice will transfer the cost to control pollutions from enterprises to society.

External sources and property rights. The Coase theorem can link the external resources with the ownership relation. The theorem states that "if there are no transaction costs, bargaining will lead to an efficient outcome regardless of the initial allocation of property rights. However, the actual transaction cost will never equals to zero, so it is very necessary to clarify property rights, including the right of use in laws." Take the air pollution of factories as an example. The theory actually means that if the property right has been clarified, whether factories with the pollution right or residents with no right to pollute, either of the party involved can find out the most effective solution through market mechanism (to minimize the transaction cost, of course). All useful resources with clear property rights will obtain rational utilization and protection. Contrarily, for public resources with an ambiguous boundary, people will exert efforts to gain profits by usage, or even abuse of public resources (Tianyong, 2006).

4.1.2. *Problems and solutions of property rights of resources and environment in china*

What problems lie in the property rights of resources and environment in China and how will they be solved?

Ambiguous property right of grassland and forestland and solutions. The following points shall be noted: (1) Owing to ambiguous state-owned or collectively-owned property rights in some areas, every household hopes to obtain more benefits from public land, leading to the repetitive cutting down of forests and devastating grazing in small state-owned forests, and collectively-owned forests and grassland; (2) As the property rights and the rights to the usage of desert, gobi, and barren hills belong to the state or cooperative, no one is willing to invest or protect these areas, so they are left deserted; (3) Since the foundation of New China, forest planting has been carried out for many years. According to official statistics of the tree-planting area and survival rate, China should have made the land green over five times, which obviously disagrees with the fact. In addition to the false result report, ambiguous property rights also contribute to the situation, which lead to no operation or protection.

Fewer people will invest and operate the green forests owing to the shorter time of the right to use. China shall clarify the property and the right to the usage of grasslands, woodlands, forests, and wetlands. For the desert, barren hill, gobi, and grassland areas, anyone who invests in, makes the land green with plants, and protects them shall own the property right. The usage period for barren hills, desert, and gobis shall be extended to 1,000 years. The property rights of woodlands, grasslands, and other facilities shall go to the investor. People who have the right to the usage of land and property right of woodland and grassland can plant economic forests, or inherit, mortgage, or transfer these rights under the supervision and regulation of the amount of growing stock, as allowed by the law (Tianyong, 2007).

Ambiguous property right of mineral resources and solutions. Currently, mineral resources belong to the state, while only the exploration right and the right to the usage of explored minerals are transferred to the investor and the operator of the mine. Herein lies a problem: the state does not transfer the mineral resources reserves, but only the right to the usage of the mine to the investor and operator. Therefore, the investor and operator will only explore the mineral resources that are of high grade and are most easy to explore, but abandon the resources that are of low grade and are difficult to explore, which results in the low utilization factor. Meanwhile, frequent accident occur owing to their disregard of production safety. To solve this problem, the ore body and the minerals shall be split apart. The ore body including the land shall be owned by the state. The period for the usage of the land of ore body can be regulated according to the exploratable life of the mine, but the property right will not be transferred. However, the property right of minerals that are found within the ore body can be sold to the investor and the operator of the mine according to the amount of reserves available, instead of auctioning the exploitation right of the mine.

4.2. *Negative consequences of the low price of resources and solutions*

The current prices of many resources and environmental products in China do not reflect the degree of scarcity or the cost (such as the sewage discharge fee generation at the time of the utilization of fresh water). Considering the rise of general prices and residents' capacity, the increasing prices of resources and environmental products are regulated. Actually, this strategy failed to produce favorable results, but only led to the negative consequences of saving resources and protecting the environment.

4.2.1. *Price mechanism for resources and environmental products*

Do resources such as land, forests, and water have their own values and prices? According to modern economics, environment can be utilized for many purposes. When the marginal cost of an environmental factor exceeds zero, the factor is considerd to be in short supply. The scarcity results in the competitive usage of a product, thereby, it is necessary to adjust the supply and demand, by implementing changes to its prices, which leads to the generation of its value. After the scarcity of the product is revealed, if the positive contribution of environmental products to human welfare is still not reflected in the price system, the abuse of environmental products will appear in the market economy competiton. In addition, since the abuse of environment will lower the cost of production, enterprises are more inclined to abuse the environment.

Therefore, it is necessary to set a price for environmental objects. First, the rise in cost will exert more competitive pressures on producers and force them to adopt advanced production technologies and management to lower energy and material consumption. Second, when the resource-intensive products are too expensive for people to maintain their traditional consumption structure, the public has to adjust the consumption structure due to high pressure in the increase of prices, hence they tend to transform from energy-intensive to energy-efficient lifestyles, and finally form a lifestyle in accordance with sustainable development. Third, the technologies for saving resources and protecting the environment cannot be achieved, promoted, and industrialized without raising the prices of scarce resources or charges being levied on the usage of environmental objects or services, such as charges on pollution discharge etc. Therefore, the price mechanism of resources and environment is actually the most efficient tool for adjusting the application of new technologies. It is recognized that a pricing system favorable to the sustainable development of the nation is necessary for the formation of a lifestyle that goes well with the sustainable development (Tianyong, 2006).

4.2.2. *The low price of resources and environmental products*

The prices of most resources and environmental products, such as electricity, water, gas, and agricultural products are too low in China. The low price provided for land expropriation and the high assignment price do not reflect the supply and demand relations, leading to no rational profits and may even result in a loss for enterprises. The negative effect includes high consumption of resources and environment in China.

Excessively low prices of resources and resource products will incur the following dangers as well: (1) The price of non-resource products increases while the price of resource products decreases. The reason for the constant increase in the price of non-resource products is due to the appreciation of RMB and inflation without government restrictions. However, the price of resource products is under government control and therefore is restricted and relatively lower, and it often becomes the method to stabilize the price of commodities, especially during inflation. The gap between the prices of non-resource products and resource products is becoming wider and wider, reflecting a very distorted pricing system; (2) The low price and high cost of resources and resource products can earn few profits, or even suffer a loss, so social capital will not be used for the development of the sector and as a result, the favorable development of some industries are restricted. For example, the investment and the production of agricultural resources are affected adversely due to the price restrictions imposed by the government. Peasants working in grain production may earn an even lower income than those working as waiters in urban restaurants; (3) Government subsidies are necessary because of the low price of resources and products, which paves way to financial crisis. However, leakages and corruptions exist in the government subsidies and render them very inefficient. The financial subsidies cannot guarantee rational profits for the production of many resource products, but can only help them to earn a slight profit, or break even. It is a waste if similar industries abandon these technologies, but they cannot earn significant profit from them; (4) The long-term low price of resources and resource products will disable the prices to reflect the supply and demand for resources and resource products, so the over-demand on resources cannot be inhibited. The excessively low prices of resources and resource products prevent some resource-saving technologies and alternate resources from being researched, applied, promoted, and industrialized.

4.2.3. The idea and task of rationalizing the prices of resources and resource products

In the 30 years after reform and opening up, China first adopted the double-track price system reform, i.e., left more and more products to be priced by the market, and later conducted the reform on price system mainly on integrated double-track system. Therefore, more than 95% of products are currently priced by the market supply and demand. Some products related to the national economy and people's livelihood are still priced by the government, such as electricity, gas, agricultural products, fresh water, expropriated land, and some agricultural means of production. Despite the small amount, these products occupy a large proportion and important status in economic society. As mentioned above, the low cost has led to a series of damages. Therefore, the second round of price reform mainly focuses on the rationalization of the price system of resources and resource products should be conducted.

The aim of the second round of price reform is to rationalize the relationship among the prices of resources and resource products, the capacity of the masses, and the rise in price to the end consumer. First, the reform on the price system of resources and resource products shall be firmly carried out. Second, some supporting reforms and system constructions are necessary for the steady reform of the prices of resources and resource products. China should promote the competitiveness in production and the supply of resources and the resource products, consider people's capacity in the price reform and provide appropriate subsidies to a few residents with low incomes and those in the agricultural sectors. The government should ask the enterprises of monopolies of production and supply of resources and resource products to open their finance conditions and accept people's supervision, strengthen the monitoring of the enterprises of production, and supply of resources and resource products.

4.3. *Taxation mechanism to protect environment and save resources*

Resource and environment taxes are considered an important economic measure for the government to adjust the resource utilization and protect the environment. The proportion of the current resource tax in China is very low, while the tax on environment is incomplete and unorganized, which is far from the goal of promoting scientific development with taxes. Many problems currently exist in the system of government administration over resources and environment. A set of rational tax systems shall be designed and the current system shall be reformed to facilitate resource saving and environmental protection.

4.3.1. *Role of resource and environment taxes*

A certain proportion of resource taxes shall be collected in the utilization of land, minerals, and fresh water. The functions of resource taxes include the following: (1) The collection of land use tax, including on land for different uses, inhibits the construction of low density and low utilization rate; (2) Different types of resource taxes are collected on high grade and low grade ore, which would prevent enterprises from only extracting high grade ore, but abandoning low grade ore and enables fair competition among mining enterprises of different levels; (3) The sustainable development fund shall be founded for mines, which will reserve part of resource taxes and contribute them in the land reorganization of the mine, infrastructure construction, and the adjustment of industrial structure in the future; (4) Space resource taxes shall be collected, including telecommunication channel, in order to facilitate the rational allocation and utilization of space resources. The income shall be applied to control pollutions, that occurs due to the advancement in telecommunication and noise pollution, to turn the negative externality of air and telecommunication enterprises to their cost and facilitate the interiorization; (5) Places of river sources or rich mineral resources often belong to places of processing industry and underdeveloped areas with an unbalanced industrial structure. A certain proportion of resource taxes are collected for the protection, development, and production of mineral resources and the water resource taxes levied on the water users at a low level play a significant and practical role in balancing the development of different regions and narrowing the difference between the East and the West.

The environment tax is collected over the emission (CO_2) and pollution discharge by manufacturers and residents that seriously affect the environment. Its functions include the following: (1) It can turn the negative external loss generated by discharge and polluting production and activities to the cost of acting enterprises, families, and individuals; (2) It shows that environment is a scarce resource, so the cost shall be paid for the usage of the environment, which is incorporated into the cost and price of the products; (3) Enterprises, families and individuals will reduce emission or discharge to lower the expenses by spending some extra money on the improvisation of the equipment, so that the discharge or emission is low, thus protecting the environment; (4) Environmental tax is the main source of capital to be utilized for preventive care and treatment; (5) A part of the environmental tax is used to establish funds to cope with the environmental emergencies.

4.3.2. *Problems in resource and environmental taxes*

Problems currently exist in the collection of resource and environmental taxes.

In addition to the low tax rate, the taxes are replaced by unorganized charges, and many a times, they have not been collected on wastages and pollutions. The charges are not compulsory enough, and many collections have not been able to save resources and inhibit pollutions, but have actually shown a negative effect. The low rate of resource and environmental taxes and chaos in levying fees have led to insufficient investment, construction, and operation of resource saving and ecological protection as well as the accumulation of debts in the process of improvisation of ecology and environment.

Bibliography

Anonymous (2004). China shall establish a complete system of green taxation. Environmental Protection Sector of Huicong Net. Accessed on 17 August 2004.

Anonymous (2008). American lifestyle needs reform the most. *Chinese Commercial News* (*L.A.*), 1 November 2008.

Bai Meiqing. Carefully summing up experiences of reform of grain prices and serving for the grain safety in new period. Available at http://news.u88.cn/zx/shipinzixun_mimianlei/765798.htm.

Baidu Baike. Industrial water-efficient technologies. Available at http://baike.baidu.com/view/2441870.htm

Baidu Baike. Seawater desalination. Available at http://baike.baidu.com/view/22173.htm.

Comprehensive summary of the Huicong Water Industrial Network (2009). Analysis of the causes of rise of water prices and call from various circles, 2 December 2009.

Dong Xin and Ge Rongxi. First batch of four sets of equipment for seawater desalination of the first stage of Beijiang power plant are put into operation Available at http://news.china.com.cn/rollnews/20100–6/15/content_2692283.htm. Accessed on 15 June 2010.

He Degong (2005). A trend in Japan: Abandoning the lifestyle of great productive consumption. *China Youth News*, 12 July 2005.

Kong Weichao (2010). Analysis of the causes for the loss of power enterprises and solutions. *Wealth*, 1.

Lin Boqiang (2010). Problem of the change of the price of natural gas, not compared to international level. China Economics Net. Accessed on 1 June 2010.

Liu Chunxiang (2008). Crazy increase of steel prices, development of alternate materials springs up. *Daily Economic News*, 4 March 2008.

Ma Jianping (2009). Link relations among income increase, environmental policies, environmental-friendly technologies and pollution intensity. *Economics and Management*, 10.

News report (2002). *Guangming Daily*, 12 August 2002.

The Ministry of Agriculture (2010). Answers to questions on genetically modified technologies and bio-safety. *Website of the Ministry of Agriculture*. Accessed on 15 March 2010.

Xiaoyi (2008). Renault applies Noryl GTX in replacement of steel materials. *China Trade Net*. Accessed on 25 December 2008.

Yang Guanghe and Wu Haibao (2010). Typical railway transportation network — the breakthrough in core technologies of the high-speed railway of China. Accessed on 19 April 2010.

Ye Zefang (2003). On China's selection of the mode for progress of agricultural technologies. *Economic Review*, 2.

Yu Chenglie (2008). Several points on the technologies to control water pollution Available at http://club.china.alibaba.com/forum/thread/view/220_25851145_1.html. Accessed on 12 November 2008.

Zhao Shubo (2009). Small effect of the rise of environment rate on GDP. *China Taxation News*, 17 June 2009.

Zhou Tianyong (2006). *New Development Economics*. China: Renmin University Press.

Zhou Tianyong (2007). How to make China's barren hills and desert green. *China Economic Times*, 25 June 2007.

Zhou Tianyong (2007). The current system will only lead to more and more serious environmental pollutions in China. *China Economic Times*, 3 July 2007.

Zhou Tianyong (2010). *China's Way Out*. Beijing: People's Daily Press.

Zhu Jiaxian (2010). How to build the market of transaction of emission allowance in China. *China Environment News*, 2 June 2010.

Zhu Liuhua (2010). Actively and steadily promote the improvement of rural land. *People's Daily*, 19 Sept 2010.

Chapter 6

The Focus of the Second Reform: Fiscal and Taxation System

During the 11th five-year plan China's finance expenditure structure started to orient toward public service. However, it is still featured with investment and construction-oriented finance that only aims to satisfy people's basic livelihood needs. In addition to taxes, there are also too many charges, the income has not been wholly incorporated into budget management, and no balance between income and expenditure has been maintained among people, the People's Congress, and the government. In addition, a series of problems exists in the unregulated fiscal and taxation system, such as the unfair income distribution, constant rise in housing price, huge profits from the real estate sector, very low property incomes of peasants, wasteful use of resources and serious environmental pollution.

1. Reform of the Government Income System

The author considers that the following aspects should be included in the reform of fiscal and taxation system during the 12th five-year plan until 2020.

1.1. *Thoroughly modify fees and charges and alter necessary fees to taxes*

Income from charges and fines under the budget amounted to 896.22 billion yuan in 2009. Known fees and fines out of the budget have reached 790 billion yuan. The fees and fines without proper statistics are estimated to be about 510 billion yuan. The three items above equal up to 2.1962 trillion yuan and account for one-third of taxes. The author thinks that a five-year cleanup plan shall be implemented during the 12th five-year plan while supporting the reform plans of various departments, especially with regard to the fees and charges of governmental departments and administrative organizations, including the arbitrary imposition of fines.

First, during the first year of the 12th five-year plan, a general check-up is expected to be conducted on the item and scale of fees and charges. Second, the reform of incorporating administrative fees into taxes and then transforming the same is expected to be carried out. Third, the charging and penalty rights of most government departments and administrative organizations, and the system of "separate management of administrative charges and incomes," would be abolished. The system of "bonus for excessive income" and fines shall be prohibited, but then would be changed to the tax office's system of collecting taxes and financial appropriation. Fourth, the reform of county and township government institutions, government logistics, consumption of publicly-owned cars, entertainment of civil servants and public institutions, complemented step-by-step based on cost estimation and risk assessment, would be carried out. Fifth, the party and the government would give consideration to the business startups and employment of people and take actions to solve the problem i.e., collection of fees and charges by all government departments and administrative organizations. Sixth, the government would actively clean up the fees and charges and form a system to prevent arbitrary fees and fines, under the supervision of the National People's Congress. Seventh, the 12th five-year plan would formulate a plan to solve the problem of arbitrary levy of charges and fines.

1.2. *Establish an integrated and complete national financial revenue system*

In the current governmental revenue system of China, except for a few taxes and charges, a great part of the fees and charges, the social security fund, profits of state-owned enterprises, revenue from land transfers, the transfer of exploration and mining rights, lottery sales, and charges of public examination are not incorporated in the fiscal budget of the government. The author thinks they shall be gradually brought into the unified budget management.

1.2.1. *Social security shall be collected as taxes and incorporated into budget management*

Due to the indifferent legal sense of Chinese people and a large informal employment and presence of many medium and small-sized private enterprises, social security should be compulsively collected as taxes, which the government would save for personal accounts on behalf of the people.

Management of the social security fund relating to the administration structure of the State Department. The type of social security fund management is determined by the kind of governmental system that the state department would build. In view of the efficient and stable structure, and the unity of government administration, the social security funds shall be brought into the unified financial budget management: (1) Presently, the social security funds are administrated by funcational departments, which have actually formed a second "Ministry of Finance" in China; (2) Under the current special administrative governance structure of China, the financial budget shall be integrated and centralized in order to prevent several departments from owning large amounts of funds. Therefore, the management of social security funds shall be gradually centralized from the local level to the central government and from different departments to the government, thus forming a mode of horizontal division of labor for all links, including the collection of social security taxes, budget management, operation of funds, check of social security, socialized delivery, and monitorization of the third party.

1.2.2. *State-owned industrial, commercial, and financial assets and their profits shall be incorporated in financial budget*

The state-owned economy shall be incorporated into the financial budget administration. Though the government has contributed huge investments in state-owned enterprises, these enterprises submit a low profit, so it is necessary to incorporate the state-owned assets and their profits into budget management; (1) Different proposals are provided for the choice in the budget management of operational state-owned assets, including independently organizing the management and submission to the National People's Congress for approval, or including the profits or losses of enterprises into the national financial budget and submitting to the National People's Congress for approval; (2) Non-operational state-owned assets shall also be incorporated into the unified budget management.

1.2.3. *The administrative organization for state-owned financial assets shall be established*

Currently, a large amount of state-owned financial assets have accumulated in the state-owned financial system, especially the two aspects of state-owned net assets. First, enormous profits from state-owned or state-holding banks, insurance, securities, funds, and other financial enterprises in the financial system have accumulated because they have not submitted profits to the government. The second is the seigniorage profit of the People's Bank. As the profit of state's sovereignty on issuing currencies, the seigniorage profits have constantly grown along with the increasingly large scale of the actual sphere of circulation of Chinese currency. The management systems, including assets management organizations and legal systems, have not defined to whom these assets belong to, how to use them, and the possible results of such usage, thus, leaving these assets to secret operations.

1.2.4. *Other revenues shall be categorized, reformed, and incorporated into the financial budget*

In addition to the social security tax and profits from state-owned enterprises, many revenues have remained outside of the financial budget, which shall be gradually cleaned up, changed from charges to taxes, and incorporated into budget management. The first profit outside the financial budget is the current transfer of exploration and mining rights. The rights shall be reformed to be the transfer of ore body (such as the area and depth), while the property rights of minerals in the ore body shall be auctioned with the auction revenue submitted to the state's treasury. The second is the transfer of land. Currently, only the government can sell land and accept invitations for bids. The system shall be reformed to enable all lands to enter the land market and share the same price standards and enable the government to collect the transaction value added taxes (VAT) and use tax of land and submit them to the state's treasury. The third is the fees and charges. Unreasonable and illegal fees and charges shall be cleaned up and abolished; partly unreasonable but legal fees and charges shall be gradually cleaned up and abolished; and some rational fees and charges, such as charges on the usage of channels for communication companies and the usage of space for aviation, shall be transformed from fees to taxes. The government shall regulate a rational tax rate, or improve the original tax rate, and incorporate the tax into the financial budget. The fourth is the revenue from the issuance of lotteries and fees on national examinations, which shall be incorporated into the financial revenue of the state and the budget management.

1.3. *Adjust and reform the structure of revenue sources*

Enterprises are the main objects of taxation in the current Chinese taxation structure. It is actually a tax policy that encourages occupying profits based on assets and using resources in a wasteful way, but discourages business startups or the creation of wealth. This tax and fee structure fundamentally runs counter to the socialist value idea of common prosperity and scientific thought of development. The revenue sources in the future should be decided by the factor prices, scarcity degree of resources and environment, and accumulative distribution of wealth, and the adjustment and reform of the structure shall be conducted accordingly.

How, then, is the structure to be reformed? First, the maximum tax rate of individual income tax should be lowered below 30%. The second measure is to levy the property tax. The third is to collect taxes on resources and environment and raise their rates. Fourth, the consumption tax shall be levied to protect resources and environment and encourage conservation. In conclusion, fees shall be transformed into taxes based on governmental income structure. Regarding the taxation structure, the first measure is to gradually lower the rate of taxes on startups, investments, and enterprise operations; the second is to gradually increase the rate of personal income tax along with the constant rise of labor cost and accumulation of human capitals; the third is to collect property taxes and raise the rate of house taxes, inheritance taxes, and gift taxes; and the fourth is to adjust and collect taxes on resources and environment and raise them to a rational level in consideration of the scarce resources and limited environmental capacity.

The following measures are required in the taxation system reform: transforming current tax collections, mainly on enterprises and capital factors, to taxes on enterprises and capital factors as well as labor factors; transforming current tax collections, mainly on production and service to taxes on behaviors (such as conservation or waste, protection or pollution); transforming tax collections mainly on the enterprise exchanges to taxes on communications and even retail link; transform taxes mainly on enterprises to taxes on both enterprises' production and service and residents' wealth; and from taxes on channels with legitimate accounts and cash flow to taxes based on account taxation and reports and declarations of personal income. A series of supporting systems shall be designed, established, and carried out on residents' identity, driver's license, passports, income record, social security, bank account and current, control of cash transaction, registration of building property, credit and tax records, income and property monitoring, and report and record of tax evasions and so on.

2. Reform of the Government Expenditure System

The task of the financial expenditure reform is to lower the proportion of expenditure on the government and party's public affairs, and administration expenses, separate the general budget and construction budget based on the modern national budget system, transform into a public service-oriented financial expenditure structure, and change the invoice reimbursement system to a system of allocation according to the budget and cancellation after verification.

2.1. *Joint reform of the budget system and compiling system*

In 2007, the proportion of expenditure on the public affairs of the government and party and the administration expenses had actually reached 44% of the total expense of the government, (Zhou Tianyong, 2010) higher than the administration expenses of many other states. China still follows the vicious cycle of raising people by finance, raising people to collect fees, and collecting fees to raise more people. The financial expenditure system and compiling system shall be jointly reformed, or otherwise only the administration system reform or the financial system reform will lead to the future expansion of organizations and personnel and finally result in the vicious cycle of "simplification, expansion, more difficult simplification, and greater expansion".

More importantly, all fees and charges shall be transformed into taxes; administration, law enforcement, fees and fines shall be separated from department interests; and governmental organizations of official businesses, administration, implementation, and law enforcement shall be supported by financial appropriation. Small amounts of fines shall be directly submitted to the state's treasury, isolated from salaries, welfare, or other interests of organizations and personnel of administration, implementation, and law enforcement organizations. The setup of organizations and increase of personnel shall be submitted in advance to the Finance and Economics Commission of the National People's Congress for advice. The party's committee cannot propose to establish organizations or discuss the positions of leaders; the organization's department cannot nominate or check cadres; the compiling department cannot compile organizations or personnel; and the personnel department cannot provide positions for civil servants or public institutions without financial appropriation. The government shall not provide for officials, civil servants, personnel of public institutions, and temporary personnel of government and public institutions without financial appropriation.

2.2. *Separation of general financial budget and construction budget*

How are the construction and regular budgets of the government at all levels to be separated? Proposals to carry out this separation are as follows: (1) All public government construction projects shall raise funds by issuing debts; the government at all levels shall separately prepare for this level of the construction project budget and submit it to the National People's Congress for check and approval. Accordingly, the general financial budget shall set up an interest payment item. The construction scale of the stage is restricted by the repayment ability of this stage. In central and West China, the expenses on the interest repayment of the project construction shall be taken into consideration in the financial transfer; (2) The procedure and mechanism for issuing debts shall be regulated. First, the administration department of the construction shall propose the project, and then the financial department will put forward the proposal on the budget and issuance of debts and submit their proposal to the People's National Congress for discussion, which has the right to veto or approve the proposal. Second, a neutral credit rating organization will rate the credit of the government, including the revenue, debt, and deficit of the government, the estimation of government's income and repayment ability in the future and the government's previous performance in the payment of interest and thus rate the debt issued by the government. Then, the government will entrust a securities broker to issue a governmental bond through the bank; (3) Macrocontrol shall be conducted for the debt issuance for construction. Considering the republic system of China, local government needs the approval from the higher authority of the Development and Reform Commission to issue debts. According to the standard, the debt cannot exceed the current debt proportion line in the financial revenue of the current level and the proportion line of the debt balance in the financial revenue of that year, with the growth of financial income in the future and interest repayment ability taken into consideration; (4) The in-advance demonstration and the procedure, mechanism, and time for approval of the construction project shall be regulated.

Finally, the budget act of the government is formed based on the integration of the general financial budget, social security budget, state-owned assets budget, and construction project budget of the central government, and the regular budget and construction project budget of provincial or country governments. Then, the budget shall be prepared, discussed, checked, approved, carried out, and monitored according to the law.

2.3. Construction of a public service-oriented budget

China's current financial system was transformed from the previous planned economy. The traditional financial system in the planned economy served both production and construction. Along with the transformation from a planned economy to a market economy system, the financial system shall transform from the production and construction-oriented finance to public service and social management-oriented finance, presenting the idea of assuming power for the people in a financial aspect.

2.3.1. Confirm the budget item according to public service-oriented finance and different budget

The public budget mainly covers public products and public service, with the core idea of people orientation and the focus on people's livelihood. Budget items with greater expenditure include social security tax, education, medical care, low-income subsidies, ecological and environmental protection and improvement, fire control, and public security. Therefore: (1) The budget items of governments at all levels of a public service-oriented government shall be designed according to the idea of a government for the people and public service; (2) Some items shall be adjusted along with the deepening reform; (3) The items featured with characteristics of a planned economy shall be cancelled; and (4) Special categories and income and expense accounting shall be set up for social security, state-owned assets (or budget on state-owned capitals), and construction projects, if necessary.

2.3.2. *Reduce the administration expenses*

According to Ren Yuling, a member of the Chinese People's Political Consultative Conference (CPPCC), from 1978 to 2003, China's expenditure on administration within the budget has grown 87 times. The proportion of the administration expenditure under the budget in the total financial expenses rose from 4.71% in 1978 to 19.03% in 2003, which is 16.65%, 14.84%, 13.97%, 12.53%, 11.93%, and 9.13% higher than 2.38% of Japan, 4.19% of the United Kingdom, 5.06% of South Korea, 6.5% of France, 7.1% of Canada, and 9.9% of the United States. Actually, the expenditure out of the budget and administration expense comes from local domains revenue. Therefore, as mentioned in the above report, the *Law on Supporting Personnel of State Power and Public Institutions* shall be formulated.

During the 12th five-year plan, there would be a medium and long-term firm plan on reducing the proportion of the administration expenditure of the party and government in the total actual cost from the current 40% to about 18% by 2020. The goal to reduce the proportion by more than 2% each year shall be set up and practically implemented. By 2021, the proportion of the administration expenditure of the party and government in the total actual cost shall be lowered to the level of Italy, so as to reflect the party and government's objective of depending on people and serving people, while assuming the power for the people.

2.3.3. *Ensure the rapid and steady growth of expenses on public service items*

Based on the analysis of the current financial expenditure structure, the following adjustments shall be made on the structure of expenditure on public finance: (1) Raise the proportion of expenditure on education in the total financial expenditure, reform the education system in order to improve the education efficiency, gradually reduce the items of school charges, lower the price of education, strengthen the management of the capital outside the financial budget, incorporate the education capital outside the budget in the unified financial budget management, and integrate the education capital inside and outside the budget and use them in a well-planned way; (2) The second is to raise the expenditure on public health in the total actual expenditure and aim to raise it from the current 4.23% to over 10%, which is the level of developed countries; (3) A considerable part of financial income growth, including the operation of state-owned assets and realization profits, will be applied to fill the gap in social security; (4) Increase financial investment on social stability; (5) Increase the input on environmental protection, science and technology, and agriculture.

In short, it is necessary to gradually cancel the expenditure on investment and construction project in the regular budget, and reduce the proportion of administrative expenses and raise the proportion of public service-oriented projects, such as education, health care, social security, public safety, fire control, ecological environment, and agricultural science and technology, in order to establish a people-oriented and public service-oriented financial budget system.

3. Rationalizing the Fiscal and Tax Relations Between Central and Local Governments[1]

The fiscal and tax relations between the central and local government is an economic problem, as well as a political problem, involving the national governance structure and the distribution of central and local interests. A debate on how to design the relations between the two has been made in theoretical circles, while academic circles have proposed on how to reform the relations. The author's opinions and designs are put forward here.

---

[1]This part was jointly completed with Doctor Gu Cheng from the Institute of Finance of Dongbei University of Finance & Economics.

3.1. *Division of the affair and expenditure scope of central and local governments*

A scientific and rational division of central and local affairs is the pre-condition to coordinate central and local relations and stimulate the enthusiasm of the local government, as well as the foundation to improve the financial transfer and payment system that matches the central and local financial strength and responsibilities. Therefore, the expenditure scope of governments at all levels shall be defined based on their own responsibilities. According to different levels of public products, the division of governments' functions, and the principles for the division of responsibilities and expenditure liabilities among governments, the division of expenditure liabilities of central and local governments shall follow the idea as below.

First, the central government shall be responsible for public expenditure that represents the interests of the whole nation, nation-wide availability of public products that shall be arranged all around the country, while the funds shall be provided by central financing. Second, local governments shall provide local public products shared by local residents. Third, the central government shall be involved in trans-regional or external public projects to a certain degree. Finally, it is the central government's responsibility to adjust the income distribution among regions and residents, such as social welfare, and adopt a unified standard in China.

Regarding the expenditure obligations of the central government, provincial government, and the country government, most financial expenses shall be centralized in the provincial or lower level. The expenses of cities and counties account for 50% to 55% of the total financial expenses, the provincial expenditure occupies 15% to 20%, while the central expenses account for 25% and 30%. Therefore, the financial transfer payment is bound to become an important integral part of the financial system.

3.2. *Reform of the tax system: Division of the income scope*

The system of tax division is a key content of the financial management system and provides support to the central macrocontrol system. The key point of the tax division system is to strengthen the central regulation and control, with the clear definition of responsibilities of governments at all levels as the precondition, and the improvement of the administration and service ability of local governments as the focus. In order to change the unmatched relationship between China's current system of tax division and the responsibilities of central and local governments, China shall divide the functions between the central and local governments with "economic adjustment and market supervision" for central government and "public service and social management" for local government. It will follow the basic trend of downward movement of the management service focus, maintain and consolidate the proportion of central financial income, improve the proportion of financial income of counties and villages (towns), and reduce the financial income proportion of provinces and prefecture-level cities.

The categorization of taxation items shall correspond to the functions and characteristics of various taxation items and the functions of governments at different levels. Specifically, the following principles shall be followed: (1) The function of the taxation item shall be in accordance with the functions of the governments at all levels; (2) The categorization of taxation items shall not inhibit the reasonable nationwide flow of production factors, in order to maintain the uniform national market; (3) The categorization shall improve the efficiency of tax collection.

3.2.1. *Taxation of the central government*

The central government mainly relies on social security taxes and also includes tax items related to state sovereignty, fair market environment, overall benefits, stability of national economics, social order, and adjustment of income distribution as well as some mobile and unevenly-distributed taxes, such as tariff, VAT and consumption tax, securities transaction taxes, personal income taxes, enterprise income taxes, and taxes on offshore oil. The taxation of the central government shall be higher than 50% of the national income.

3.2.2. *Taxation of the provincial government*

As the main body of local finance, the provincial finance is responsible for the economic adjustment and control at the intermediate level, income redistribution and construction of infrastructure of large investment scale, and the beneficial scope. Therefore, the provincial finance shall maintain its strength to a certain degree and incorporate some local tax items with regulatory functions. The income of provincial government mainly relies on the business tax, as well as taxes on resources, taxes on urban mainenance and construction, VAT, enterprise income tax and local proportion of personal income tax. It shall take up about 15% of the national income.

3.2.3. *Taxation of the municipal and county government*

Municipal and county governments mainly include taxes on real estate, as well as contract tax, land VAT, inheritance tax, effluent tax, urban construction and maintenance tax, and license tax of vehicles and vessels and other taxes of low liquidity and detailed requirements on the information that are easier to be controlled by the basic level, in addition to small taxes, except national and provincial taxes. Its total income shall account for about 30% of the income of the whole country.

3.3. *Allowance and scientific control of debt issuance of local governments*

In order to facilitate the transformation of local governments from production, construction, and administration-oriented governments to public service-oriented governments and to control the current chaos in local governments' debt release, the local government shall be allowed to raise debts for the construction of public facilities based on regulations.

First, it shall be regulated that no financial deficit is allowed for local governments. They can issue local debts for large construction projects and list them under the item of debt repayment for the construction project in the budget. Second, it is illegal for main leaders to decide on any major construction project, and all construction projects shall be approved by the National People's Congress regardless of the possibility of construction and the cost. Third, for major local construction projects, the NPC shall organize a hearing on the necessity, feasibility, and budgeting of the construction, invite engineering experts, economists, budget experts, accountants, citizens, NPC representatives, governmental officials, builders, auditors, and engineers to discuss feasibility, plans to control expenditure, and the risks and fiscal capacity, which will be widely reported by the media and accepts social supervision. Fourth, regarding the debt release by the local government, a neutral credit rating organization will rate the credit of the debt and publish the credit rating of the government. The credit rating will decide the price of the bond, so the investor can decide whether to buy and how many, and at which price to buy. Fifth, the liabilities of local governments shall be cleaned up. Local governments will not allowed to get into debt in a disguised form, while all debts shall be open and normalized. Only bond release would be allowed for local governments, and other forms of debts would be prohibited. Sixth, the approval of the Development and Reform Commission of higher authority and financial department shall be obtained for the bond release to local governments.

The control and reduction of local debts is very important for the adjustment of the relationship between central and local governments. The following measures can be employed: (1) To check, regulate, and control the borrowing of local governments; (2) To prepare the financial report of the government; (3) To check up on local debts; and (4) To solve local debts based on an integration of several methods. In addition, the debts can also be offset by the income from the sale of leading locally state-owned enterprises, operational facilities, land, and non-profit state-owned assets of the government, which shall be auctioned or sold according to the credit rating and offset against the debt. The debt shall be listed under the long-term credit repayment item of the regular budget, i.e., the long-term solution for debts. In some frontiers and poor areas of financial poverty, the central government will not directly assume their debt, but provide subsidies of special transfer payment to the interest repayment item in the regular budget.

3.4. *Establishment of scientific, fair, and open transfer payment*

The transfer payment from the central government to the local government aims to solve the unbalanced development between different regions, maintain authority of the central government, maintain the unification of China, and establish people's trust and dependence on the state and highlight efficiency and openness. To be specific, the following shall be considered when normalizing the current transfer payment system of China.

The first is to integrate the current "mixed" transfer payment system of China. The current "mixed" transfer payment can be integrated into two forms: the general transfer payment and conditional transfer payment. The second is to place the standard income and expenditure and the formula as the basis of distribution of transfer payment, which can be calculated in two modes: the simple proportional factor method and the income and expenditure balancemodel. The third is to establish the local general transfer payment system. The fourth is to accelerate the legal construction of the transfer payment system among governments. China should draw lessons from the advanced experiences of the world to solve problems in its current transfer payment system. Legislation of the transfer payment system should be promoted in China to provide legal guarantee to transfer payment.

4. Promote the Democratization of Finance

The problems in China's current financial and tax balance system include the following. There are too many unreasonable fees and fines in the laws, regulations, and rules of various departments, and the governmental departments, even the administration units, can collect fees only by issuing documents. For taxation, the great power of decision by governmental financial and taxation departments does not reflect on the balance relationship between tax-payers and the government. Regarding the expenditure, too many civil servants, personnel, administration units, and temporary and assisting personnel are raised by finance; the budget submitted to the NPC is difficult to understand; considerable governmental incomes are not incorporated into the management and have not been submitted to NPC for approval; the powerful departments can obtain a greater amount of the budget when compared to the weak ability of the public service department to push for the budget; and the transfer payment is non-transparent and unfair.

The core of the reformation of the financial system is to promote the democratization of the financial income and expenditure, which aims to make finance open, fair, and transparent, inhibit the excessive power of the government in financial income and expenditure, prevent the consumption of financial income by the party and government, and transform the finance to provide public services to the people. Therefore, the reform of the financial system forms an integral part of the reform of the economic system and the reform of the political system.

4.1. Reform of NPC and CPPCC that is related to the reform of the financial system

The reformation of the financial and budget system should be jointly carried out with the reformation and improvement of the NPC and CPPCC systems and relevant legislation work.

The Fund Raising and Budget Committee should be set up respectively in NPC and CPPCC; This should be divided into Fund Raising Committee and Budget Committee that would be responsible for regular examinations. The establishment of the Fund Raising Committee and the Budget Committee will balance the relationship between financial income and expenditure, while officials, experts, and scholars engaged in macro-management and finance, or the teaching of and research in economics, taxes, finance, accounting, audit, and laws, can be employed to work for the Fund Raising Committee and the Budget Committee, and professionals in taxes, finance, audit, accounts, and laws can be employed to work in the office.

NPC shall be transformed from the current meeting system to a full-time and permanent system, gradually reducing the number of meeting representatives, and increasing the number of permanent representatives. To balance the NPC and the government and prevent governmental officials and civil servants from affecting the fund raising and budget act, meeting representatives of the government and the Supreme People's Court and the Supreme People's Procuratorate should be reduced and finally eliminated from their representation in the NPC and CPPCC (except CPC leaders serving the government and the Supreme People's Court and the Supreme People's Procuratorate).

Since NPC allocates the quota of representatives according to population proportion, the representative structure of CPPCC shall be established as the "multi-party plus provincial region" structure in order to enable the transfer payment to the underdeveloped regions to pass the approval. The number of representatives shall be averagely distributed, regardless of the nation, party, number of party members, population, and the area of the region. As with the CPC, the CPPCC too shall reduce the number of representatives, change the current meeting system, change to a full-time and permanent system, and gradually reduce the number of representatives from the government and the Supreme People's Court and the Supreme People's Procuratorate. CPPCC shall be given the legislative authority to discuss, examine, and approve the act on fund raising and budget. The joint conference system shall be established between NPC and CPPCC to discuss fund raising and budget.

Of the same importance, China shall strengthen its monitoring over financial implementation and form the scientific feedback system of "preparation, discussion, check, and approval; implementation and supervision; and adjust the preparation" for the budget. In order to reach this goal, China shall, first, strengthen NPC's supervision over the budget implementation; second, reinforce the momentum on the audit of the budget implementation of the government; and, third, increase administrative and criminal punishment for any violation against the budget act or abuse of the budget.

In terms of legislation, China shall facilitate the revision to the budget law and coordinate the law with the budget reform. The draft, discussion, and release of specific laws shall be accelerated, such as the transfer payment law, law on the permission of charges by governmental departments, law of budget of social security, law on budget of state-owned assets, and law on budget of public construction projects. The budget law shall be coordinated with the accounting law, audit law, criminal law etc. — to enable the budget law to turn into a real law in order to take effective penalizing actions against illegal activities. Relevant enforcement regulations of the budget law and other relevant laws shall be formulated by relevant departments in detail, which shall be submitted to NPC and CPPCC for examination and approval, in order to prevent various departments from misinterpreting the spirit of legislative bodies and ensure the fairness of the law's enforcement.

4.2. Two legal proportions of governmental financial income and expenditure

The two proportions mentioned here refer to the proportion of total governmental income in GDP and the proportion of the expenditure, respectively, on the party, government, and administrative affairs in total governmental expense.

4.2.1. "Two proportions" of developed and developing countries

Developed countries and countries of greater civic welfare often share a higher proportion of governmental income in GDP when compared to the lower proportion shared by the developing countries and countries of weaker civic welfare. Financial income takes up between 35% and 45% of GDP in developed countries, which have the strong ability to collect resources, owing to high productivity and surplus wealth. These countries often work for the welfare of their people, covering education, medical care, unemployment, work-related injury, care for the aged, and housing. They have the ability to centralize the financial strength and use them mostly in people's welfare.

In most developing countries, the financial income takes up between 18% and 25% of GDP. First, these countries are lower in productivity and are unable to collect funds. Too many taxes affect people's enthusiasm in business startups, investment, and operation and may reduce job opportunities and increase unemployment rate. Second, developing countries provide their people with weaker public service and welfare, lower welfare coverage, and fewer welfare items. In conclusion, objectively, developing countries have no fundamental conditions to centralize financial resources, and, subjectively, they show less attention to public services and people's welfare than those of the developed countries.

Regarding the proportion of expenditure on governmental administration in total governmental expenditure, Japan is 2.4%, the lowest among developed countries; Italy is 19%, the highest; and America is around 14%. Among developing countries, those adopting complex democratic system are lower in proportion, while those under greater authority of presidents or serviceman dictatorship have a much higher proportion of expenditure on governmental administration in total governmental expenditure, but low proportion of public service expenditure.

4.2.2. *China's problems in the two proportions*

In terms of the relationship between China's financial income and national economy, and between financial expenditure and the people, problems exist in the two proportions: The first is the high proportion of total governmental income in GDP (around 35%) which does not meet China's basic condition, a developing country of low productivity; the second is too high proportion of expenditure on party and governmental administration in the total governmental expenditure.

4.2.3. *Restrictions on the two proportions by legislation*

Two important tasks of the reform of financial system shall be completed. The first is to stabilize and control the proportion of governmental income in total GDP and gradually lower it to a rational level. The second is to control the proportion of the expenditure on the party and governmental administration in the total expenditure and reinforce the momentum to lower the proportion at a rapid rate.

4.2.3.1. The total legal governmental income shall not exceed 30% of GDP

The system shall be changed and the budget law shall be revised. Based on the new budget law, all governmental incomes shall be incorporated in the budget management. Considering the rational income distribution among the government, residents, and enterprises, especially the low proportion for residents because China is a developing country with low productivity, the total income shall take up less than 30% of GDP before China becomes a developed country. Based on strict legal restrictions, China shall capably handle the relationship between the growth of financial incomes and the growth rate of GDP and between the growth of national incomes and increase in the residents' income. The growth rate of annual financial income shall be controlled to ensure a financial income occupying lower than 30% of GDP.

4.2.3.2. The proportion of expenditure on party and governmental administration shall not exceed 15% of the total governmental expenditure

The restriction shall be confirmed as a legal rule that the proportion of expenditure on the party and governmental administration shall not exceed 15%. The *Law on Supporting Personnel of State Power and Public Institutions* shall be formulated and released to restrain the unlimited expansion of government organizations and personnel.

In order to reduce the large proportion of expenditure on party and governmental administration, it is necessary to simplify party and governmental organizations, socialize the logistics for them, transform public institutions into enterprises, open and embody public consumption, and socialize the social security. It is an arduous task to complete these reforms which will definitely encounter many obstacles. However, it will be very difficult to reach the goal of building a public service and social administration-oriented government if these reforms cannot be carried out, the budget on supporting officials cannot be lowered, charges cannot be reduced, and relevant approvals and permissions cannot be decreased. In addition to reforms, a law shall be formulated to restrain the expansion of party and governmental organizations and personnel.

The *Law on Supporting Personnel of State Power and Public Institutions* shall be formulated and released. The law requires fixing the position and personnel, regulating standards, establishing an indicator system, strictly controlling the budget appropriation, forming the method of check and supervision, and confirming the procedure to increase the personnel in order to strictly control the expansion of governmental institutions and personnel supported by the finance.

4.3. *Establish and improve the system of examination and approval of the budget by NPC and CPPCC*

One of the important characteristics of a socialist political civilization is that the people are the masters of the country. In a socialist society, after citizens transfer part of their power and wealth to the country, an extremely transparent system shall be established to enable citizens to know and supervise how the public power is functioning and how the money is used as the tax and charge payer. Therefore, whether the finance is open and transparent and whether the people are responsible for approval and supervision is an important symbol for a socialist civilization.

The power to decide taxes, charges, and fines shall be given to NPC, and governments and governmental departments' power in this respect shall be cancelled. The fund raising committee shall be established in NPC and CPPCC, which would be responsible for the proposals and terms on taxes, charges, and fees submitted by governments and governmental departments.

4.4. Desperate need to build the system for governments at all levels to submit financial report to CPC

In addition to the rationalization of the financial relation between central and local governments, openness and standardization of local governments' borrowings, reform and clean up of the charge and fine system, and reform of finance in land sales, it is very important to build the system for local governments at all levels to submit financial report to the CPC.

First, local governments shall prepare the reports on governmental finance, regularly report to NPC at the same level every year, and disclose this information to society. Based on international experiences, market economy countries can comprehensively and systematically disclose all government debt information in the governmental financial report. The governmental financial report in China shall improve the disclosure of the government debt information. For government debts that meet the affirming conditions and measurement standards of the debts under the accrual basis, the accounting confirmation and measurement of the total financial budget accounting shall be conducted according to the accrual basis, which will be disclosed in the relevant items of the balance sheet; while for implicit debts that do not meet the specific affirming conditions and measurement standards and therefore cannot be quantified, the relevant information will be disclosed in the notes to the financial report of the government to comprehensively and systematically disclose all of the government's debt information. According to relevant laws and regulations, the governmental financial report will incorporate all debts and borrowings of governments at all levels — governmental departments and their agencies. For any item not incorporated in the administration, the borrower shall burden himself, while the government will not assume the obligation to repay the debt, in order to restrain the borrowings of governmental officials.

Second, strict restrictions, regulations, and checks shall be conducted on governments at all levels and governmental departments, especially for their debts. Laws or the state council regulations shall be established at the first opportunity to regulate local governments to not run into debts arbitrarily in order to contain the borrowing expansion of local governments. Borrowings are forbidden for regular items and social security items but allowed in construction projects, which is subject to advice from the government, approval of the NPC at the same level, examination and approval of the higher authority, the rating from the credit rating organization, and the method of market release. In addition, it is prohibited to get into debts in methods that are not included in the laws. Debts for construction projects are not allowed to be issued without the approval of NPC at the same level or the examination and approval of relevant higher authorities.

4.5. *Transfer the leadership authority of national audit, national assets, and compiling system to NPC*

Problems in the current audit system are rooted in the mutual relationship between the audit organization and the government, meaning that the audit office is the internal audit organization under direct control of the government. Problems mainly include the lack of independence, inhibitions in disclosure of audit results, unstable audit focus, and goals that make it more difficult to play the auditor's role of supervision, blank space for audit supervision, and formality of the budget audit.

The audit office shall be transferred to NPC to reveal the superiority of China's NPC system, so that the people can directly manage the government and their financial behaviors and directly supervise the financial budget. The spirit of this change is how the government is responsible for the people, which reveals the following: (1) It reveals the constitutional thought of people becoming their own masters; (2) It is favorable to prevent government officials' corruptions; (3) It accords to the environment after China's entry into the WTO, when the financial system has to run transparently and efficiently; and (4) It represents tax payers' requirements to supervise the management of public capitals.

State-owned industrial, commercial, and financial assets belong to the people. However, the principal-agent relations between "people and NPC, NPC and government, and government and enterprises" have not been clarified. People's power to supervise assets is not reflected in the current situation of the government's direct management of state-owned industrial, commercial, and financial assets. State-owned and state-holding enterprises are favored by the government in terms of systems and policies. In addition, the state-owned industrial, commercial, and financial assets and the profit distribution are non-transparent, directly managed by the NPC. The party and governmental administrative organizations and personnel have expanded and it is impossible for them to control themselves. Therefore, the compiling system shall be managed by the NPC, which will inhibit the expansion of the party and governmental organizations.

Bibliography

False invoices reflect the loopholes in financial management system. *The Beijing News*, 25 June 2010.

Lai Yingxuan (2005). Focus of the reform of personal income tax, efficiency or fairness. *China Economic Weekly*, 15 August 2005.

Li Jingrui (2009). Half of fees on real estate development in nine cities go to government according to all-China federation of industry and commerce. *The Beijing News*, 6 March 2009.

Li Weiling (2005). 45% tax rate of personal income tax actually equals to no tax revenue. *International Finance*, 30 September 2005.

Liu Hong and Fang Liang. On the problems in the budget preparation of China. *Paper China Net*. Available at http:/www.pp -cn.com/. Accessed on 12 June 2006.

Man Yanyun, Zheng Xinye, and Zheng Ying'er (2009). China's environmental taxes have exceeded average level of developed countries. *First Financial Daily*, 14 December 2009.

Xu Wenxiu (2010). Overview on the process of study on profit distribution of state-owned enterprises. Net of Party School Library of Zhejiang Provincial Party Committee, Column of modern field of view on social sciences, 12 April 2010.

Yang Xiaochang and Xiao Zezhong. Investigation, problems and reform of China's audit system. Available at http://www.66wen.com. Accessed on 14 September 2006.

Zhao Fengbin and Han Li (2008). Fair profit distribution of state-owned enterprises. *Economic Guide.*

Zhou Tianyong (2005). Suggest to formulate the 11th five-year plan to clean up governmental charges. *Economic Information Daily*, 11 July 2005.

Zhou Tianyong (2010). *China's Way Out.* Beijing: People's Daily Press.

Zhou Tianyong (2010). *Manage the "Money Pocket" of Tax Payers.* China: Friendship Publishing House.

Zhou Tianyong and Gu Cheng. Report on study of the fiscal and taxation relation between central and local governments, Project of the European Institute of the Chinese Academy of Social Sciences.

Zhou Tianyong, Wang Changjiang and Wang Anling (2008). Report on the research on the reform of Chinese political system, Construction Corps Press, Xinjiang.

Note: Relevant data from the website of the State Statistics Bureau.

Chapter 7

Elimination of Polarization and Realization of Common Prosperity

What is socialism? An important characteristic of socialism is to avoid polarization and realize common prosperity. This is the opinion of the authors of classic scientific socialism, the ideal of Chinese socialists and the people involved in the horrendous 100-year struggle as well as the dream of most of the Chinese. The following is the blueprint of China's ideal future socialist society: to give full play to all its people and to the positive roles played by the labor, technology, and capital; conduct the primary distribution of wealth based on the contributions; to protect ecology and environment, and save resources; conduct the secondary adjustment by the government and society; ensure the socialist democracy, fairness, and justice; guarantee employment, education, medical care, concern for the aged, and relief for the disabled and impoverished; narrow the gap between the rich and the poor by facilitating more contributions from the higher income groups; create harmonious living environment for all people irrespective of their age, occupation, and caste or creed; and to establish a healthy society of high employment rate.

1. Scientific and Comprehensive Understanding of the Factors Contributing to Uneven Distribution

The key to the adjustment between income distribution and pattern of ownership is to figure out the profound and multiple factors contributing to the income gap between the poor and the wealthy. Different opinions exist in the academic circles on the reasons for this gap. In author's view, all these opinions are understandable, but a comprehensive and in-depth discussion is needed, in order to strategize and formulate an effective policy.

1.1. *Profound structural factor of the income gap in China*

The reason for this income gap is rarely contemplated from the perspective of the structural factor-utilization of the wealth creation and development mode of a country.

Only few scholars have studied the relation between the structure of enterprise scale in terms of industrial organization and the income gap, but there are few rare researches on the reasons for the income gap in terms of unbalanced rural and urban structure, proportion of industries, and industrial structure. This lack of research is indeed regrettable for theoretical purposes and to carry out policy analysis which would otherwise help China in narrowing the income gap by structural adjustment.

1.1.1. *Structure of factor-utilization and income gap*

Factors that create wealth include labor, capital, land, technologies, management, minerals, and other resources. For the primary distribution and value creation, the process of creation of wealth is a part of the process of distributing new income. The input prices of various factors, such as the salaries, social security, interests, land rent, patent prices, remunerations for managers, and profits of the mine owners will form the newly-increased value of commodities and service. Such input prices form the primary distribution pattern among different owners.

Which development model should be adopted in the study of income distribution: Capital and energy-intensive economic development mode; or the mode of balanced capital, resources and labor; or the labor-intensive economic development mode? There is a law that states that labor cannot be fully utilized in a country preferring capital and resource-intensive development mode, because capital and resources lead the creation of wealth and many labor may be left unused. That is the reason for the large proportion of income distribution to the owners of capital and resources, and small proportion of distribution to labor, leading to the income gap between the two.

A reflection on China's development mode is needed. In order to lead economic growth, many regions in China are interested in attracting investments in infrastructure development. Labor has been replaced by capital in the creation of wealth and not fully utilized. Indeed, capital is vital to promote economic growth. However, for China, a country of large population, the capital and resource-intensive economic development mode would result in a high unemployment rate, that, combined with the low salaries for labor, will necessarily lead to an increasing income gap between resource owners and labors. Therefore, mode of balanced capital, resources and labor would work well in China's development.

1.1.2. *Slower urbanization and increasing income gap between rural and urban areas*

The gap between urban and rural areas has been constantly widened since China's reform and opening up. In 1983, the income ratio of urban residents comparatively to rural residents was 1.82:1, as that of 3.33:1 in 2009, with a growth rate much higher than developed countries as well as the developing countries such as Brazil and Argentina. What is the reason for the increasing urban and rural gap? As an objective tendency, the proportion of agricultural added value in GDP has been constantly declining, which requires rural population and labor to accordingly migrate to urban areas and non-agricultural fields and to enable the decreasing rural population to meet the declining rural and agricultural added value. Seen from statistics, the proportion of agricultural added value in GDP has dropped from 33.4% in 1982 to 10.6% in 2009; the proportion of rural population has decreased from 78.87% to 46.59%; while the employment rate of the primary industry has only declined from 68.1% to 38.1%. Compared to the rapid decline in the proportion of wealth production in rural areas and agriculture, the excessively slow transfer of rural population and labor to urban areas and non-agricultural fields will lead to the comparatively less and less agricultural added value distributed to relatively more and more rural population and labors. This would lead to an increasing gap.

In the late 1990s and early 21st century, the labor economy, i.e., peasants working in urban areas bringing their incomes back to the agricultural sector increased the income of rural areas. However, improvements in the knowledge levels of peasant workers leads to drastic changes in their ideologies and lifestyles which ultimately increases the living standards of the rural people in urban areas, there-fore it is highly impossible for the peasant workers who are born after the 1980s to bring their incomes back to their hometowns, as com-pared to the peasant workers of the 1960s and 1970s. This has resulted in the imbalance of rural and urban incomes.

In addition to the above-mentioned problems, factors such as peasants having no income from land, and the unreasonable prices of agricultural products, such as grains, also contribute to the expanding urban and rural gap. First, rural assets cannot bring huge profits. Urban residence and land for enterprise use can be mortgaged for funds, rent, or even sold, and thus bring asset profits. Contrarily, Chinese peasants' arable land, forest land, and residence land cannot be realized or mortgaged for funds, and cannot bring any income as assets except for the production of agricultural products. In addition, some peasants face poverty owing to the irrational land requisition and compensation system. Second, the macro control of commodity prices has distorted the price system of industrial and agricultural products and transferred parts of interests to urban residents owing to the comparatively low price of agricultural products. In the 30 years after reform and opening up, macro control has placed the stability of general prices as the main goal, but an important means to stabilize the commodity prices is to control the rise in the prices of grains. The rapid growth rate of non-agricultural products, including the means of production for agriculture and relatively slow growth rate of agricultural products have transferred a part of the interests from rural areas to urban areas owing to the low prices.

1.1.3. *Lower proportion of the tertiary industry and smaller distribution to labors*

The industrial structure has changed three times, the law of which is summarized below. In total GDP, the proportion of the primary industry has been constantly declining, which will finally reduce to below 5% from the original 80% to 90%; the added value of the secondary industry increases in the beginning, maintains at about 30% to 40%, and finally declines to 20%; the tertiary industry is constantly increasing, from the original 15% to the final 75% or even higher. Regarding the employment structure, the proportion of labor in the primary industry will decline from 80% to below 5%; the labor in the secondary industry will reach the peak of 35% and drop to about 15%; and the labor in the tertiary industry will finally rise from 15% to 80%. Then, two problems in income distribution will emerge: (1) Under the distorted production structure and labor allocation structure of the industries, the different labor productivity will lead to a gap in the income distribution. Labor of the industry would match the added value created by the industry. For the primary distribution, labor creates wealth and distributes the wealth it creates. Therefore, the mismatching industrial added value and its corresponding labor scale and the different labor productivity will lead to the income gap among various industries; (2) The second problem lies in the different degrees of utilization of the production factors. In a macro view, the capital-intensive industry has been production-intensive. The too-low added value and employment proportion of the labor-intensive tertiary industry indicate the large proportion of the secondary industry and the capital in the creation of wealth. If more incomes go to capital owners, the labor will end up with a smaller proportion of total incomes, leading to the increasing income gap between the capital owners and the labors.

According to general regulation, the added value of the tertiary industry in countries and regions of per-capita GDP of 3,500 USD often accounts for 60% of GDP, while the employment rate takes up 65%. China's per-capita GDP was 3,400 USD in 2009, but the added value of the tertiary industry only takes up 42.6% and the employment rate is 34.1%, respectively 20% and 30% lower than the world average level. Economically, it refers a large number of labor in the primary industry and part of labor in the secondary industry that should have been, but have not been, transferred to the tertiary industry that are left unused, so they have not created wealth and therefore cannot get the wealth distributed accordingly. Most wealth is created by the capital-intensive secondary industry, so a large proportion of wealth has gone to the capital owners. This situation leads to the unbalanced income distribution between capital owners and labor owners.

Along with the rising cost, such as salaries and social security, the organic composition of the capital in the secondary industry will improve, which means that capital will further replace labor owing to technological progress and automation and reducing percentage of labor will promote higher percentage of capital. Under these circumstances, if production and employment are not improved in the tertiary industry, the unemployment rate will increase when excessive labor remains unused; the income distribution between capital and labor will be further worsened and the income gap will widen.

1.1.4. *Relatively fewer enterprises and expanding income gap*

The industrial structure can be divided into proportional industrial structure and organizational industrial structure. The former mainly refers to the industrial and regional distribution, such as the production structure and employment structure of industries, while the latter refers to the concentrated degree of industries, such as the structure of enterprise and scale, including extra large, large, medium, small, and micro-sized enterprises. The structure of the enterprises' scale and the number of enterprises per thousand people are closely related to the structure of income distribution among capital owners and the labor class.

In terms of factor and industrial distribution, most extra large and large enterprises, and a considerable number of medium-sized enterprises, belong to capital-intensive enterprises, which are mainly engaged in the secondary industry. Some medium, and many small and micro enterprises are involved in the tertiary industry with a less number of small and micro enterprises in the secondary industry providing production support and service to the tertiary industry. Therefore, the former enterprises are capital intensive; where the law of the capital organic composition is developed, while the latter are labor-intensive. Capital occupies a large proportion of the creation and distribution of wealth by the former, whereas labor is considered an important factor by the latter.

The larger proportion of small enterprises in the enterprise scale will result in a greater number of enterprises per thousand people, a higher labor intensive degree, more medium and small investors, a lower unemployment rate (since the labor class is fully utilized), and a smaller income gap. On the contrary, the presence of more numbers of large enterprises will result in lesser investment in small and micro enterprises, less number of enterprises per thousand people, worse utilization of labor, fewer medium-income people, more poor people owing to unemployment, and increasing income gap.

The rate for Chinese undergraduates to start business in three years only accounts for 2%, compared to 20% in developed countries. If five commercial households are calculated as one enterprise, according to optimistic estimation, the number of enterprises per every thousand people is about 12, compared to 45 in developed countries and 20 to 30 in developing countries. Insufficient business start-ups and fewer small and micro enterprises contribute to the large income gap in China.

In conclusion, without the change in the development mode or in the structural adjustment, the problem of the uneven income distribution can hardly be solved simply through minimum cost of living, rise in salaries, public service, transfer payment, and reformation of the distribution system.

1.2. *Historical and time reasons for the income distribution gap*

Historical causes and the Matthew effect during the process of re-earnings and the accumulation of wealth lead to the gap of income and wealth distribution.

1.2.1. *Historical causes since the reformation and opening up*

Reform and opening up began after the Third Plenary Session of the Eleventh Central Committee in 1978. At that time, China suffered popular equalitarianism, low productivity, low standards of living, and had a national economy on the brink of collapse, so the party and the government proposed the policy to allow some people and some regions prosper before others. Among these people, some became rich through hard work, innovation, and with the application of knowledge, technologies, operation, and proper management. Examples of such people were common laborers working overtime or working for more than one unit and technicians of state-owned enterprises, and research and development institutions who worked in township enterprises on Sunday, known as "Sunday engineers." Some people who were good at running businesses engaged in long-distance transportation of sale and obtained profits from the price difference of commodities in different regions; some people consulted for enterprises and teams and gained profits by management; and some individual businessmen earned profits through effective production and operation.

However, some groups of people accumulated wealth by exploiting the imperfect laws and regulations, systems, and policy management. Some of them resold the governments' certifications and approvals to earn profits, such as the approval to invest into specific projects, quotations for import and export, and special certifications for certain projects. Second, some utilized the dual-track prices of many materials and products under the planned economy by abiding to the market regulation and earned considerable income. Third, some speculated on foreign exchanges and earned profits based on the price difference between the official prices of foreign exchange control and the black market. Fourth, some people earned huge profits by smuggling, bankruptcy, and through reforms of the state-owned enterprises and funding. Fifth, some people obtained profits simply through buying and selling of lands. Many developers and other investors made use of the gap between the supply and demand of land and in the rapid growth of their values; buying land from the government when the price was comparatively low, or even for free of cost, and earning huge profits simply by changing the usage right of land, and adjusting the plot ratio accordingly. This is the "original sin" of the capital accumulation of some private enterprises, which had been fiercely discussed several years ago.

1.2.2. *Rise of the price of real estate in the time course*

In addition to the study on how wealth is created based on the factor combination, economics also places focus on the study of time economics, because wealth is created based on both time and other factors. Certain amount of wealth will be accumulated over a period due to the rise in prices. The value of some assets would increase gradually leading to an increase in wealth accumulation. For example, some people bought commercial residential buildings or purchased houses out of their working units during the reforms in the pricing of state-owned houses in the early years. The prices of these houses or the compensation for demolition have significantly grown. For example, a resident of Beijing bought a house at 2nd Ring Road in 1997 with a unit price of 4,500 yuan per m², which may have risen to 45,000 yuan per m² by 2010, so the price of a house of 120 m² will increase from 540,000 yuan to 5.4 million yuan over a period of time. However, the residents buying houses on mortgage in 2010 need to pay for the high housing prices and bear the burden of both principal and interest. Therefore, the variation in asset prices also contribute to the gap in income and wealth distribution between the residents who bought houses in the early years and the residents who are buying houses in recent times. In addition to houses, the prices of land, stocks, gold, diamonds, and curios also continue to rise. Residents who own these assets will accumulate more and more wealth along with the variation in prices over a course of time.

1.2.3. *Re-earnings and accumulation of wealth investment in the course of time*

As another important aspect of time economy, investment and accumulation, as well as re-earnings and re-investment, are also available to increase the wealth accumulation by compound interest. Residents who own assets can use them to gain profits and accumulate more wealth. For example, residents who own several houses can rent some out; or people can invest in stocks and real estate, purchase the original issue stock or newly develop commercial houses to gain premium income; or buy the secondary stocks or houses at a lower price and sell them at higher prices; or re-invest with the accumulated wealth to set up factories and gain profits from production, operation, and management. In conclusion, wealth can be invested for profits and this process can be repeatedly carried out.

Therefore, the Matthew effect exists in the distribution of people's wealth in the time economy, a phenomenon whereby those with more wealth will earn relatively more wealth, and those with less money will gain relatively less wealth. Apart from the above mentioned reasons, the polarization between the rich and the poor also result from the education being provided to the children that belong to different income groups, which will make the later generations respectively inherit their wealth or poverty. Later generations of the rich will continue with their high social status and connections, and work opportunities, which is one important aspect of the Matthew effect.

1.3. **State ownership becomes the important force to promote polarization**

In addition to the above-mentioned structural, historical, and time reasons, the defective systems also contribute to the uneven distribution of income and wealth in China. The national income, i.e., the wealth needs to flow, allocated and distributed among the governments, enterprises, and individuals according to the wealth distribution systems. China has encountered the following problems in the system of income flow and distribution.

1.3.1. *State-owned monopoly economy promotes polarization*

The state-owned economy includes state-owned industrial and commercial enterprises, financial institutions, and the system of state-owned land. In the original public ownership and planned economy, industrial and commercial enterprises, banks, and other financial institutions and land were state's and collectively-owned, as the basis of equitable distribution. The fairness and the rationality of the system, whether the system has promoted the development of productivity will not be discussed here. The problem to be discussed here is that the socialist public ownership under the market economy, in contrast with the plan of traditional socialist theory, has contributed to the unfair income distribution and polarization.

The process and mechanism for the formation and distribution of wealth in monopoly state-owned industrial, commercial, and financial enterprises. How do state-owned economies obtain resources, form wealth flow, and distribute wealth evenly? A specific and objective discussion shall be made: (1) According to the estimation, the state-owned industrial and commercial enterprises with a value of more than 30 trillion yuan, including large-scale state-owned financial assets, are entirely under people's ownership; (2) More than 10 trillion yuan have been invested to rescue the state-owned enterprises in the middle and later periods of the 20th century; (3) State-owned enterprises are estimated to gain more than 10 trillion yuan after 1997, since they do not submit profits to the government; (4) State-owned enterprises also obtain 10 trillion yuan of monopoly interests by market access, resource monopoly, by submitting a few taxes and expenses to the government, and transferring the cost of pollution that shall be borne by themselves to the government; (5) Since the number of staff is reduced, fewer people in the state-owned economy are enjoying the achievements of the reform, which reduces the reform cost of each person, so they save about 10 trillion yuan in this way.

1.3.2. *The state-owned monopoly banking system promotes polarization*

In addition to the investment made by the self-owned enterprises, debt capital is also necessary in the asset structure of business startups and enterprises. The debt ratio of industrial and commercial industries generally ranges from 40% to 60%. On the whole, debt is necessary to expand the scale of enterprises and ensure capital turnover. Some enterprises also invite capital in the market by listing in stock exchanges. The financial systems, especially banks, securities, funds, guarantee, and some other financial organizations, distribute social capital to various enterprises through certain channels. The different distribution patterns of the financial systems in collecting, adjusting, and distributing social capitals to various industries and enterprises decides the conditions for the financing of extra large, large, medium, small, and micro enterprises, the conditions for the financing of capital-intensive and labor-intensive enterprises, and the conditions for the financing of the secondary industry and service sector.

Where, then, does China's state-owned financial system allocate the social capital? Most are distributed to extra large, large, and medium-sized enterprises, capital-intensive enterprises, and secondary industry. Only a few loans go to small and micro enterprises, labor-intensive enterprises, and service industry, which can give birth to a large amount of middle-income groups and create ample job opportunities, so these enterprises obtain 70% to 80% of debt capitals from underground or informal financial channels, usury, and even through illegal gang activity. In China, the state-owned banking system has dominated the savings resources and distributed most resources to state-owned enterprises, large-scale private economies, foreign-owned enterprises, capital owners, and the minority groups, but distributed only a few to small enterprises, service industry, modern agriculture, pioneers starting up small and medium enterprises, skilled labor, peasants, and low-income groups. Actually, it is impossible for the state-owned monopoly financial system to provide loans to individual, micro, small, labor-intensive enterprises which can enrich people, or provide loans to the service industry that can absorb great amount of labors owing to the difficulties in assets mortgage.

The state-owned financial system distributes little or even no loans to most people that create and distribute wealth, but provides favorable loan conditions for a small number of people, which is a more distorted system than the financial system in capitalist countries and significantly contributes to the large income gap and polarization.

1.3.3. *The state and collective-owned land system promotes polarization*

China adopts a state-owned system for urban land and collectively-owned system for rural arable land, forest land, residence land, and pasture land. This is the basis for the socialist public ownership, when all assets belong to the state or the cooperative, where employment problem of the labor class is solved by the government and the cooperative, the revenues through production and consumer goods are allocated according to the plan, and salaries and prices are under unified regulations of the country. However, the land system in the market economy has been changed to the following process of interest allocation.

First, the local finance system earns profits from transferring land and collecting fees and taxes from real estate owners, which actually satisfies the peasants of low income and other people in the low income group that plan to purchase houses. The government requests land at a low price and invites to bid at a higher price; thus earns profits from peasants and the house buyers by raising the price of houses. Second, peasants can only earn money from agricultural production without any asset income as per the current land system. Third, the government can vigorously increase the price of land owing to the monopoly land supply system under administrative control, so the estate agents can gain huge profits from the great gap between supply and demand and the price rise. In addition, some speculators buy houses at a low price and sell them at a higher price to earn huge profits and accumulate wealth at a premium level.

1.3.4. Reflections on the relationship among the ownership, operation environment, and wealth flow

Based on the analysis, the state and collectively-owned economy under the planned economy system is fairer, despite the low efficiency and living standards, since the country controls the production and its prices and most laborers serve in state and collectively-owned economy. However, only fewer people are working in state-owned economies under the market economy, while a large number of them are serving for the non-state and collectively-owned enterprises. Profits from assets of state-owned economies are not submitted to the government for allocation. The loan resources of state-owned banks are distributed to enterprises containing small employment, instead of economies providing more job opportunities, so fewer and fewer people can enjoy the interests from the state-owned economy and loan resources. Even the land requisition system that changes collectively-owned land to state-owned land becomes the mechanism to compulsively gain interests from low-income groups.

As a conclusion of the above three aspects, irrespective of public or private ownership, a system that concentrates upon social resources and interest benefits to a small number of people will necessarily lead to unfair distribution and polarization. A paradox has emerged between socialist theory and practices since the reform and opening up; the theoretical socialist public ownership conflicts with the fair distribution and common prosperity in practice. This means that the socialist public ownership, which shall be the theoretical basis for the fair distribution and common prosperity, has led to the practical result of unfair distribution and polarization.

According to the above analysis, in the recent 30 years, especially after the socialist market economic system was established in the early 1990s, the state-owned economy, banks, land, and collectively-owned land, which were previously the basis of the socialist system, have become the mechanism to seek profits for fewer people and promote polarization. The tough question today is whether or not the public ownership, to be specific, the state-ownership, and collective land ownership is the basis of socialism under market economy in terms of fair distribution and common prosperity.

1.4. The imperfect modern system for adjustment and plugging of income distribution

In addition to the three major reasons mentioned above, the imperfect income distribution adjustment system and unreasonable leakages in the process of income distribution also contribute to unfair wealth distribution.

1.4.1. No wage consultation system

Labor and capital form a unity of oppositeness. The government and laws shall protect and check both parties and establish a functional chamber of commerce and labor union during the creation of wealth. Otherwise, the labor force may grow too strong, conquer bigger percentages of profits owing to high wage requirements, and lead to the bankruptcy of enterprises; or, if the force of capital is too strong, workers would risk exploitation.

Some local governments set up a very low minimum wage for workers in order to create a low-cost place to attract investment. Some places even regard the low salary as a policy to attract investment from other places. The government lowers the wage level, but the labor union cannot be given full play owing to the weak organization and the sound force of capitals, so there is no room for workers to negotiate the price of labors and capitals.

1.4.2. No proper adjustment of the government

The government, on the one hand, re-distributes the excessive wealth from high-income people by taxation and other levers, and on the other hand, seeks for the fairness in social income and wealth distribution by social security, equal public service, and transfer payment.

As mentioned above, China does not collect real estate taxes from people, who possess many houses but compulsively requests land from peasants at a low price and sells to low-income people who are buying houses on mortgage, and thus earn huge profits. In the process, the real estate agents also obtain considerable profits. For residents with more houses, they may gain great profits by speculating on houses — buying houses at a lower price and wait for the value to rise before reselling them, or rent houses to gain profits. Therefore, they become richer within a limited timeframe. By 2009, China had not implemented the inheritance tax or gift tax. The income from real estate taxes only accounted for 0.59% of the total income of the government. In the entire taxation structure, heavier taxes are levied on business start-ups and enterprises that can increase employment, but lighter taxes are collected on wealth, resources, and environment, which substantially encourage the rich to accumulate profits by occupying the wealth of others, waste resources, and pollute the environment.

Every resident, no matter rich or poor, should enjoy equal welfare through education, health care, and social security based on equal distribution of public resources. The previous governmental organizations on education and healthcare only served urban residents and established social security in cities alone, while the distribution of public resources, such as education and health care, as well as the distribution and coverage of social security in urban residents, remained ill-balanced. The situation has improved in recent years along with the establishment of urban and rural minimum living standard security system, initiating urban education for the children of peasant workers, and leading old-age security in rural areas. However, it takes great efforts to realize fair distribution of education and health resources to urban and rural residents and full coverage of rural and urban social security due to the the existing system of public expenditure.

1.4.3. *Corruptions and semi-overt income*

Doctor Wang Xiaolu has conducted a special in-depth analysis on the semi-overt income. He considers that the huge profits from power-money deals, corruptions in public investment and approval (such as contract of projects, transfer of land, public purchase, and transfer of mines), land incomes, and monopoly incomes become the semi-overt incomes of high-income residents. Between 2005 and 2008, the invisible income outside the statistics grew by 91%, with an annual growth rate of about 20%; 2% of people at top levels take away more than 80% of wealth. The semi-overt income closely related to power-money deals and monopoly interests has reached 5.4 trillion yuan.

With these semi-overt incomes taken into consideration, the income gap among residents is even wider. The maximum urban family income in 2008 was 26 times greater than the minimum urban family income, which is only shown as 9 times according to the state statistics bureau (Website of State Statistics Bureau). Considering both rural and urban areas, 10% of families with highest per capita income was 97,000 yuan in 2008, compared to 1,500 yuan of the top 10 families with lowest per capita income, with a gap of 65 times, which is presented as 23 times according to state statistics bureau (Wang Xiaolu, 2010).

Scholars of the state statistics bureau have discussed the above analysis made by Wang Xiaolu. They pointed out that the per capita disposable income of urban residents was 32,154 yuan in 2008 according to Wang Xiaolu's report, which is double the amount as per the state statistics bureau; and the disposable income of national residents reached 23.2 trillion yuan, 9.26 trillion yuan higher than the national residents income estimated based on the investigation on rural and urban residents conducted by the state statistics bureau and 5.3 trillion yuan higher than the disposable income in the national cash flow table of 2008. According to them, Wang Xiaolu had obviously overestimated the rural and urban residents' lifestyles. According to Wang Xiaolu's calculation, the disposable income of residents in 2008 should have accounted to 73.9% of GDP, and 72.6% of total disposable income. Meanwhile, in the same year, the national financial income occupies 19.5% of GDP and the disposable income of the government takes up to 21.3% of the total national disposable incomes. Based on this, calculations say that the disposable income of enterprises only accounts to 6.1% of total national disposable incomes, which is obviously unreasonable (Shi Faqi, 2010).

2. New Ideas and Strategies to Solve the Income Distribution Problem

It is very important to solve unfair distribution, narrow various gaps, and enrich people in terms of strategies and policies for construction of a harmonious and rich society. Brand new ideas shall be proposed to solve these problems and appropriate strategies shall be formulated.

To lower the proportion of distribution to residents in the GDP and improve the proportion of the residents' income in the GDP, the correct idea is to improve the distribution ability of the labor factor in the GDP, stabilize and adjust the capital factor distribution in the GDP, and control the expansion of the proportion of distribution to the governmental power in the GDP.

To control and narrow the income gap among residents and lower the Gini coefficient, the correct idea is to spur employment through new startups, increase the population of medium-income groups, reduce low-income people due to unemployment and poverty, and ensure the basic living conditions of the poor by providing minimal living facilities through equal distribution of wealth.

To control and narrow the distribution gap between the rural and the urban residents, urbanization should be promoted, excessive labor in agriculture should be transferred to cities leaving capable fewer laborers to share the decreasing total value of agricultural production. Simultaneously, efforts should be undertaken to modernize agriculture, reduce the taxes and fees on agriculture, increase investment on "agriculture, rural areas and farmers," and provide necessary public service to peasants and rural areas.

To control the gap in development in various regions and gradually eliminate the unbalanced regional development, it is recommended to promote the migration of laborers and population from central and west China to places of rapid economic growth that require labor. It is further recommended that the reforms in administrative and economic management system should be facilitated and efficient policies to promote capital and industries in the underdeveloped regions should be formulated. Investment on infrastructure and public services in underdeveloped regions should be enhanced along with general transfer payment, especially to frontier and impoverished places and places of ecological protection.

To rationalize the relationship between the ownership structure and the creation and distribution of wealth, it is recommended that the government deals with the relationship between the large state-owned enterprises and small-scale private individuals; administer the relationship between capital intensive state-owned economies absorbing fewer labor and the labor intensive small private economies generating medium-income and fully making use of labor; and properly deal with the relationship between the state and collective ownership and establishing balanced distribution of asset profits under market economy.

To eliminate the income gap based on historical reasons and to improve the wealth distribution adjustment and plugging system, higher taxes may be levied on the rich, tax coverage of medium-income people may be expanded, and people of low income may be protected by redesigning the systems and mechanisms on taxes, transfer payment and prevention of corruption, so as to realize the goal of achieving small proportion of high income and low income groups and a large proportion of medium income group.

In conclusion, in order to solve the unfair distribution and low proportion of distribution to residents in the GDP during the 12th five-year plan, China needs to: (1) Consider, from the perspective of economic laws and tendency, social transformation, change in its economic structure, and regional population flow into cities; (2) Encourage business startups, increase employment, adjust the structure and learn experiences from East Asia to develop small enterprises to increase the medium income group, enhance employment, and reduce poverty in order to prevent the rise of the Gini coefficient in the transformation of an agricultural society to urban society based on the self-balance income distribution system and forces; (3) Give full play to people's enthusiasm in business startups and creation, make full use of the government's role in adjusting the income distribution, and coordinate in the construction of harmonious society; and (4) Coordinate the relationship between national taxation level and social vigor in startups, between startup and employment distribution and secondary distribution, between the regional population flow, and industrial capital transfer between the social self-balanced distribution and government adjustment, and between the social welfare level and the national financial ability. Thus, a brand new strategy to increase the distribution to residents in the GDP could be formulated that would narrow the income and development gap and enrich people in the period of the 12th five-year plan and a longer period afterwards.

3. Some Major Strategies on Fair Distribution and Prosperity of People

According to the above analysis, directional adjustments shall be made and the following major strategies shall be proposed in order to comprehensively solve the problems of unfair distribution, declining proportion of distribution to residents in the GDP, and unbalanced regional development.

First, formulate and implement the strategy of urbanization and population flow among regions. It will be necessary to change the backward urbanization situation in China, which is 15% behind countries of per capita GDP of 3,200 that shares the same development level with China; and promote the transfer of excessive labors in agriculture to urban areas, promote excessive labors in the Central and Western areas to transfer to cities of developed coastal areas, to the secondary industry, and particularly to service sector. It is suggested to collect taxes on abandoned arable land, which will enable peasants to transfer the arable land to large grain producers when they get transferred to urban areas. It will improve the scale of agriculture and labor productivity, increase the agricultural added value for fewer labors and population involved in agriculture, thus increasing the income of peasants. Peasants who have transferred to cities can gain greater incomes than the agricultural profits in rural areas, thus inhibiting the rise of urban wages. This can strategically reduce the income gap between rural and urban residents as well as the income gap of residents in different regions.

Second, formulate and carry out the 10-year strategic plan to promote the development of small enterprises. If five commercial households are calculated as one enterprise, the number of enterprises per every thousand people is about 11, compared to 45 in developed countries and about 25 in developing countries. Insufficient development of small enterprises is an important factor for the growing number of poor people due to unemployment, low wages owing to few demands on the labor force, unfair distribution, and high Gini coefficient. Therefore, a 10-year plan should be immediately formulated to facilitate the development of small enterprises in order to expand employment, improve people's livelihood, and stabilize society, which is an important strategy to increase the population of medium income, reduce the number of unemployed, and poor people and lower the Gini coefficient.

Third, formulate and implement the strategy of facilitating the development of the service industry. The service industry can greatly absorb labor force. Compared to the countries of the same development level, China's proportion of the added value of service sector in GDP is 20% lower than the average international level, and the employment proportion of service industry accounts for 33% of total employment, 27% lower than the international average level. Employing available skilled labor force from rural areas in the service industry will significantly reduce the unemployment problem increase incomes, and lower the Gini coefficient. Therefore, it is necessary to formulate a strategic plan that can practically promote the development of the service industry and corresponding system reform plan, meanwhile enhancing the improvement of systems and policies of various departments and truly enabling the service industry to attract labors and increase residents' incomes.

Fourth, draw up and carry out a long-term strategic plan to improve the wellbeing of the nation. Though China is a large country with huge population, it has excelled other developing countries with its economic strengths in the process of development. China shall gradually raise the living standards of the people by providing the minimum comfort levels to the rural and urban population that live below the poverty line, establish and improve social security on medical care, endowment, unemployment, and disability in both rural and urban areas and build a modern socialist welfare country of competitive vitality, considerable wealth, and fairness.

Only significant adjustments on these strategies can comprehensively solve the problems, including low proportion of distribution to residents in the GDP, large income gap between rural and urban residents, high Gini coefficient, and unbalanced regional development, in order to build a country of common prosperity.

Bibliography

Li Junru (1995). Deng Xiaoping's answer *to* "What is socialism". People's Daily, 15 June 1995.

Liu Guoguang (2010). Basic ideas on realizing fair income distribution. *Xinhua Net*. Accessed on 30 June 2010.

Shi Faqi (2010). On doctor Wang Xiaolu's "Semi-overt incomes and distribution of national incomes". *China News Net*. Accessed on 2 August 2010.

Wang Xiaolu (2010). Semi-overt incomes and distribution of national incomes. *Comparison*, 3.

Yin Zhongli (2010). Distorted prices in financial market showing great influence on income distribution. National Business Daily, 23 August 2010.

Zhou Tianyong (2010). *China's Way Out*. Beijing: People's Daily Press.

Zhou Tianyong and Tan Xiaofang (2009). Financing of medium and small-sized enterprises and development of small banks. Research report submitted to the All-China Federation of Industry and Commerce.

Chapter 8

Improving the Economics Systems: Reform of Land, Finance, and State-owned Economy

Important unfinished reforms in the economic systems of China include the reform of the resource pricing system and the finance and taxation system. However, more reforms shall be further conducted. First, reform of the current land system is important to meet the demands of the normal operative system of the socialist market economy and urbanization. Second, reform of the current financial system should be carried out to meet the demands of the fair allocation of resources such as loans and social funds to various industries and enterprises. Third, reform of the current state-owned enterprises is necessary to break up the monopoly, ensure equal competition, improve efficiency, enable enterprises to submit reasonable profits to the government, and prevent unfair distribution by controlling the interiorization of the state-owned economy. The reforms of the five economic systems shall be promoted in the next 10 years, in order to establish a perfect socialist market economic system by 2020.

1. Amendments to Laws on and Reform of the Land System

How to reform the land system and fix the system through legislation in the 12th five-year plan, and in the future plans? Currently, the revisions to, and legislation of, the land management law are hotly debated, and the design of the land system is being formulated, and will be confirmed by, legislation. The author believes that this is the right opportunity for land reforms.

1.1. *Goal of the reform and legislation of the land system*

Though it is necessary to implement land system reform by amending existing laws, it is crucial to confirm the goal of the system after the reform and legislation. The author adds that the goal of the land system reform shall be further clarified.

First, the land system shall be regarded as part of the socialist market economic system. Though land is significant than any other resources, it shall also be allocated mainly based on the principle of market economy, instead of administrative practices. Second, the land system shall be established to facilitate the transformation of the dual structure of urban and rural areas, and the urbanization and modernization of agriculture. The reform of the system and legislation shall not inhibit the transfer of excessive rural labors to urban areas, the circulation of land, or large-scale agricultural operation. Third, the efficiency in the allocation of land resources should be improvised. Fourth, the housing prices should be lowered to enable most urban residents, including labor and migrating population from rural to urban areas to afford housing in cities. Fifth, distribute urban and rural land according to the well-laid plans in a scientific and democratic manner. Sixth, the reform and legislation of land system shall place emphasis on people's livelihood and interests. The government shall not fight against its people particularly peasants for the collection of taxes.

1.2. *Idea and plan of the land system reform*

The idea of the land system reform is to extend the term and similar property rights, enable the rural collective land to be exchanged in the market equally as other types of land, and change the fees to taxes while not changing the ownership.

1.2.1. *Reform and establish a reasonable financial income from land and houses of local governments*

According to the Ministry of Land and Resources, the total volume of land transfer in China amounted to 2.7 trillion RMB in 2010, with a growth rate of 70.4% compared to 2009. It is believed that land would be mostly used for urbanization that may lead to irrational interest distribution, acute social conflicts, therefore, it is important that the land reform system and law are perfected. (The Ministry of Land and Resources). It is believed that important factors contributing to the rise in housing prices also include the increasingly higher fees on the land transfer, other taxes and expenses levied by governmental tax departments and relevant departments dealing with real estate, and the responsibilities of the land agents to bear the public installations. Some research suggests that the transfer fee, taxes, and various expenses collected by the government have taken up half of the total price of urban houses. The All-China Federation of Industry and Commerce proposed a report on *Reasons for the High Housing Prices in China* in CPPCC in 2008 and indicated that 49.42% of total expenses (i.e., the cost of land and total taxes) have been transferred to the governments according to the investigation of *Development Costs of Real Estate Enterprises* conducted in nine cities in 2009 (Li Jingrui, 2009).

Regarding the current finance on real estate, the economic development and tax collection are actually funded by peasants and low-income people. In 2009, the total sales volume of commercial houses amounted to 4.39945 trillion yuan. Based on the proportion of 49.42%, the government will obtain 2.174208 trillion yuan as transfer fees and taxes for the provision of housing facilities. There are two main sources of government income. The first is the difference between the low cost of land requisition and the high price of sale, which actually intrigues the peasants while the second one is the low-income people who wish to buy their first house out of their own savings, as well as through bank loans.

It will be necessary to allow different ownerships of land; permit legal or genuine owners market their lands without any discrimination; change the current monopoly market system of the government, and form multiple subjects for land supply. As an important rule of market economy, collective and state-owned land shall share the same price based on same conditions, while the land requisition and compensation cannot be applied.

1.2.2. *Extend the term for the use of land and form stable land rights*

The author believes that, in the collectively-owned land system of rural areas, the reform and legislation shall accord to the principle that the usage right of land shall remain unchanged, as proposed in the 3rd Plenary Session of the 17th Central Committee, which means that the right to use collectively-owned lands in rural areas and suburbs, including their contracting arable land and housing sites, except for public use, permanently belongs to peasant households. Moreover, except when the government requests land for the welfare of public, peasants can transfer, rent, mortgage, buy shares with it, and even sell the long-term usage right of land provided they meet the requirements on the usage of the land.

The author considers that it is practically impossible to ask householders to pay transfer fees again at the end of a term due to several reasons, so it is better to ask land users to assume their responsibilities to the state by changing to permanent or long-term use of land, employing inheritance system, or collecting taxes of real estate. The current system, which specifies a transfer period of land of 50 to 70 years and the payment for 50 to 70 years, shall be reformed.

The term of land use shall be extended. For example, the term for urban residential land can be extended to 500 years, while the enterprise land can be extended for 300 years. A one-time reform of the transfer fee to taxes on real estate such as residence, office buildings, commercial complexes, hotels, etc.; taxes on land use i.e., land used to build factories; or two taxes collected at the same time, e.g., for cottages. Genuine owners or tenants can trade their remaining land use term in the market, instead of returning it to relevant governmental departments, when they decide to quit or transfer land usage. By abolishing the current system of fees on land transfer, and in addition to the transfer fee when the government land is transferred to others for the first time, the government can collect transaction VAT on the real estate and lands that are traded within the term and levy the real estate taxes and land use taxes for the real estate and land in use. In the current policy, the land must be returned back to the government before the government decides on its transfer, which shall be reformed later on.

Similar property rights have been formed upon the extension of the term of land use. An important way to clarify the property rights is to record and release the certificate of the long-term use of peasants' contracted field and residential site, rural public and village land, and land used by owners and tenants in cities, in terms of the contract system.

1.2.3. *Collect VAT on real estate transaction, tax on real estate, and tax on land usage*

Using the above as the basis, China should reform the taxation system and the local finance on real estate, replace transfer fees and other expenses with taxes, and change the income source on real estate of local governments. In addition, it is necessary to clear up various taxes and expenses on real estate, abolish expenses and simplify taxes into three types: VAT on real estate (changing the land transfer fee to VAT and collecting VAT on real estate transaction); tax on real estate; and land use taxes owing to over occupation of land. Despite a lower rate, the taxes shall be firstly levied on residence, while the rate of the real estate tax shall be confirmed by local governments. The governments can provide subsidies to the low-income people who shall submit the taxes on real estate in a reasonable range, but the government would never exempt anyone of taxes. Progressive taxes shall be collected from people who exceed a certain living area when their living standards are up. However, the wages or subsidies shall be increased for personnel in enterprises, public institutions, social groups, and organizations of self-controlled income and expenditure before the collection of taxes on real estate is conducted.

In summation, the author considers it necessary to reform the oligopoly of government on land and form several subjects for land supply, extend the term of the land usage and form stable property rights of land, reform the taxation and local finance system and change the income source on real estate. It is necessary that the reforms in the current system should promote economic development and establish real estate's financial income by collecting fees and taxes from rich residents.

In conclusion, the reform and legislation of the land system shall accord to the people-oriented spirit, implement laws that support economic and social development, and facilitate improvements in the socialist market economy. Such reform should also consider the particularity of the allocation of land resources, and the historical continuity and operability of the land system into account, by encouraging involved parties to submit their opinions.

2. Promote the Reform of the Financial System with the Development of Small Banks as the Breakthrough Point[1]

The current monopoly by state-owned financial system prevents credit funds from being fairly distributed to private, small, and micro enterprises, leading to difficulties in business startups, insufficient development of small and medium-sized enterprises (SMEs), high unemployment rate, fewer medium-income people, and further unfair distribution of incomes. Therefore, the key is to break the monopoly by large state-owned banks on social credit funds by developing small banks.

---

[1] This is part of the research report submitting to the All-China Federation of Industry and Commerce, based on the cooperation with Dr. Tan Xiaofang.

2.1. *Financing difficulties of private, micro, and small enterprises*

By now, China has more than 40 million SMEs and privately or individually-owned businesses, absorbing about 75% of the urban population that includes migrated labor from rural areas, contributing over 60% of GDP and 50% of taxes, owing 65% of patents, and producing 80% of products. However, the financing problem of SMEs has not been solved for a long time. As influenced by America's financial crisis, about 7.5% of nationwide SMEs had stopped operation or were shut down by the end of 2008. SMEs, most seriously affected by the financial crisis are unable to finance or establish businesses due to shortage of funds than ever before.

The financing problems of SMEs mainly occur due to the following structural conflicts.

(1) In terms of financing sources, SMEs show an over-dependence on internal financing, but lack external financing SMEs in China highly depend on internal financing, but it is inhibited by the development status of the enterprises themselves.

(2) In terms of external financing, SMEs show an over-dependence on indirect financing, but relatively lack direct financing. The volume of direct financing of China's SMEs, i.e., the sum of bonds and equity financing, takes up less than 1% of total financing, which is very little or equal to nothing. The main channel among all indirect financing methods for SMEs to obtain credit capitals is through folk loans and bank loans. Folk loans, though popular in some regions, are considered "illegal" loans.

In the near future, the main channel for the financing of SMEs will still be bank loans, instead of equity investment. Therefore, the problems in financing SMEs mainly lie in the degree of difficulty in obtaining bank loans.

After more than two decades of reform, the current financial system of China is still featured with government monopoly, where the government retains the power to allocate financial resources.

The four state-owned banks have occupied majority shares in the banking industry, whose financial assets took up to 51% of total assets of all commercial banking organizations by the end of 2008, and loans and deposits occupied more than 51% of the total amount of all financial organizations (see Table 8.1). State-owned commercial banks own most of the widespread branch offices, which are the main suppliers of credit funds, or substantially the monopolistic suppliers of credit funds in a certain sense. Medium and small-sized financial organizations in China only include 136 urban commercial banks, 22 rural commercial banks, 163 rural cooperative banks, 91 village banks, 6 loan companies, and 10 rural cooperation funds. State-owned commercial banks are the leaders of majority of financial resources, while local financial organizations, which serve SMEs, only share fewer financial resources due to smaller numbers and scale.

Table 8.1.   Total Assets and Liabilities of Financial Organizations by the End of 2008 (Including Home and Foreign Currency within China).

Financial Organizations	Total Assets (100 million yuan)	Proportion (%)	Total Liabilities (100 million yuan)	Proportion
State-owned banks	318,358.0	51.0%	298,783.6	51.0%
Joint-equity banks	88,130.6	14.1%	83,683.9	14.3%
Urban commercial banks	41,319.7	6.6%	38,650.9	6.6%
Other types of financial organizations	176,104.7	28.2%	164,897.2	28.1%
Total	623,912.9		586,015.6	

Date source: website of the China Banking Regulatory Commission.

Note: State-owned commercial banks include Industrial and Commercial Bank of China, Agricultural Bank of China, Bank of China, China Construction Bank and Bank of Communications. Joint-equity banks include China CITIC Bank, Everbright Bank, Huaxia Bank, Guangdong Development Bank, Shenzhen Development Bank, China Merchants Bank, Shanghai Pudong Development Bank, Industrial Bank, Minsheng Bank, Prudential Bank, Zheshang Bank and Bohai Bank. Other financial organizations include policy banks, rural commercial banks, rur al cooperative banks, foreign-invested financial organizations, urban credit cooperatives, rural credit cooperatives, finance companies for enterprises and groups, trust investment companies, financial lease companies, automotive finance companies, money broking companies and postal saving banks.

2.2. Difficulties of small-loan companies

After one year of operation, the small-loan companies have played their positive role in relieving the financing problems of SMEs to a certain extent, though it is far behind the expected outcome. However, small-loan companies have found themselves in an awkward position.

First, they are able to earn only little money. Owing to policy restraints, many regular businesses of financial organizations cannot be carried out, such as note discounts etc.. Therefore, interests from the small loans are their only source of profits. The second problem is the limitations on the source of credit funds. More importantly, loan companies see no future for their development. The financial industry is a monopolized industry in China with a high entry threshold, so the small-amount loans are no doubt the best springboard to the financial service industry. According to the *Temporary Provisions on the Management of Village Banks* released by the Banking Regulatory Commission, small-loan companies have the chance to transform into village banks, which draws the blueprint for the enterprises with the business circle entering into the financial industry. However, according to another regulation in the *Temporary Provisions on the Management of Village Banks*, the biggest shareholder of village banks must be formal financial organizations, such as banks, which greatly disappoint the applicants of village banks, including many companies hoping to upgrade from small-loan companies to village banks.

2.3. Slow development of pilot banks and irrational governance structure

Village banks are an innovative solution to the omission of financial service in rural areas. A village bank plays a significant role in facilitating the formation of a new rural financial system and in strengthening it. However, the newly born village banks have encountered barriers and obstacles which failed them to play their functions and roles.

The first reason is the limitations of the policies. Village banks have not obtained any response on their bank number from the People's Bank of China (PBC) nor have they joined the large and small-amount payment system of PBC. The second is the conflict between the target and sustainable development. The third is the restraints on the qualification of the main founder. Same with loan companies, the main founder of village banks shall subject to current bank organizations. The fourth reason is the irrational governance structure. Due to all these reasons, the village banks see a slow development far behind the demands of SMEs.

2.4. The way-out of the financing of medium and small-sized enterprises and the development environment for the medium and small-sized enterprises

The current financial system of China was established at the beginning of the reform and opening up, which was mainly based on state-owned banks that serve the state-owned economy, but lacked the medium and small-sized financial organizations that support SMEs. Along with the rapid development of SMEs, the economy becomes increasingly diversified, without confirming the corresponding relationship between economic and financial subjects, leading to the asymmetry between the economic structure and financial structure and between the credit structure and financial demands. SMEs mainly with private economies as their main bodies cannot find corresponding service departments in the financial system and are therefore placed in a weak position in the current financial system. Therefore, it is impossible to find a solution to the financial problems of SMEs in the current financial system, hence traditional financial system or old mode of thinking are still applied.

2.4.1. Medium and small financial organizations: the fundamental solution to the problem of financing medium and small-sized enterprises

The profound reason for the difficulties that lie in the financing of SMEs' is the monopoly of banks catering to large enterprises in the current banking market structure and insufficient development of medium and small financial organizations. Therefore, China has no choice but to vigorously develop medium and small-sized financial organizations to solve the problems of SMEs. The *Report on the Implementation of Monetary Policies in the 2nd Quarter of 2008* published by the Central Bank discussed SMEs' difficulties in financing and pointed out the solution to the difficulties, i.e., to vigorously cultivate and develop medium and small-sized financial organizations.

This is the right time to facilitate the foundation of small and medium-sized financial organizations. The first condition is the availability of abundant social capital. Second, China has already cultivated a large number of financial personnel. Third, the market demand on small and medium-sized financial organizations is strong. Finally, China can draw experiences from many other foreign countries. Developed countries often go by the solution of vigorously developing small and medium-sized financial organizations, and therefore it provides rich experiences for China. America owns more than 7,000 small banks with a capital less than 1 billion USD, which mainly serve small enterprises. In Korea, the SMEs bank, one of the three major policy banks, has reached assets of 111 billion USD and can serve 160,000 SMEs. Therefore, it is necessary to emancipate the mind, vigorously develop small and medium-sized financial organizations in many aspects, strengthen the reforms in the financial system based on the spirit of reform and innovation, and practically give full play to the important role of small and medium-sized financial organizations in solving SME's difficulties in financing.

2.4.2. *Different opinions on the development of small banks*

When the development of small banks is mentioned, some scholars and relevant departments will immediately mention the large number of bad debts previously incurred by the rural cooperative funds and stock funds in China's financial system, as well as the frauds in societal financing. Therefore, an objective opinion shall be employed to consider these questions and distinguish them from small banks.

(1) The previous problem in rural cooperative funds mainly resulted from the ambiguous property rights, which cannot be compared to non-governmental small banks. Rural cooperative funds and the property ownership have regulated the governance system and operational mechanism of rural foundations. Cooperative funds originally belonged to collectively-owned financial organizations, however, in most places, the transformation of the community joint-stock cooperative system with relatively clearer property rights, has not been adopted after the all-around responsibility system was employed. Regarding internal management, no supervision system has been established for the foundation owing to the "omission" of the real owners. However, the private stockholding economic organizations, represented by many rural cooperative funds in Wenzhou, are featured with clear and normative guiding theories, principles, regulations, composition, and specific operation, but they were put down when the government required the closure of rural cooperative funds. Therefore, since the current financial system cannot solve the difficulties that arise in the financial structure of the SMEs, it is necessary to moderately open the market and allow medium and small-sized financial organizations with clear property rights to enter the market to facilitate adequate competition in the financial market based on historical experiences and lessons.

(2) Large-scale frauds in financing and small-scale non-governmental banks share different ranges and degrees of risks. The large-scale frauds arise as a result of raising funds from the public for three or four years, tempting people with high interests, investment returns, or profits. The most representative case is the case of illegal fund raised by Wu Ying, a rich woman in Dongyang of Zhejiang, at the beginning of 2007. Non-governmental banks in small scales only assume small-scale and low risks.

(3) The problem also lies in the policy environment for medium and small-sized financial organizations. Compared to the operational orientation of big banks, small and medium-sized financial organizations are more willing to provide financial services to SMEs. On the one hand, they cannot afford to provide financial service to large enterprises due to their limited capital, and on the other hand, they enjoy

advantages on the information for serving SMEs. As local financial institutions, small and medium-sized financial organizations mainly serve SMEs in the same region. The long-term cooperation enables small and medium-sized financial enterprises to increasingly understand the operation of SMEs, and thus avoid the information asymmetry between small and medium financial enterprises and SMEs. Therefore, the efficient method to solving the financing problems of SMEs is to establish and reform the small and medium-sized financial organizations.

After several years of development, small and medium-sized financial organizations have accumulated funds for the upgrading of its foundation, improved the risk resistance capacity, and enhanced the operation and development level. Despite the favorable prospects, these financial organizations also face a series of problems. First, the property rights of current small and medium financial organizations, such as the rural credit cooperatives, village banks, and loan companies are not easily understandable. Second, they lack sufficient capital. Owing to simple capital source, small and medium financial capitals are weak in their self-supporting ability. The third is the difference in policy environment.

2.5. Small banks: attaching equal importance to development and supervision

The only way for the provision of loans to individuals, micro, and small enterprises is to break the monopoly of large state-owned banks, vigorously develop rural and urban non-governmental banks, and develop the efficient and practical supervision system and method.

2.5.1. Vigorously develop small non-governmental banks and guarantee system

In addition to the development of small banks and guarantee companies, the finance shall support small enterprises with the help of interest subsidies.

(1) Develop Small Banks

The current number of banks in small and medium-sized financial organizations can hardly satisfy the needs of the development of so many SMEs in China, so it is necessary to vigorously develop non-governmental banks. First, China should expand the range of access capital through guidance and encourage the non-governmental capital to establish small banks that provide financial services to local SMEs, and supports non-governmental capital to buy shares of small and medium-sized financial organizations. Second, China should control the scale of small banks. Third, the functions of small banks shall be specified clearly.

(2) Improve the Guarantee System and Expand the Scope of Collaterals

Currently, the indirect financing of SMEs is mainly in the form of guarantee loans, especially in the form of real estate mortgage loans. Insufficient insurance and collaterals will lead to the difficulty in obtaining loans for the SMEs.

In order to change the 'inferior position of SME guarantee companies with banks, it is necessary to build multi-level SME loan guarantee funds, guarantee organizations, and vigorously promote the development of commercial guarantee and mutual guarantee organizations based on the establishment of policy guarantee organizations. Local governments can also set up policy SME re-guarantee companies for the benefit of commercial guarantee and mutual guarantee organizations. The scope of collaterals shall be further expanded due to the small capital scale of SMEs and limited collaterals.

(3) Governments Mainly Support SMEs by Interest Subsidies

Governments have several ways to support the financing of SMEs: (1) Establishing counseling centers for financing of SMEs; (2) Providing diagnosis and operational guidance services; (3) Setting up special organizations to provide information and counseling service; (4) Carrying out the financing guarantee policies for SMEs; and (5) Adopting the policy of interest subsidies. Interest subsidies refers to providing loans to SMEs with an interest rate lower than the market rate, which is adopted by various governments to provide fund support to SMEs. The loans with interest subsidies enable provision of social funds to aid SMEs and thereby benefitting them to obtain loans, so the governments mainly rely on interest subsidies. The government shall first provide subsidies for the long-term loans of SMEs, thus helping to obtain credit funds; and secondly increase the proportion of the interest subsidies and expand the applicable range of the policy of interest subsidies.

2.5.2. *Legalization of underground finance*

According to the *Investigation of Underground Finance in China* released by the Central University of Finance and Economics in 2006, China's underground financial credit ranged between 740.5 billion to 816.4 billion yuan, with the average index of underground financial scale of 28.07, which means that the scale of underground finance accounted for 28.07% of the financing scale of the normal channels. The underground finance has played the supplementary function for SMEs and agriculture that obtains lesser support from normal financial credit. As shown in the survey data, about one-third of the loan provision made to SMEs are obtained from informal channels, while over 55% of credit loans for agriculture comes from informal channels. On one hand, large-scale underground finance has huge potential risks and shall be incorporated into the financial supervision as soon as possible. On the other hand, the positive role of underground finance in solving the financing problem of SMEs cannot be ignored. Underground finance should not be allowed to develop freely, but should be legalized along with the development of non-governmental financial organizations as a necessary replenishment of China's financial system and incorporated into the financial supervision system. This is the best option undertaken to overcome the problem of financing.

3. How to Transform State-Owned Enterprises and the Supervision System

By now, significant changes have occurred in the status of state-owned enterprises, the pattern of supervision and management of state-owned enterprises, their internal governance structure, and their positions in national economy. For example, the reform of state-owned enterprises has consumed a large quantity of national resources. More than 6,000 staff members of state-owned enterprises have been laid off, transferred to other enterprises, or retired. State-owned enterprises have not distributed profits to their investors since more than 10 years, and only the state-owned enterprises controlled by the central government have reached assets of 21 trillion yuan and seen profits of 815.1 million yuan in 2009 and 618.86 billion yuan from January to July 2010, which was estimated to exceed 1 trillion yuan by the end of 2010. The academic circle holds many opinions about the reforms in the state-owned enterprises, such as "state-owned enterprises advances while private sector retreats," highly dejected with the monopoly of state-owned enterprises, and its irrational distribution. Then, how will further reform be conducted?

3.1. *Continue the socialization of state-owned capitals and the reformation of industrial organization*

For state-owned industrial, commercial, and financial enterprises, the aim is to further promote the reforms in the capital society and acilitate the competition and continue anti-monopoly.

3.1.1. *Further socialization of state-owned capitals*

In most fields, the objective of reforms in large state-owned or state-holding enterprises is to socialize the capital held by the state-owned enterprises. There are three major capitals from different sources — family and private capitals, state-owned capitals, and social capital. Social capital refers to the capital of the enterprises invested by many investors, but are utilized by the authorized persons. Social capital includes enterprise capitals, joint-stock, and joint-stock cooperative capital, unlisted enterprise capital, capital of listed companies, capitals of fund investment organizations, and enterprise capital of collectively-owned groups. Reforms in large state-owned enterprises should not aim to turn state-owned capital to family or individual capital, or strengthen the state-owned assets, rather socialize these capital.

3.1.2. Reform of the industrial organization

Except for the problem in the unsocialized state-owned capital with respect to capital composition and enterprise system, China also has disadvantages in the industrial organization, such as the over monopoly in electricity grids, railways, and other fields, and the small scale and low concentration ratio of enterprises and facilities in the production of steel, oil refining etc. Therefore, it is necessary to conduct anti-monopoly for some industries where it is needed to lower the concentration ratio and fight against monopoly, and increase the concentration ratio and expand the scale for some small industries. Even for the industries in need of higher concentration ratio, the key to solving problems incurred by the system of monopoly is to socialize the capital, establish public companies, and put them under the supervision of the society. In addition, the system of supervision and inspection by a third party shall also be set up.

3.2. Separation of administrative supervision, investor supervision, and capital operation

Actually, the government should supervise and manage the state-owned and state-holding enterprises in multiple levels. The first is the common supervision and management, such as the industrial and commercial registration, quality monitoring, discharge management, and tax collection. Every enterprise shall accept this kind of common and fair supervision regardless of its ownership. The second is the government's supervision and management over the state-owned and state-holding enterprises as the investor, including the safety of state-owned assets, profits from the investment, and distribution of profits. The third is the specific operation of assets. As the representative of the investor, the government cannot operate state-owned assets. The operator of state-owned assets alone would have the rights to complete the operation of state-owned assets, such as the merging, sales, and entry and exit of assets in the industry.

3.2.1. *Cancel the particularity in supervising and managing state-owned enterprises*

In terms of the particularity of state-owned enterprises in China, some monopolistic state-owned enterprises in tobacco, postal services, and petroleum or petrochemical industries indirectly exercise the power of administrative control. Many state-owned enterprises receive special care from banking and other systems, such as assets stripping and cancellation of bad debts after verification. The government also states that only state-owned enterprises can enter into certain fields. This is unfair to non-state-owned enterprises, including foreign-invested enterprises. Therefore, the reform shall further clean up the obvious and invisible administrative power of monopolistic state-owned enterprises in market competition, cancel the special care given to state-owned enterprises with respect to their systems and policies, and enable equal competition among state-owned, private, and foreign enterprises and ensure fair treatment to the market access of state-owned and private enterprises.

3.2.2. *Management functions of the investor and prevention of the reversion of administrative management*

The responsibilities of the investors of state-owned enterprises are to ensure the operation of state-owned assets in certain fields, maintain and increase the value of these assets in these fields, and produce certain profits. However, it should be pointed out that the state-owned enterprises are special in some areas. First, state-owned enterprises cannot exist in all economic fields. Second, state-owned enterprises shall assume social responsibilities for public interests in addition to valued maintenance and appreciation of assets. For example, some assets of state-owned enterprises can be transformed into social security funds. Third, the government shall require state-owned enterprises to invest and research in long-term scientific and technological progresses regardless of the earning rate of the assets.

For the management of state-owned assets, the administrative management and the operation of state-owned assets needs to be further separated. A State-Owned Assets Supervision and Management Committee should be established as the chief representative of the property rights of state-owned assets at the top level, with the state-owned assets management office set up under the committee as a permanent administrative body. The second level establishes the state-owned assets operation company, with the welfare of the state-holding companies as its key objective. Substantial changes have occurred in the relationship between the governments and enterprises after the foundation of state-owned assets operation companies. Five steps must be taken: (1) Clarify the subjects of investment; (2) Separate government functions from enterprise management; (3) Conduct capital operation. State-holding companies can adjust the product structure, industrial structure and enterprise organization structure, revitalize stock assets, optimize assets allocation, and improve the operation quality and efficiency of assets by manipulating capital and exercising functions of the strategic planning, investment decision-making, ascertain profits of the assets, and act as the representative of property rights; (4) Assume the liabilities on assets. The primary responsibility is to ensure the value maintenance and appreciation of state-owned assets.

The current problematic question is: Should state-owned assets operation companies be established in various regions of the country for various industries? Or, Should only a head state-owned assets operation company be set up under the State-Owned Assets Supervision and Management Committee? The Committee is planning to establish a new asset management company to operate and manage central-governments' assets, in order to enhance the operation quality of state-owned assets, facilitate the strategic adjustment on state-owned enterprises, strictly separate the capital operation and actual operation of state-owned assets, and avoid administrative intervention. In the current design, the assets management company will adopt a slow strategy, which will only place some shares of these state-owned enterprises to this new company. This equals to a company controlled by the Committee (Zhong Jingjing, 2009). Of course, the reform will necessarily prejudice the power and benefits of many state-owned enterprises. The birth and fate of the head of State-owned Assets Operation Company will be decided between the Committee and the large-scale enterprises and the attitude of the central government and the state department.

3.3. *Reformation of the budget and profit distribution of state-owned assets*

The reforms in the management and profit distribution practices of state-owned industrial, commercial, and financial assets has been partly mentioned in the reforms of financial and taxation system. In addition, profits from state-owned assets shall be submitted to the central and local governments and the following reforms shall be carried out.

3.3.1. *Establish the system of the financial report on state-owned assets submitted to NPC*

In addition to the establishment of the budget for state-owned assets in state-owned industrial, commercial, and financial enterprises, the system of financial reports on assets and liabilities of state-owned enterprises submitted to governments and NPC shall be established, which shall include the following contents: (1) Manage the property rights and profits rights of state-owned assets of state-owned enterprises and other enterprises using state-owned resources and assume the responsibilities to maintain and increase the value of state-owned assets. The financial report must report about the efficient management and maintenance of state-owned assets to the information users; (2) The financial report shall incorporate the information on fixed assets owned by state-owned enterprises and administrative organizations. Currently, the efficiency of the usage of fixed assets of state-owned enterprises, governments, and administrative organizations is low, while repeated purchase and construction can be commonly seen, causing major losses. Therefore, the financial report shall strengthen the supervision over the state-owned fixed assets and provide the users with complete information on the status of state-owned assets. At the same time, it shall also properly disclose the investment in infrastructure constructed by the state-owned enterprises and governments; (3) The report shall include the creditor's rights and liabilities of state-owned industrial, commercial, and financial enterprises as well as administrative organizations. The state-owned liabilities include domestic and foreign liabilities, liabilities of other subjects (except the subjects of the financial reports), real, and clear liabilities, and the potential and contingent liabilities; (4) The report shall also include the financial information on the governmental procurement funds. Along with the increasingly in-depth reforms in the financial management system and the further implementation of these systems for government procurement and treasury concentrated payment, the governmental procurement funds will become an important content of the financial activities (Finance Bureau of Dawa County).

3.3.2. *The system of deciding the wage and remunerations for the managers of state-owned economy*

First, remuneration for the persons in charge of state-owned industrial, commercial, and financial enterprises should be confirmed. The performance of state-owned enterprises determines the salaries of staff in charge of these enterprises, and such salaries will be examined and evaluated. Second, the difference between the salaries of foreign staff members and enterprise managers in the state-owned enterprises, as well as the special policies on the monopolistic operation of the state-owned enterprises, will be considered. It is irrational to confirm the remunerations of the board of directors, board of supervisors, and management teams of state-owned enterprises which would be even higher than in developed countries. Before profit distribution, state-owned industrial, commercial, and financial enterprises shall submit reasonable resource taxes, effluent taxes, and investment and operational profits of state-owned assets.

3.3.3. *Supplement social security by socializing state-owned assets*

The task of "adopting several methods, including transferring part of state-owned assets to supplement social security funds" had been listed in the report of the 3rd Plenary Session of the 16th Central Committee. However, the transfer has not yet been implemented. The transfer of state-owned assets to supplement the social security funds will facilitate the socialization reform of state-owned assets, the accumulation of social security funds, and the improvement of capital markets.

The state-owned assets will be gradually socialized and will gain revenues by selling assets in the market to supplement the social security funds. Previously, China did not accumulate social security funds for staffs, but requisitioned land and purchased grains at low prices that damaged their ability to accumulate savings, so the socialization of state-owned assets shall be adopted to correct the previous unreasonable policies. State-owned assets will be gradually transferred to supplement social security funds and give full play to its advantages in long-term investment, which will significantly help the reforms in state-owned enterprises, as the government will hold the shares of some major enterprises for a long period. In addition, the social security funds hold the state-owned shares as a shareholder, which will inhibit the situation of "single-large shareholder" and thus promote the improvements in the management of state-owned enterprises. The possibility of social security funds encountering the risks of fluctuation in stock prices or bankruptcy of some state-owned enterprises after the funds obtain some shares deserves attention. Therefore, an efficient risk management system shall be established for the social security funds (Fu Ning, 2005).

3.4. *Promote the democratic supervision of state-owned assets*

State-owned enterprises, as the public assets, accumulate profits from the taxes submitted by people, making use of the price differences in industrial and agricultural prices, and requisitioning peasants' land at low prices. People entrust the country and government to manage state-owned enterprises and assets. Therefore, people have the right to know and the right to supervise the value maintenance and appreciation of state-owned assets, operational status of state-owned assets, and the profit distribution. Democratization of finance and taxation is important aspect of people's democracy.

3.4.1. *State-owned assets supervision and management committee subjects to the management of NPC*

The following are plans on how to manage state-owned assets: (1) People entrust the NPC, and NPC in turn entrusts the government to exercise the power of investors, supervisors, and managers; (2) The Audit Administration and Central Organization Committee Office is subjected to the management of NPC. If the first plan is adopted, it needs to handle properly the relationship among the public assets, NPC, the ultimate investor of state-owned assets, and the government, as the agent and supervisor. However, based on the practices of the committee since its establishment, the more thorough second plan shall be employed, so the committee subjects to the management of the NPC.

The chairman of the board and president of the board of supervisors of the state-owned enterprises and banks shall be selected upon the suggestion of relevant professional departments, State-Owned Assets Supervision, and Management Committee and the NPC. Some regions have created the procedure for the NPC nomination of "eight steps:" "understanding and investigation, examination of laws, talk with leaders, post report, inquiries, discussion and vote, democratic evaluation, and release of certificates." These can be regarded as the system for NPC investigation and nomination for the chairman and director of the state-owned industrial, commercial, and financial enterprises.

3.4.2. *Democratization and openness of the management of state-owned assets*

Apart from the financial department and other state-owned assets administration departments submitting the financial report on the budget of state-owned assets and the state-owned economy, the cost of state-owned industrial, commercial, and financial enterprises shall be audited by a third party, as an important content of the democratic management of state-owned assets.

It is believed that, in addition to state-owned industrial, commercial, and financial monopolistic enterprises, the cost of non-monopolistic state-owned enterprises, state-holding enterprises, and the state-owned shares in other enterprises shall be audited by an independent third party. In order to reach democratization of management of state-owned assets, NPC shall hear, or organize, social hearings on the annual salaries of leaders of state-owned enterprises, wages of staffs, cost accounting, and price adjustment. In addition, any economic information of state-owned enterprises, including the annual salaries, wages, annuity, cost, major investment, profits, and losses and costs, except those related to national security, shall be disclosed through government notices or websites for people to look up.

In conclusion, the reform of the state-owned economy includes the reform of state-owned land system, state-owned industrial, commercial and financial economies, and state-owned administrative and public assets management. And this reformation will continue socializing the assets, establishing, and improvising the budget for assets operation of state-owned enterprises, necessitate state-owned economies to submit profits to the government, and place the state-owned enterprises under the management of NPC. Such reforms will enable NPC to nominate the enterprise mangers and fix their salaries; encourage submission of budget and financial report by the state-owned enterprises to NPC, and open the state-owned assets, operation and the wage management to public.

Bibliography

Anonymous (2007). Serious monopoly leading to problems in 30% power supply enterprises. *Electric Products Net*. Accessed on 7 December 2007.

Anonymous (2010). Pollutions of Zijin minerals kill 1.89 million kg fish, not the first time. *Yangzi Evening*, 14 July 2010.

Baidu Baike. Explosion of Dalian oil-pipe.

Cai Jiming (2008). Thoughts on the principles of the land system. *Finance and Economics Net*. Accessed on 25 May 2010.

Chang Hongxiao (2010). The first key step of the reform of land system. *Finance and Economics Net.* Accessed on 20 October 2008.

Chen Yicong (2010). No delay for the reform of power grid. 21st *Century Economic Report*, 18 August 2010.

Finance Bureau of Dawa County (2010). On the establishment of the financial report system of China's governments. *Dawa Finance Bureau Net.* Accessed on 22 June 2010.

Fu Ning (2005). Three advantages of transferring state-owned assets to social security. *China Security News*, 9 September 2005.

Han Baojiang (2010). Protect peasants' rights and benefits, the right time to deepen the reform of land system. *Outlook*, 22 November 2010.

He Zhaocheng and Yu Baodong (2009). New thoughts on the power reform and power market construction. Available at www.serc.gov.cn/jgyj/ztbg/. Accessed on 27 November 2009.

Li Jingrui (2009). Half of expenses on real estate development flows to governments according to the all-China federation of industry and commerce. *The Beijing News*, 6 March 2009.

The decision of the CPC central committee on several issues concerning the rural reform and development. Approved by the Third Plenary Session of the 17th CPC Central Committee, 12 October 2008.

The Ministry of Land and Resources (2011). Pilot reform of land auction in this year. *Daily News.* Available at http://news.dichan.sina.com.cn. Accessed on 28 January 2011.

Wen Xiaocai (2010). Selection and design of the mode of the management of state-owned financial assets. *Reform and Strategies*, 3.

Wen Yiyan (2006). Monopolistic enterprises shall be forced to open their information. *Yanzhao Urban Newspaper*, 13 June 2006.

Xia Qing (2010). Steel enterprises in meager profits, with more rapid reorganization of steel industry. *China Security News*, 28 August 2010.

Ye Xiangsong (2002). Comparison between two different management and operation methods for state-owned assets. *Modern Finance and Economics*, 4.

Zhong Jingjing (2009). The state-owned assets supervision and management committee plans to establish a new assets management company to manage the assets of the central government. *The Beijing News*, 3 March 2009.

Zhou Tianyong (2003). Reflections on the development of private economies and the direction of the monetary policy. *China Business Times*, 24 July 2003.

Zhou Tianyong (2008a). Developing small and medium banks better than developing financing securities. *Hexun Net*. Accessed on 19 September 2008.

Zhou Tianyong (2008b). It is an illusion to count on large banks to provide loans for small enterprises. *China Financial and Economic News*, 2 September 2008.

Zhou Tianyong (2008c). Only the development of rural and urban community banks can rescue small and medium-sized enterprises. *Financial Circles Net*. Accessed on 24 October 2008.

Zhou Tianyong (2009a). Narrowing the gap between rural and urban areas and permanently giving the use right of rural land to peasants. *Economic Information Daily*, 21 October 2009.

Zhou Tianyong (2009b). The key is to develop financial organizations that provide financing service for small and medium-sized enterprises. *Hexun Net*. Accessed on 22 January 2009.

Zhou Tianyong and Zhang Mi (2005). *Assault on Reform of State-Owned Enterprises*. China: Water & Power Press.

Chapter 9

Route Map of China's Road

Many parts of the book entitled *Chinese Dream and China's Road* have been published in *China Economic Times,* which is sponsored by the Development Research Center of the State Council. After the completion of the previous eight chapters, Mrs. Bai Jingwei, the famous journalist and the Editor in Chief of the theory section of the *China Economic Times,* suggested that I conclude the whole book and propose a map of China's road to development, to enable readers to have a clear understanding about the structure of the book. This chapter is composed in a form of an interview.

1. Propose and Clarify Some Key Theories on China's Road

1.1. *Further innovation and development socialism through practices*

Bai Jingwei: The selection of road often relates to theoretical researches. A theoretical misjudgment may lead to a misapplication of practices. What theoretical researches are mentioned in your book and what are their roles in confirming fundamental policies for future practices?

Zhou Tianyong: You're right. Some ambiguous theoretical understandings may mislead China's development road in the future. These vague theories will result in undefined key tasks and development focuses. This book conducts theoretical researches in the following aspects:

First, we will learn how to understand socialism. What is the main task of the socialist society in the next three decades? In general, the goals and tasks of the socialist society include how to improvise productivity in order to maximize wealth, and to fairly distribute the wealth in order to reach common prosperity. In the previous 30 years, China has made great achievements in the improvisation of productivity, but showed weak performances in fair distribution and common prosperity. In the next 30 years, China shall attach the same importance to fair distribution and common prosperity in addition to the improvisation of productivity and creation of wealth.

Bai Jingwei: Some believe that it is necessary to go back to ownership that is large in size and collective in nature and strengthen the planned economy in order to realize fair distribution and common wealth. What do you think about this opinion?

Zhou Tianyong: In the traditional socialist theory, the socialist society has two important features: the public ownership and the planned economy. First, the cost, efficiency, feasibility, and practical rationality of the planned economy shall be discussed. Except for Korea, more than 30 countries that adopted the planned economy system have transformed into a market economy since 1950s and 1960s, including Vietnam and Laos. The ideal planned economy system in the traditional theory has almost globally stepped down from the historical stage. I wrote an article The *Predicament of the Planned Economy and Reform Towards the Market Economy* published in the *Study Times* on 29 September 2008 that discussed the plan of the planned economic theory and the causes of its failure in terms of resource allocation.

Bai Jingwei: Then, does the current difficulty facing Chinese lie in what ownership structure shall be selected to realize the fair income distribution and common prosperity under the economic system of market-oriented resource allocation?

Zhou Tianyong: Yes. My first finding in the theory on the relationship between the ownership structure and income distribution pattern is that without the corresponding system construction and balance, despite the public ownership of assets, the country with a high concentration of large enterprises and high capital organic composition of productivity will suffer unfair distribution and polarization, similar to the private economy of large capitals. More and more industrial, commercial, and financial state-owned assets have been accumulated, however, controlled by a very few practitioners, so without the rationally defined budget, distribution, and democratic monitoring of public assets, public ownership will actually promote polarization. The chapter *Elimination of Polarization and Realization of Common Prosperity* discusses this in detail, so no further explanation will be given here.

Bai Jingwei: I found that you also mentioned that the state-owned and collective-owned land system also contributes to the unreasonable income distribution. Can you explain that in brief?

Zhou Tianyong: My second finding in the theory on the relationship between the ownership structure and income distribution pattern is that the current public ownership of land distributes more profits to high-income people and allocates more national income to the government. This public-owned land system actually robs the poor and helps the rich while centralizes national incomes in governments.

Bai Jingwei: I have read your research on the development of small enterprises and come to the conclusion that the society with more numbers of small enterprises will enjoy fairer income distribution and lower Gini coefficient. Is this right?

Zhou Tianyong: This is my third finding in the theory on the relationship between the ownership structure and income distribution. A society with more private, micro, and small enterprises will embrace a fairer income distribution and lower Gini coefficient. I conducted the data calculation and comparison in my last book, *China's Way-Out*. In conclusion, since private, micro, and small enterprises are mostly labor intensive and large enterprises are capital intensive; more small enterprises will lead to more income distribution to the labor, more medium-income people, fewer poor unemployed people, and a wider scope for the collection of social security funds. When the large enterprises dominate, it will result in more distributions going to capital owners and large capital investors, more high-income people, relatively more poor people due to unemployment, low employment rate and large gap in the collection of social security funds.

Bai Jingwei: Then, to be brief, what is China's socialism in your opinion?

Zhou Tianyong: In my opinion, for the ownership structure, China should socialize and publicize the assets of state-owned enterprises, socialize the capitals of large private enterprises, create a relaxed system for business startups, and employment and fair opportunities, give priority to increasing private, micro, and small enterprises and to solving the unemployment problem and making efforts to pursue fair and just income distribution. For the distribution relationship, China should collect reasonable income taxes and property taxes and adjust the high-income groups. The government shall improve its public service, provide equal service, and employ transfer payment for underdeveloped areas. The social security system shall be established and improved. Therefore, this kind of socialist society can develop productivity while achieving common prosperity.

Bai Jingwei: Why did you analyze the relationship between the ownership and common prosperity in the book *Chinese Dream and China's Road*? What is the practical meaning?

Zhou Tianyong: After three decades of practices and setbacks after the foundation of the state, we had come to realize that socialism should develop productivity and improvise the economy. After three-decades of reform, opening up, and development, we further understood that the basic economic system of socialism should develop and change along with practices. We shall be practical, emancipate the mind, continue innovation and reformation on various systems, adapt to the market economy system, and build a modern society of common prosperity, affluent people, and strong country.

1.2. *Urbanization: irresistible objective tendency*

Bai Jingwei: In your book *China's Way-Out*, you analyzed the ideas, systems, and mistakes of urbanization since the foundation of New China and designed a plan to promote urbanization. Why do you emphasize on the facilitation of urbanization?

Zhou Tianyong: It is an objective tendency of human society transforming from a rural economy to industrial and service-oriented economy or urban society, which is pushed by the internal economic laws such as the economies of scale and concentration, saving of labor, costs of cooperation and transaction, externality and economy of scope. Whether the population would transfer to cities or not the speed of transfer is independent of man's will. The structure will be distorted if urbanization is artificially inhibited.

Bai Jingwei: Has a consensus been reached on the above ideas in academic circles, including the political circles?

Zhou Tianyong: Despite an increasingly clear understanding of urbanization, the academic circles and relevant departments also have some ambiguous ideas on strategies and fundamental policies: (1) Some wrongly believe that urban construction has occupied and wasted too much land. Actually, the rural population had decreased by 62.46 million in 2007 comparatively to 1978, while the rural land had increased by 196.28 million mu. In the same period, the urban population had increased by 421.34 million, but the urban built up area, including towns had only increased by 50.43 million mu (Zhou Tianyong, 2010); (2) It is necessary to balance rural and urban development, reduce and remit rural taxes, increase the inputs on rural areas, and build the new socialist countryside. However, some departments and regions ignore urbanization and rigidly understand the construction of the new countryside. It shall be pointed out that no matter how the government supports agriculture, the proportion of the total output of agriculture and rural areas in GDP will constantly decline. It is the worldwide trend that villages will decay along with the population transferring to cities. The government shall improve peasants' living levels by transferring more rural population and labor from rural areas to cities. The construction of the new countryside refers to achieving a balance between rural and urban development by establishing large communities in the countryside and cancelling small villages; (3) There has been no scientific estimation nor any preparation for the future rapid transfer of rural population to urban areas in the following three decades. According to my prediction, at least 80% of the rural population will live in the cities by 2040. By 2040, most aged rural population will live in rural areas, where the low living costs will lower the financial burden, thereby providing comfort living to a large number of aged people. The scales of cities and the distribution of urban systems are independent of man's will and are determined by the market adjustment, though the government may exert some influence.

Bai Jingwei: Academicians and policy-making departments may concern themselves with the employment and accommodation for so many people being transferred to the cities; hence who will cultivate the rural land?

Zhou Tianyong: Yes, this problem is often discussed, illuminating the following points: (1) In reality, the secondary and service industries may create most job opportunities. The development of the service industry is actually in direct proportion to the level of urbanization. More concentrated population may create more jobs; (2) In China's road to development, the urbanization process is inseparable from the development of individuals, micro, and small enterprises. Most labor transferred from rural areas will work in these enterprises. For China, the development of individuals, micro, and small enterprises may be more important than the construction of the new countryside; (3) Agriculture, especially the grain crop farming, shall be transformed from the previous labor intensive to technological and land intensive industry. Only when the scale economy of land is formed, modernization of agriculture can be realized. Therefore, except for those who have already transferred to the cities, about 330 million agricultural labors are still planting 1.8 billion mu of land. The number of agricultural labors is too large, when compared to Latin America, U.S., Europe, Japan, South Korea, or even Chinese Taiwan.

Bai Jingwei: I read that you compared the mode of urbanization in China, Japan, South Korea, Chinese Taiwan, Latin America, and India and considered China's road of urbanization to be full of risks. Can you briefly explain that?

Zhou Tianyong: Except the discussions on whether to develop large, medium, or small-scale enterprises in academic circles, the more important topic in the road of urbanization is the procedure for the urbanization of the rural population, i.e., how would this population exit rural areas, whether they can enter into cities easily, what would be the status of their employment, residence, and public service, and whether they can enjoy social security. Urbanization can only be regarded as positive when the procedure is complete and moderate. The procedure varies in different countries.

Bai Jingwei: It seems that different countries have different characteristics. What is China's current mode?

Zhou Tianyong: The urbanization of rural population in China is summarized as below. Based on the collectively-owned land system, residential land, forest land, and arable land cannot be relinquished through the market system, but can only quit at a low cost in the form of removal. Despite the household restraints on access, the temporary residence system has solved the problems of access to a large extent. Due to the insufficient development of the service industry, China has too many restraints on access and operation in developing small enterprises and levies heavy taxes and fees. Some private, micro, and small enterprises fail to find finance, incurring great pressure on the employment of labor being transferred to the cities. The slums are not allowed and rural assets cannot be realized. The housing price in cities and the growth rate are far higher than the income level of peasant workers and the growth rate of rural areas. Many people who transferred from rural areas can only rent houses of poor conditions. It is almost impossible for the government to provide housing for the current 200 million peasants in cities and the 600 million peasants in the future. The government has started to attach importance to the public service and social security system for peasants migrating to cities.

Bai Jingwei: What are the main problems and risks in China's urbanization road?

Zhou Tianyong: To be brief, the major risk lies in the living and employment of 800 million peasants that have entered or willing to enter cities. Owing to the growing cost of wages and social security, appreciation of RMB, and increasing organic composition of capital, along with the industrial upgrading, the absorption of labor into active employment is decreasing. For the sake of GDP and taxes, local governments show more attention to investments in large-capital projects and the development of large enterprises. The overstaffed party, government, and administrative affairs exert a great burden on the national economy. Private, micro, and small enterprises face many difficulties and the service industry is not developing in an ideal way.

Bai Jingwei: Then what about the risks in residence after peasants migrate to cities?

Zhou Tianyong: We haven't found scientific and clear ideas, strategies, systems, and policies to solve the settlement of 800 million peasants that have entered or willing to enter cities. They cannot realize their rural assets, so they cannot afford houses in urban areas. Amphibious residences in both rural and urban areas will lead to great wastage of land. Since no slum is allowed, commercial houses are too expensive and it is impossible for the government to build houses for 800 million people. The only result is that most of the 800 million people migrating to cities live without definite residence, while the aged may return to rural areas or become trapped in cities. Most of the migrating households do not have adequate rental or purchasable housing options from the 200 million urban population. Therefore, urban residents become the proprietary class that live on rents, while the proletariat has to submit one-third of their income to house owners or be troubled about the rent if they are unemployed and about the rising cost of rent. As there is no method to solve the residence of 800 million people, it is a risk as serious as the employment problem of these people. The current mode in China will create greater risks than the mode of slums in Latin America and India if no adjustment is made.

1.3. *Innovation of theories and policies on income distribution*

Bai Jingwei: Increasing the income gap is a vital problem that may affect the current and future social stability of China. Solutions can only be proposed based on the theoretical understanding of the causes of the problem. Then, how will the causes of the problems be analyzed?

Zhou Tianyong: The theory on labor and wages under the market economy mainly analyzes income distribution under the current structure and system. The proposed reasons for the increasing income gap include the weak bargaining power of labor in the management–labor relations — the monopoly of state-owned enterprises — and corruptions. It is suggested to strengthen the power in planning and adjustment, improve the minimum salary and the wage level, reform state-owned enterprises, provide fair public service, establish social security and fight against corruptions. However, it is actually difficult to analyze and solve China's income gap based on the theory of "labor and wages" under the Western structure and stable system.

Bai Jingwei: Then, how are the analysis angle and method to be innovated?

Zhou Tianyong: First, it is necessary to analyze the formation of China's income gap in the process of space-time and structural trans-formation, i.e., the structure under fierce changes. Therefore, a framework shall be established to analyze whether the structural change and income distribution are balanced. Based on the situation in the 30 years after reform and opening up, a dynamic analysis on the income distribution shall be introduced in the theory on the economic development and structural transformation.

Bai Jingwei: What is the internal relationship between structural change and income distribution?

Zhou Tianyong: Seen from the structure of wealth created by rural and urban areas and the primary, secondary, and tertiary industries, the proportion of wealth created by rural areas and agriculture in GDP has been constantly declining. The growth of industries was fluctuating at first and became stable later, while the proportion of the service industry has been constantly increasing, from 70% to 80%. To organize and maintain the structure of labor employment, a dynamic and proper re-allocation of funds created by rural and urban areas and as well as the industries shall be conducted in order to maintain a balanced structure of wealth distribution. An important structural factor contributing to the huge difference between the urban and rural areas and high Gini coefficient is the advancements in industrialization, backward urbanization of rural areas, and seriously distorted production and employment structures. All these factors led to comparatively lesser wealth created and distributed to larger population and labor in rural areas involved in agriculture, whereas more wealth was created for distribution to fewer people and labor in urban areas.

Bai Jingwei: The structural analysis method for the causes of the income gap really makes sense. In addition to the distorted urban, rural and industrial structures, are there any other structural factors contributing to the differences in greater income distribution?

Zhou Tianyong: Yes, there are. The industrial organizational structure is gradually progressing in developing countries. In China, the industrial organizational structure, the backward development of the service industry and the slow development of individuals, micro, and small enterprises result in an unbalanced creation and distribution of wealth to the nation's capital and labors. This is another profound reason for the increasing uneven income distribution gap in China.

Bai Jingwei: Is there any other factor contributing to the income gap? How should problems in strategies, systems, and policies be solved?

Zhou Tianyong: Of course, the distorted structure is not the only reason for uneven income distribution. I believe that complicated reasons have brought about the increasing gap in income distribution. To solve the problem of uneven income distribution, the revenue structure in the urban and rural areas, industries and enterprises needs to be adjusted; reforms have to be carried out in finance, taxation and other systems; a balanced system for the negotiation between labor and capital should be established as well as building up of a public service-oriented finance and social security system. Also, the problem of uneven income distribution cannot be fundamentally solved only through the reformation of wage system or by any other means without adjusting the structures.

2. Route Maps in Four Fields

Bai Jingwei: You have discussed about the Chinese dream and China's development road with more than 400 thousand words. Can you summarize the route map for China's development road here?

Zhou Tianyong: China's road to urbanization shall be discussed in four aspects, development; resources and ecological environment; improvement in people's livelihood and reformation of the economy, which also includes the key factor known as logical progression within the stipulated time.

2.1. *Route map for development*

Bai Jingwei: What is your opinion about the development?

Zhou Tianyong: The route map for the development of China would be agricultural modernization, urbanization, upgrading of industrial structure, technological progression, development of small enterprises, completion of the first phase of modernization and facilitation of the second phase of modernization.[1]

---

[1] He Chuanqi's research group believes that the content of the first modernization of the society refers to the transformation of a rural economy to an industrial society, which is featured in the urbanization, welfare, circulation, specialization, mechanization, electrification, automation, technicalization, standardization, justification, compulsory primary education and public communication, etc. The content of the second modernization of society refers to the transformation of the industrial society to a knowledge-based one, which is featured in the knowledge, information, suburbanization, rural and urban balance, greening, ecology, nature, innovation, internationalization, diversification, leisure, individualization, rights and benefits of women and children, higher education and life-long education (see Li Bin). Reported by Li Bin, Xinhua Net. Accessed on 7 February 2006.

Bai Jingwei: What are the main tasks and key points of the road map for development?

Zhou Tianyang: Owing to backward urbanization when compared to industrialization, the core and most important task in China's development route is to facilitate urbanization. In addition, the key point is to enhance the development of small enterprises in the process of urbanization, especially the development of small enterprises in the service industry and absorb and balance employment as the industrial capital organic composition improves. Urbanization is the key to defining China's development in the future while small enterprises determine people's livelihood and stability of China.

Bai Jingwei: What do you think about the role of large enterprises in the road map for development? Are they unimportant?

Zhou Tianyong: No, large-scale industrial enterprises, in particular, play a very important role in the development of China. I didn't list them in my book because industrialization in China, paved way for the development of heavy industries well in advance. Owing to the role of GDP and local taxation system, though the large capital and enterprises are not emphasized in China's development road, they are paid much more attention than the private, micro, and small enterprises in terms of strategies, systems, and policies. Under the current system, it is not difficult to make the country rich by improving financial structures, but the problem of unemployment and enriching the lives of the people is very serious. Therefore, the development of small enterprises in the future is much more important than the large enterprises in the facilitation of urbanization of China.

2.2. Route map for resources, ecology, and environment

Bai Jingwei: Based on the large population and relatively scarce resources, what does China think about the relationship between development and lifestyle, and resources, ecology, and environment?

Zhou Tianyong: The route map for resources, ecology and environment of China shall be the development of a strategy for the preservation of resources and emission reduction — frugal, low-carbon, suitable for living and consumption; progress in technologies on protecting resources, ecology, and environment; forming a society of favorable ecology, clean environment and sustainable utilization of resources. Production is the basis for consumption, while consumption reacts to production methods. Therefore, on the development road, the key for the solution to the conflict between large population and scarce resources and environment is to form a frugal and comfortable consumption method.

Bai Jingwei: How is the frugal and comfortable consumption method to be understood?

Zhou Tianyong: China shall inherit the vegetable-based traditions of Chinese nations for the diet structure to maintain adequate balance of the nutrients. Regarding the residence structure, China shall save land and energies, protect the environment, and ensure heat insulation. China shall rely on public traffic of energy and land conservation and emission reduction. In terms of administration and public service, methods for resource conservation and emission reduction shall be formed. China would aim to lead the mutual effect between the economic structure and the method of production, exchange, and consumption, by demands based on the frugal, low-carbon, and comfortable consumption method, so as to establish a society that saves resources and protects the environment. Of course, it is also very important to achieve progres in technologies to overcome the bottlenecks in resource shortage and preserving environment.

2.3. Route map for people's livelihood

Bai Jingwei: It seems that people's livelihood has not been adequately discussed in China's previous development road. Is China not paying enough attention to people's livelihood?

Zhou Tianyong: Yes. The previous China's mode or road mainly involved the development of a comprehensive national strength, but considered less on improving people's livelihood. We are not aiming for the sole development of the nation, but for the livelihood of the people as well. Therefore, an important aspect in the 12th five-year plan is that over the next decade or even three decades, people's livelihood will be strongly considered. The route map for people's livelihood shall be by encouraging business start-ups; assuring employment; assuring that urban residents own their own homes; implement favorable public services and acceptable social security scheme; fair income distribution and wealth allocation; forming a dynamic society that can offer safe living conditions.

Bai Jingwei: What is the key to this route map?

Zhou Tianyong: There are two key points in the route map. The first is to encourage business startups in order to increase employment because employment is considered as the basic factor for the enrichment of people's livelihood. The second is the role of the market and government in people's livelihood. What public service and social welfare role shall be assumed by the government? How will the social security system be built? Can the government satisfy the demand for the provision of housing to about 800 million people in the future? Special attention shall be paid to the relationship between efficiency and fairness and the market and government.

2.4. *Route map for reforms*

Bai Jingchang: In addition to the development, balance of resources; ecology and environment; and people's livelihood, a great number of reforms are necessary to build a harmonious society in China. Are these reforms an integrated part of China's development road in the future?

Zhou Tianyong: Yes. The route map for reforms shall be emphasizing its reforms in the financial and taxation system, rationalizing the resource price system, reforming and innovating the land system, breaking the monopoly of the financial system, and further deepening the reform. According to practices of reforms, a single reform often ends up in a failure without the support from other reforms. The order of reforms cannot be confirmed, so the government has no other choice but to give priority to the key points, take all factors into consideration and coordinate with the task of promoting reforms at the same time.

Bai Jingwei: Why is the reformation of the financial and taxation system the main focus of the future reform?

Zhou Tianyong: The importance of reformation of the financial and taxation system is revealed in the following aspects. First, the environment for the development of individuals, micro, and small enterprises that can absorb a lot of labor is closely related to the system of fee collection by the government as well as the reform, adjustment, and the reduction of taxes. Second, the reformation of the financial and taxation system would clearly define the responsibilities of the central and local governments and is the base for the rational actions of the local governments. Third, many reforms are linked together, such as the relation between the reformation of the state-owned enterprises and the financial budget system; between the reformation of the land and taxation systems; between the control and reform of the party and government personnel and their expenses; and the reformation of financial budget system. Fourth, the reformation of the financial and taxation system, especially the democratization of financial incomes and expenses can greatly promote the political system reform. Many other reforms connected to the reformation of the financial and taxation system are not listed here.

Bai Jingwei: Why do you think these reforms shall be integrated?

Zhou Tianyong: According to the experiences, a professional department can formulate a very ideal and perfect reform plan, but fail in the implementation. Why? It is because of the internal relations of the systems and various affairs. The reform will fail without a clear understanding of the relationship between the reform and other aspects, which will result in the changes possibly incurred by the reform.

Therefore, the reforms can only succeed when the government designs an integrated plan to organize various reforms at the same time.

3. Coordination of the Development Roads in Different Fields and the Expectations

Bai Jingwei: Any expectation on China's development road?

Zhou Tianyong: I think there should be. CPC has been involved in the revolutionary struggle for 28 years since its foundation, installed order out of chaos of the Cultural Revolution in 1978 (30 years after the foundation of new China), and spent another 30 years in reforms and open-up. It is believed that the economic and social development of China will dominate the next three decades, from 2011 to 2040.

3.1. *Coordination of the development roads in different fields*

Bai Jingwei: How to effectively coordinate the roads of development, resources, ecology and environment, people's livelihood and reforms?

Zhou Tianyong: The overall planning and consideration of various fields is the key point. For example, in order to enable the population migrating to cities to be able to afford housing, it is necessary to allow the distribution and realization of rural assets, encourage business startups generate employment and maintain growth rate where the incomes are higher than the rapid increase in housing prices, so a unified plan shall be made, including the reformation of the rural land system, reformation of financial and taxation system, and promotion for the development of small enterprises. In order to build a society for resource conservation, ecology and environmental protection, it needs to reform on the pricing system of the resource products, reform the financial and taxation system and promote the technological progresses on new energies and materials. In addition, the fundamental reform of the monopolistic financial system and its supervision is to promote the development of small enterprises; otherwise it is impossible to break the financial bottleneck that hinders the development of small enterprises which can absorb much labor.

3.2. Expectation of the road of reform

Bai Jingwei: Is there an expected timeline for the completion of these tasks?

Zhou Tianyong: Yes. I think there should be a proper strategic expectation on the reformation of economic and administrative system, including the political system which inhibits economic development. It is believed that five years will be spent to assault the difficulties in the reformation of financial and taxation system since 2011. Deng Xiaoping had proposed a trick for the reforms, where every reform has "a certain time limit" (Deng Xiaoping, 1993).

3.3. Expectation of the urbanization road

Bai Jingwei: What is your expectation on the speed of urbanization, the main line of China's development road?

Zhou Tianyong: The process of urbanization is the most important key in China's future development road. It is very likely that the urbanization of China will reach 80% based on the development from the late 1970s to the late 2040s, which means assuming the population would reach 1.55 billion during this period, 1.24 to 1.32 billion people will live in cities. Urbanization will be facilitated between 2011 and 2020, a high growth rate is anticipated between 2021 and 2030, a gradual decrease in the growth rate by 2031, and a steady growth after 2036. The industrialization will be basically completed by 2020, and at the same time, the marketization will also be complete. Informationization will come in the later stage by 2040. However, the most important trend in China's economy and society over the next 30 years is the huge continual influx of population and labor (about 800 million) from rural and agricultural areas to urban areas and from the secondary industry to the service industry.

3.4. *Expectation on the business start-ups and development of small enterprises*

Bai Jingwei: You have mentioned business startups, employment, and development of small enterprises in the route map for the development of the nation and people's livelihood. What is your expectation in these fields?

Zhou Tianyong: As urbanization may be facilitated in the future, if more attention is not paid to it between 2011 and 2020, the development of individual, micro, and small enterprises cannot be raised to a high strategic level as the construction of an innovation-oriented country, employment for several hundred thousands of laborers will lead to high unemployment rate, and unstable incomes. Even if the unemployment rate is controlled at 10%, 70 million to 100 million labors will remain unemployed, affecting the lives of 200 to 300 million people, which will necessarily incur social disturbance. Therefore, we appeal for a 10-year development strategy to encourage business startups and promote the development of small enterprises and consider the strategy as the first priority of the country. The departmental interests and prejudices shall be overcome. Practical reforms shall be conducted in the departments of access, approval, and supervision, finance and taxation. Practical measures shall be adopted to encourage business startups and development of small enterprises, in order to enable the country to get through the risky period of the urbanization.

3.5. *Expectation of the solution to the living problem*

Bai Jingwei: According to you, it is very important to solve the problem of livelihood. Do you have any expectations on this?

Zhou Tianyong: Residence is just as important as employment, and there should be a strategic expectation. In a socialist society, it is an important part of common prosperity that enhances people's living standards. If 20% of families in urban areas lease their houses to 80% of people who are without houses, two social ranks will be formed, thereby not conforming to the principle of common prosperity under socialism. The increasing housing prices lower the hopes of tenants to buy their own houses. In addition, it is impossible for the government to provide houses for 200 million people living in cities and the 600 million people that will migrate to cities, based on the productivity and finance conditions.

Bai Jingwei: Then, how do we solve this problem?

Zhou Tianyong: Practical plans shall be formulated and relevant reforms shall be carried out. First, allocate land correctly for the use of planting grains and residence only. Transform the 600 million mu of saline-alkali mudflat to support the process of urbanization and residents' demands, to restrict the housing price from sharply growing due to insufficient supply of land. Second, reformation of the rural land system should be carried out to enable families migrating to cities to realize their assets, in order to increase the ability to purchase houses in urban areas. Third, reform the current land and finance system, extend the definition for the usage of land, enable land to go to the market equally, abolish the monopolistic sale of land by the government, allow the auction of land, form the system of transfer of land for about 40 to 70 years, and replace the transfer fee with taxation, i.e., pay equal attention to the increase of land supply and system reform to solve the problem of high housing price.

3.6. *Expectation on the transformation of the living and consumption method*

Bai Jingwei: What is your expectation on the development road of resources, ecology and environment?

Zhou Tianyong: As discussed above, the conservation, improvement, and protection of resources, ecology, and environment is mainly dependent upon the transformation of the lifestyle and public consumption. We believe that it is necessary to make a decision to strictly carry out the reform on consumption by the party, government, and administrative organizations who at all levels shall apply a frugal method of public consumption to set an example for the people. Efforts should be undertaken to to cancel the unreasonable automobile use by the party, governmental, and administrative affairs by 2015 and gradually change the entertainment method during 2010 to 2020 to save the consumption of public entertainment. In addition, use of office facilities and the government square should be restrained, in order to save paper and communication costs and energies and land resources.

Then, by 2040, it is possible for us to improve and maintain a favorable and beautiful ecological environment and satisfy people's demands at a medium and high development levels, based on the frugal lifestyle.

3.7. *Expectation on the future technological progress*

Bai Jingwei: In addition to the strategic expectations on the main tasks in the major development roads, any other important things you want to talk about in the future development?

Zhou Tianyong: There are many tasks to be completed in the above four fields. In addition, it should be noted that the comprehensive national strength is the basis to building a rich country and the technological progress is the core of competitiveness. Based on the demands on technological progresses by the state, first, enhance the scientific and technological progresses that can increase China's scientific, technological, economic, and national defense competitiveness to great heights, such as the mobile communication, space, and cloud computing technologies. Second, promote the development of technologies demanded by the scarce resources and ecological environment, such as the technologies on new energies, energy conservation, emission reduction, restoration of ecological environment, and ecological agriculture, etc. Third, innovate and adopt technologies based on people's living standards and demands, such as the technologies on video, network and traffic. China needs to select the catch-up model in technological progress in order to build a scientifically and technologically powerful economy. The contribution of technological progresses to economic growth in China shall improve from current 40% to 50% by 2020, 60% by 2030, and 70% by 2040. According to the Lausanne Economic Academy, China has been ranked 18th among 58 world economies in competitiveness, in 2010. As calculated by the World Economic Forum, China's national competitive strength ranked 27th (World Economic Forum). China shall raise itself to the 17th by 2020, 7th by 2030, and in the top five by 2040 and become a prominent nation in terms of its scientific and technological power.

Bibliography

Selected Works of Deng Xiaoping (1993). People's Press, 3, p. 177.
Selected Works of Deng Xiaoping (1993). People's Press, 3, p. 372.
Selected Works of Deng Xiaoping (1994). People's Press, 2, p. 168.
Zhou Tianyong (2010). *China's Way –Out*. Beijing: People's Daily Press.
Zhou Tianyong (2003). Economic descriptions on the origin and evolution of cities and the city system. *Studies on Financial Problems*, 7.
World Economic Forum (2010). China's competitiveness rising to the 27th, two ranks higher than the previous year. Report on the Global Competitiveness 2010–2011. Finance Sector of Phoenix Net. Accessed 9 September 2010.

Epilogue

Everyone has a share of responsibility for the fate of the country. By October 1949, the CPC had struggled for nearly 30 years to establish a unitary and independent country of Chinese nations. It had also survived the disturbances of revolution, problems in economic growth, and long-term difficult living since the foundation of new China till the end of its cultural revolution. After 1978, China again experienced a 30-year period of system reform and opening up and rapid economic growth. China is now at a key turning point. Over the next 30 years, scholars need to research on major subjects of economic and social development and system reform for China.

Since mid-2006, the author, jointly with Wang Changjiang and Wang Anling, organized few domestic scholars to research the major subjects of political system reform in China. Together, they published the book *Tough Battle: Report on the Research on the Political System Reform in China*, that provides a practical, strategic, and comprehensive plan for the political system reform in the future of China.

At the end of 2007, the Shanghai People's Publishing House entrusted me to organize a research on the *30-Year Reform of China's Administrative System*, which was published at the end of 2008. The book discussed measures on how to reform the administrative system.

For more than a year since end of 2008, I studied the state of modernization in China, internal factors that contributed to the rapid economic growth for 30 years after the reform and opening up, major economic and social risks, and problems that China will face in the next three decades. I also compared China's 30-year development mode with the development modes adopted by India, Latin America, South Korea, and Chinese Taiwan. The results were published in the book *China's Way Out* in March 2010, which proposed a question to the party, country, governments, and the people: What is China's way out and what development road should China adopt?

The author only proposed problems in the book *China's Way Out,* but did not give overall solution to these problems, though some discussions were highlighted. In particular, the problems of resources, environment, and ecology were not mentioned in the book. Therefore, since February 2010, the author has started to state personal opinions on what the Chinese people need in the future, what the Chinese dream and China's spirit are, the varying tendency of resources, environment, and ecology and counter measures, how to adjust the rural and urban structure, and industrial structure, how to reform the financial, taxation, land, finance, and state-owned economy systems, and conducted in-depth research on the problems of resources, ecology, and environment in China and the future development road of China. With a year's worth of hard work, this extensive work was finally completed at the end of January 2011. The book is entitled, *Chinese Dream and China's Road*, which designs and describes a practical and integrated plan for the future development, people's livelihood, and reform of China.

The author was once asked, "Why should you conduct such a wide and difficult research?" First of all, I am grateful to the finance-centered college of Dongbei University of Finance & Economics (DUFE), where I attended school and acquired a great deal of knowledge. In addition to political economics and western economics, I also studied investment, banking, national economic plan, financial budgeting, principles of accounting and taxation, financial analysis, feasibility study for projects, industrial organization technology, basic management, and economic laws, etc. Though I did not excel in my studies, with an average score of 81 (most studies and exams failed to capture my full attention), I read many books on real estate, rural and agricultural economy, and administrative systems, etc. after my school hours, which laid a knowledge base for my understanding of systems and policies related to finance, taxation, banking, currency, industries, enterprise economies, and economic laws.

When I was in DUFE in 1987, I tenured for and finally obtained the position of Editor-in-Chief for *Development Economics* organized by the Ministry of Finance. I started to check, study, research, and teach theories on economic development based on various schools of thought, as a main part of my study and teaching career. In 2011, I published the *New Development Economics 3rd Edition* and the *Senior Development Economics 2nd Edition* through China Renmin University Press. Development economics refers to the theory on the process, laws, and tendency of a country or region transforming from under-developed to developed status. I found the theory more valuable and valid than any other theory to guide China's strategies, systems, and policies for economic development. My two books, *China's Way Out* and *Chinese Dream and China's Road*, are independent from my studies and researches on economic development theories. Personally, I believe that middle and high rank leaders will better understand the internal relations, laws, and tendency of economic and social develop-ment and more scientifically lead the economy to its success path, when they acquire more knowledge in "development economics".

All aspects are related in the economic and social life. For example, close internal relations, even multiple mutual relations, can be found in the finance and taxation system and land system, urbanization, and the problem of agriculture, rural areas and farmers, income distribu-tion and industrial structure, employment rate and small enterprises and business startups and government management. Therefore, it is necessary to become familiar with the economic and social life and system operation of the nation in order to comprehensively design China's development road by formulating new development strategies, revising laws reform systems, and releasing an overall supporting plan.

I was transferred from DUFE to the Party School of the CPC Central Committee in 1994. In the 16 years I spent at the Party

School, I found it to be an education and research organization with fine tradition where free minds from both within the Party and the country could seek truth from practices, and emancipate minds. However, as we progress through the changing times, new problems and situations are constantly emerging, so it is impossible to rationalize the ideas and formulate efficient strategies; reform systems; revise laws; and release policies based on theory or analysis. The Party school created a relaxed academic environment for scholars to conduct in-depth research on some major problems facing the country.

My experiences at the Party school as well as my stints outside of the school contributed to the completion of the book.

The following are some of my recommendations for China's second stage of prosperity. First, scholars should be just and objective in studies, explore the internal laws and tendencies, and try to be scientific by approaching the truth. These shall be the fundamental principles to discuss on economic and social problems. Second, different from propagandists and preachers, economists should pursue a pragmatic approach in studies that provides perspectives and plans to solve the problems. Third, important data and case analysis should be applied in studies. The objective situation shall be systematically and comprehensively taken into consideration for the study on internal relations between different matters. Fourth, we shall compare the different development modes and roads of various countries. China shall learn from development roads that have benefitted other countries with similar concerns as China; while rejecting any strategy, system or policy that are not wise to follow. Fifth, scholars shall propose just and objective advise on policies, maintain academic conscience, and pursue interests that benefits majority of people, especially the disadvantaged groups. Sixth, scholars shall be brave to provide suggestions on political issues and bring forward frank opinions about irrational strategy, system and policy, and the self-centered motives of the administrative sector — in order to make the strategic formulation and policy design more scientific, reform some irrational systems, enable a better social governance, maintain a healthy economy through social development, guarantee residence and employment for the underprivileged people and stabilize social politics.

The year 2010 was a very difficult period in my life due to personal reasons. I have conquered many hardships to accomplish and publish the topic by conducting research on more than 400,000 words in the year.

The part on the adjustment of the central and local relations on the finance and taxation of this book was jointly completed by Dr. Gu Cheng from the Institute of Finance and Taxation of DUFE and myself, although I made a few revisions. The part on promoting the financial system reform with the breakthrough point in development stall banks was written by Dr. Tan Xiaofang from DUFE under my guidance and with my revisions. The article written by Professor Xia Jiechang, from the Sector of Finance and Trade of the Chinese Academy of Social Sciences, was introduced in the part of systems and reforms to develop the tertiary industry, which has been noted in the reference note as well as in the epilogue.

Soon, I will organize and research, jointly with my colleagues, on the topic of "China's Development Road vis-à-vis the World," which will discuss China's road of opening up since 1978, restraints on the prosperity of the country and people, resources and environment, global fights on resources, and China's strategies and tactics, disputes between world environment, and coal tariff and the standard, war between U.S. dollars and other currencies, competition in science and technologies, conflicts between different cultures and civilizations; co-existence of conflicts and cooperation, harmonious relations within the country, and a greater China and the world pattern. The book is estimated to be published in 2012.

Professor and Doctor Jing Guilan, from the International Institute for Strategic Studies of the Party School of CPC, had carefully read the book and proposed many beneficial suggestions. Doctoral candidates Liu Peirong and Xu Xiaqian from the College of Economics and Management of the Beijing University of Science and Technology and Doctor Hu Feng from the Insurance Regulatory Commission of the Tibetan Autonomous Region have put great efforts into proofreading the book.

Mr. Zheng Xinli, the famous economist, the vice director of the Central Policy Research Center of CPC, and permanent Vice President of the International Economic Exchange Center of the National Senior Think Tank, as well as Li Junru, the former Vice President of the Party School of CPC, have delightfully written the preface of the book. Xie Shouguang, the Director, and Ren Wenwu, the Editor of the Social Science Literature Publishing, have contributed a great deal to the publishing, editing, and proofreading of the book.

Finally, I would like to thank my wife, Mrs. Zhang Mi. She assisted me in proofreading my books and supported the household as well, so as to enable me to concentrate on researching and writing this book.

Zhou Tianyong
100 Dayouzhuang, Haidian District
18 March 2013

Index